D0227905

Priests and Politics

Priests and Politics

The Church Speaks Out

Trevor Beeson

scm press

© Trevor Beeson 2013

Published in 2013 by SCM Press
Editorial office
3rd Floor
Invicta House
108–114 Golden Lane,
London
EC1Y 0TG

SCM Press is an imprint of Hymns Ancient & Modern Ltd (a registered charity)
13A Hellesdon Park Road
Norwich NR6 5DR, UK

www.scmpress.co.uk

All rights reserved. No part of this publication may be reproduced,
stored in a retrieval system, or transmitted,
in any form or by any means, electronic, mechanical,
photocopying or otherwise, without the prior permission of
the publisher, SCM Press.

The Author has asserted his right under the Copyright, Designs and Patents
Act, 1988, to be identified as the Author of this Work.

British Library Cataloguing-in-Publication data

A catalogue record for this book is available
from the British Library

978-0-334-04657-8

Typeset by Manila Typesetting
Printed and bound by CPI Group (UK) Ltd, Croydon

Contents

Preface

This is the sixth volume in a series of histories of the Church of England in the nineteenth and twentieth centuries designed for the non-specialist reader and focused chiefly on those of its leaders who made significant contributions to its developing life.

Having decided to turn finally to the Church's involvement in the political and social life of the nation, I was not disposed to waste much space arguing the case for such an involvement. The Christian religion is an ethical as well as a mystical religion. Building on the strong foundations of the Jewish faith, which was inseparable from the life of a particular nation, Jesus reinforced the belief that love of God and love of neighbour are inseparable.

This teaching, expressed in sayings and parables and above all in his own life, related to what he called the Kingdom of God and was addressed to individuals living in a particular place during a brief moment in history. But the values embodied in his teaching are universal values and, inasmuch as individuals are born to live in community, they have social as well as individual applications.

Christian history records how the Church has interpreted and responded to this second challenge. Being a community of sinners, it has not always done so successfully and sometimes seems to have made no effort at all. Yet, there have been long periods when its own life has been so intimately bound up with the life of a nation that social and political action has been routine. At other times, complacent inaction or positive support amounted to endorsement, for better or for worse, of the status quo. And the nineteenth and twentieth centuries produced some outstanding exponents of Christian social thought and action whose stories are told in the pages that follow.

A much larger book remains to be written, though not by this author, dealing with the much wider and very much more significant influence exercised by Christian lay men and lay women, often holding the highest offices in politics, finance, industry, commerce and other spheres of community life. The work of William Wilberforce and Thomas Clarkson in helping to secure the end of the slave trade would be its starting point.

This book consists of a series of essays dealing with the main issues arising during its period and makes no attempt to provide a comprehensive guide to the Church's involvement in this field, such as is contained in E. R. Norman's scholarly *Church and Society in England 1770–1970*. In spite of the surprisingly unconcealed right-wing political bias expressed in much of the author's analysis, his book is an indispensable and accessible treatment of a great deal of important material.

In order that my own political predilections should not go unnoticed, I must confess that my own Christian life was indelibly stained at an early, formative stage by the teaching of Archbishop William Temple. I am old enough to have been present in Leicester in February 1943 at the third of the 'The Church Looks Forward' meetings, when he spoke about the need for social planning. As a young bank clerk, impatiently awaiting call-up into the wartime RAF, I read with perplexity but recognition that something important was probably being said in his lecture to the Bank Officers' Guild on 'The Christian View of the Right Relationship between Finance, Production and Consumption'.

I still have a much underlined copy of his Penguin Special *Christianity and Social Order* and absorbed into my spiritual bloodstream his statement that '[t]he Church is bound to get involved in political and social affairs because it is by vocation the agent of God's purpose, outside the scope of which no human interest or activity can fall'.

Much later, Reinhold Niebuhr's writings helped to convince me that the great man's approach was not beyond qualification, and, later still, my experience as Chaplain to the Speaker of the House of Commons during the premiership of Margaret Thatcher brought me close enough to political life to recognize the complexity of the social and economic issues that politicians are daily required to face and the unavoidable compromises that decision-making demands.

Nonetheless, 14 years of ministry in a coal-mining village and a 20,000-populated council housing estate in the diocese of Durham were sufficient to confirm my discipleship of William Temple and the deep conviction that faith demands a commitment to the enhancement of the human lot through a wider embracing of justice, equality, compassion, freedom and mutual responsibility.

Once again, I am grateful to Fiona Mather for her support and candid commentary.

Romsey
Easter 2013

I

Throne and Altar

The Church of England's relations with the State at the beginning of the nineteenth century differed little from those established by the Elizabethan Settlement in 1559, when three Acts deprived the Pope of his power to appoint bishops in England, required the clergy to surrender to the Crown their legislative independence, and all to acknowledge the monarch as the only supreme head on earth of the Church of England. In principle, this was a continuation of the interdependence of Church and State that had held sway throughout medieval Europe, and it also embodied the Lutheran concept of 'a godly prince ruling a godly people'. The 1662 Act of Uniformity had prescribed the Book of Common Prayer as the only legal source of the Church's worship, and the designation 'as by law Established' was a recognition that the Church of England's ecclesiastical regulations alone were enshrined in the law of the State.

It was, however, the case that the political power of the Crown was now waning. The advance towards parliamentary democracy still had a long way to go, but it was undoubtedly advancing and must ultimately affect the mode of Church–State relations. Yet there was no suggestion that the Church of England might one day cease to embody the essential spiritual dimension of national life. In fact, fear that something akin to the French Revolution might cross the English Channel served to strengthen the conviction that this dimension was vital to the national interest.

The Church was content that this should be so. Apart from some serious problems during Oliver Cromwell's rule and a few anxieties during the brief reign of James II, it had not found its link with the Crown inconvenient. Neither had the Crown been troubled by ecclesiastical dissent, having taken care over its appointments to bishoprics and received regularly the sworn allegiance of all the clergy.

Nonetheless, the appearance in the political arena of Whig reformers was bound to raise in the minds of some of the bishops – all of whom were involved in the business of government through their membership of the House of Lords – the possibility that a Christian conscience might require them to support change. More of the lesser clergy recognized this, and of their number Sydney Smith was the most prominent as well as the most entertaining.

This ceased to be a theoretical matter when the advance of democracy required a Roman Catholic Emancipation Act in 1829 and a much wider Reform Act in 1832. In both these instances the bishops were divided – most favouring Emancipation, most strongly opposed to Reform. In the latter case, their opposition, which helped to defeat the Bill, caused considerable public anger expressed in violent demonstrations, and they were soon cajoled into support. It was soon the turn of the State to intervene in the affairs of the Church of England by the setting up of a commission to investigate a situation in which the bishoprics and cathedrals were immensely wealthy, while the Church's ministry in the new industrial towns was neglected for want of funds.

Pressure for this had come from a Whig government, but it was a Tory Prime Minister, Sir Robert Peel, who took the necessary action in 1835. The prospect of a substantial reduction in revenue was fiercely resisted by the bishops and capitular bodies, even by Sydney Smith, who was by this time occupying a more than comfortable canonry of St Paul's. A spirit of reform was, however, gathering force and the Ecclesiastical Commission was chaired by the Bishop of London, Charles Blomfield, who saw clearly that the health of the Church, and therefore of the nation, required a redistribution of its funds. He became a leading builder of new churches, with their associated new parishes, in London.

The proposals of the Commission were embodied in an Act of Parliament which, by establishing a central body to administer substantial funds for the payment of the clergy, changed the life of the Church of England for ever. That this should have required parliamentary action was not generally regarded as offensive and, in any case, the Church possessed no effective machinery for the reforming of its life since the Convocations of Canterbury and York had been suppressed in 1717, and would not be revived until 1852 in the case of Canterbury and 1861 in the case of York. Marriage and Registration Acts in 1836 made provision for civil marriages and for Dissenters to be married in their own places of worship.

Meanwhile, Church–State relations remained cordial and the sense of partnership continued throughout Queen Victoria's reign. There was some conflict over Poor Law Reform, the admission of Jews to Parliament, and legal provision for divorce in certain circumstances. The Church did not like the abolition of the compulsory Church Rate in 1868, but the Establishment was not disturbed, since no one wanted it to be. Again, the prosecutions led to the imprisonment of a few clergy, and the involvement of the Privy Council, over ritual practices during the 1880s caused concern among High Churchmen, and Canon Gregory of St Paul's told a

Church Congress that the Establishment was 'miserable and pernicious' and amounted to a State tyranny. But the intervention of the State had been at the request of the bishops, who themselves lacked power to exercise the required discipline, so the partnership was not affected.

However, the rise of the Free Churches raised an issue that was focused on education but had wider implications. The leaders of these churches had no wish to undermine the place of religion in national life, but they saw no reason why its embodiment should be confined to the Church of England, which, in terms of attendance, was in some parts of the country weaker than Dissent. In particular, why should Church of England schools alone qualify for state aid? A long battle, fought by a resistant Church, eventually brought reform. In this battle the Church of England's powers were reduced by the fact that a reinvigorated church life required the bishops to spend much more time in their dioceses, with consequent absence from the House of Lords in London. Their direct involvement in the legislative process continued to decline during the following century.

Unlike her predecessors, Queen Victoria had no great interest in politics and her long reign saw the transformation of the role of the monarchy so that it became a personal focus of national loyalty, a model of the nation's best values, displayed especially in family life, and the foremost encourager of philanthropy. In this, she had no doubt as to the spiritual dimension of the nation's life and the importance of the Protestant Church of England, which she believed should be a moderate, inclusive institution, eschewing the extremes of Evangelicalism and Tractarianism.

This generally accepted view was given significant expression shortly after her death in 1901. Although her coronation was now more than 60 years past, the fact that the ceremony had been a shambles remained in the public memory. The Sacrist of Westminster Abbey, Jocelyn Perkins, noted that the Order of Service used by the Sub-Dean of the time, Lord John Thynn, bore the inscription 'We must have a rehearsal next time'. Perkins, who had been appointed in 1899, belonged to a small group of priests who, in the wake of the Ritualist controversy, believed that the Church of England's worship should be made more colourful and dignified, while remaining faithful to the Book of Common Prayer. Described on his memorial stone as 'A Forceful Sacrist', he was at the Abbey for 59 years and largely responsible for the transformation of its worship, most of all at successive coronations which later, with the aid of radio and television (both initially opposed by the Archbishops) became international spectacles. The successors of the often reclusive Queen Emperor were on the way to becoming 'celebrities', and the bond that bound Crown and people was thereby strengthened.

Although Victoria disliked bishops as a class, appointments to bishop-rics were of considerable concern to her, since these were bound to affect the life of the Church. By this time the personal influence of the Crown had been devolved to the authority of the Prime Minister, but nonetheless they took care to consult her, especially when senior bishoprics fell vacant. Her views were taken seriously, and sometimes, but not always, prevailed. They did, however, when the Bishopric of London fell vacant in 1856. The Queen, in common with many others, was deeply affected by the plight of the Dean of Carlisle, Archibald Campbell Tait, five of whose seven chil-dren had died of scarlet fever between 6 March and 8 April that year. She believed that he should move from Carlisle to the vacant London See, and, although the Prime Minister, Lord Palmerston, was not keen to appoint someone not already a bishop to the Church's third most senior post, he obeyed the Queen's wishes. Twelve years later, though, when a new Archbishop of Canterbury was needed, she ran into much stiffer resistance from Prime Minister Disraeli over her request for Tait to be translated. In the end, she won, and he proved to be the best of the nineteenth-century Primates. On his death in 1882, the Queen asked for a lock of his hair.

The exercising of patronage in appointments to most public offices con-tinued for much of the nineteenth century and the responsibility of the State for the appointment of the Church's leaders at several different levels was not seriously opposed. When the ultra-conservative Bishop of Exeter, Henry Phillpotts, was so incensed by the appointment of the liberal theo-logian to the See of Hereford that he described the Act of Supremacy as 'a foul Act and the Magna Carta of Tyranny', the Queen suggested that he should be prosecuted. It could be, and often was, however, argued that inasmuch as politicians were conforming members of the Church of England, they were in the matter of appointments, and other matters requiring legis-lation, carrying out the responsibilities of the laity. More of this would be heard when church reform was needed in the twentieth century.

The two World Wars of that century led to a serious decline in church attendance, but while they were being waged they reinforced the Church–State partnership. National survival demanded national unity. The spir-itual authority of the Church of England in particular, but also that of the other churches, was deployed to encourage patriotism, service and sacrifice. During the First World War, the dangers in this were not always fully recognized, with consequences that sometimes involved grotesque distortions of Christian witness. These were largely avoided during the 1939–45 conflict, when, in spite of the desperate need to overthrow the great evil of Nazi Germany, a few church leaders, notably Bishop George Bell of Chichester, questioned, on grounds of Christian humanity, some aspects of war strategy.

4

The State's involvement in liturgical matters at the end of the previous century had left no one happy, and in 1902 a Royal Commission was appointed to consider matters relating to the discipline of the clergy, in particular their obedience to the requirement that it should use only the Book of Common Prayer. Two years later it concluded that 'the law of public worship in the Church of England is too narrow for the religious life of the present generation . . . It is important that the law should be reformed and that it should admit of reasonable elasticity . . . above all, it is necessary that it should be obeyed.'

The government accepted the report, and in 1906 the Convocations were instructed to prepare modifications to the Prayer Book with a view to their enactment by Parliament. The Convocations felt no sense of urgency, and the First World War intervened, so that by 1920 they had done no more than produce a revised Holy Communion service. Meanwhile a committee on Church–State relations set up at the request of the Representative Church Council and meeting under the chairmanship of Lord Selborne had recommended back in 1916 that church legislation should be initiated by the Church and subject only to parliamentary veto.

The former chaplains whose service in the trenches had revealed to them the immensity of the gap between the Church and the ordinary soldier and the inadequacy of the Prayer Book to meet his spiritual needs pressed for change, and not only supported the Life and Liberty Movement's campaign for a Church Assembly to give the Church a degree of self-government, along the lines suggested by the Selborne Report, but also demanded as a matter of urgency Prayer Book revision. The first was achieved fairly easily, it being understood that any substantial reforms, especially if related to doctrine and worship, would require parliamentary approval. Several proposed revisions of the Prayer Book were discussed by the Convocations and this led to the production of a volume for presentation to Parliament in 1927.

The revision was modest. Morning and Evening Prayer and the Psalms were virtually untouched. Slight changes were proposed to the Baptism, Confirmation, Marriage and Burial services. Pastoral usefulness was the main guiding principle and anything new was to be regarded as an alternative option rather than as a compulsory demand. A major difference arose, however, over the revision of the Holy Communion service which amounted to little more than a rearrangement of the existing material to bring it into line with the medieval pattern. But provision for the Reservation of the sacrament and a few other changes caused the Evangelical elements in the Church to believe that these constituted a change of eucharistic doctrine in a Rome-ward direction.

A vigorous campaign was therefore mounted to secure rejection of the new Book by Parliament, when it was presented in 1927. This succeeded when the House of Commons voted against it by 238 votes to 205. Consternation followed and the bishops hurriedly produced some modifications. These did not, however, satisfy the Evangelicals and, although the House of Lords again signified its assent, the House of Commons voted against, this time by 266 votes to 220.

Consternation now gave way to crisis and in July 1929 the House of Bishops passed by 23 votes to four a resolution which said that 'for the period of the present emergency' they would not take action against any clergyman who, having consulted his congregation, chose to use services in the revised book. The 'emergency' would last for more than a quarter of a century, during which time the controversial Communion service was used by hardly anyone, and the revised pastoral services came into common use. There had been no uprising of the laity in the parishes, who probably believed that the House of Commons, rather than the Church Assembly, best represented their views.

Among the bishops who had voted against the resolution was the ever-unpredictable Hensley Henson of Durham, who went on to write a book and mount a campaign in favour of disestablishment. This attracted little support, but it marked the beginning of the time when disestablishment became a reasonable subject for discussion. Dick Sheppard of St Martin-in-the-Fields and Bishop Headlam of Gloucester thought that the Establishment should be enlarged to include the Free Churches. More significant, however, was the introduction to the bishops' resolution which stated:

> It is a fundamental principle that the Church – that is the Bishops together with the Clergy and the Laity – must in the last resort, when its mind has been fully ascertained, retain its inalienable right, in loyalty to our Lord and Saviour Jesus Christ, to formulate its Faith in Him, and to arrange the expression of that Holy Faith in its forms of worship.

The doctrine of the Church propounded by the leaders of the Oxford Movement 100 years earlier was now mainstream, and the fact that the bishops' resolution was not seen as contentious by the leaders of the State was a clear indication that the days of the mystical Church–State union were ended. Yet the binding knot was to be loosened, not untied. This was not going to be easy and the next 50 years were marked by intermittent commissions, committees, reports, debates, negotiations, speeches and sermons – all treading delicately lest any proposal for reform called into question the whole relationship. In consequence, much time and paper was wasted and little was achieved, though by the end of the century the position had in many ways been significantly modified.

Meanwhile, shortly after the publication of the 1929 resolution Archbishop Davidson retired – the first Primate ever to do so – and there was no surprise when it was announced that his successor would be the Archbishop of York, Cosmo Gordon Lang. This guaranteed that no precipitate action would be taken to sever the link between Church and Crown, and it was ironic that within four years of taking office the new Archbishop was faced, in the context of an unprecedented national constitutional crisis, with, potentially, the gravest conflict between Church and Crown since the Reformation.

This involved the possible Abdication in 1936 of a new King, Edward VIII, who was faced with a choice between marrying a twice-divorced woman and retaining the Crown. Lang kept a diary of the events of that time and was deeply concerned by the prospect of having to crown a King whose personal life ran completely contrary to the teaching of the Church, of which he would be the Supreme Governor. Neither did it appeal to most of the general public.

Lang enjoyed a personal friendship with King George V and Queen Mary, and during his annual visit to Balmoral in 1935 he had 'a long and intimate talk with the King', who shared with him his concern about the company his son, the Prince of Wales, was keeping. The King died in January of the following year, and on his first audience with King Edward VIII, soon after his Accession, Lang was unwise enough to mention the conversation he had had with his father. The King resented this and thereafter regarded Lang as a likely enemy.

Although the King soon made his marriage intentions clear, and the petition for the second divorce of his future wife was lodged, the British press agreed to refrain from publishing this sensational news. Lang was well aware, however, of the drama that was unfolding, partly from political sources, but also from letters of concern he was receiving from North America, where the media did not feel constrained. At a late stage, the silence was broken in Britain when the Bishop of Bradford, Alfred Blunt, told his Diocesan Conference of his regret that the new King did not seem to take his religious duties very seriously. The press took this as their cue for breaking more serious news.

By this time delicate, often desperate, negotiations had been taking place in an attempt to avert what was seen as a possible national catastrophe. The King was determined to marry, and the Prime Minister made it plain to him that this would involve Abdication. Appeals to the King to change his mind were all rejected, and there were suggestions that the Archbishop of Canterbury should intervene. But Lang believed himself to be *persona non grata* with the King who had, in any case, said that he would listen to advice from no one apart from the Prime Minister, Stanley Baldwin. Abdication became unavoidable and took effect on 10 December 1936. On the same day, Lang spoke sensitively in the House of Lords:

> This is an occasion when our thoughts are too deep for tears, certainly too deep for words. No such tragedy of a pathos so profound has ever been enacted on the stage of our national life. Of the motive that compelled that renunciation we dare not speak. It takes us in the region of the inner mysteries of human life and nature. The heart knoweth its own bitterness, yet even we can understand in some measure the ordeal through which His Majesty has been passing and the cost of the renunciation. We can only offer him the profound sympathy of our hearts and accept with infinite sorrow the decision he has made. Was there not, my Lords, something like a stab in our hearts when we heard the words in which His Majesty took leave of his subjects?

A broadcast to the nation on the following Sunday contained, however, a few sentences of lament that appeared to be kicking the former King while he was down and, while these were applauded in Court circles, large sections of the press and public deplored them. Lang's reputation suffered considerably as a result.

The question then, as now, is how far was Lang himself involved in the proceedings that culminated in the tragedy. The impression at the time was that he had been confined to the sidelines, and there was some regret that he had not used his influence more. J. G. Lockhart, his official biographer, who had access to many of the papers, concluded that his subject's influence had been marginal. True, there had been conversations with the Prime Minister, other government ministers, Queen Mary and members of the Court, but according to Lockhart it was not until the eleventh hour, 5 December, that Lang was recalled to London to meet the Prime Minister, this being 'the only occasion on which his advice was sought and given'. Lockhart also recorded that, a few days before his death in December 1947, Baldwin told him that Lang had made no attempt to force the issue or even to press a point of view.

Subsequent biographies of Lang repeated this version of events until the publication in late 2012 of a completely new biography by the scholar and parish priest Robert Beaken. This provided a more favourable assessment of its subject's complex personality and, with the benefit of access to papers not available to Lockhart, a very different picture of his involvement in the dramatic Abdication events. Apparently he had several meetings with the Prime Minister, at which he reinforced Baldwin's view that, as the King was determined on marriage, Abdication was the only available option. As the moment of decision approached, the King suggested a morganatic marriage as an alternative. This would have kept his wife out of the coronation and public life thereafter, but Lang supported Baldwin in opposing a solution which was in any case unanimously rejected by the heads of Empire governments. At this critical moment in the history of the nation and Empire the voice of the Church of England was still important.

There had been no progress, however, in the resolving of the problems related to formal Church–State relations. A commission of peers and bishops, chaired by Viscount Cecil, set up immediately after the Prayer Book debacle, endorsed the recommendation of the 1916 Selborne Report, but these were rejected by the government. Nothing more was attempted until 1952, when a commission headed by Sir Walter Moberly recommended that the Church should be allowed a period in which to experiment with worship and doctrine changes, and that church matters should be removed from the jurisdiction of the Privy Council. It was not until 1963, however, that the latter was achieved and another two years before a Worship and Doctrine Measure authorized the first.

The issues relating to Crown appointments to bishoprics, deaneries and some other church offices had been discussed on several occasions during the late nineteenth and early twentieth centuries but there was no agreed conclusion, except that the Church should be allowed to make its views known to the Prime Minister before he submitted a name to the Sovereign. By the middle of the twentieth century, the custom by which the Archbishops were closely, though not always decisively, involved in the choice of bishops was well established and by this time the Prime Minister's Secretary for Appointments was responsible for gathering information about possible candidates for particular bishoprics. His influence was believed to be considerable, but, since the process was cloaked in secrecy, no one could tell what factors had determined the choices.

Yet, since good appointments were generally made and successive Prime Ministers showed no inclination to modify the arrangements, there was no clamour by the Church for radical change. Two actions by the Crown in the early 1960s served, however, to create disquiet. The appointment of Michael Ramsey to the Archbishopric of Canterbury within days of the announcement of Geoffrey Fisher's retirement left the Church with no time to pray, nor, it seemed, to be consulted. The fact that Ramsey's appointment was widely welcomed was regarded as beside the point. More concern came with the Crown's failure to appoint to the Deanery of the newly consecrated Guildford Cathedral Walter Boulton, who had served for some years as Provost and played the leading part in raising money and overseeing the development of the new building. This was inexplicable and, most people thought, grossly unjust. Secrecy offered no clue concerning the reason for the decision.

The outcome was the setting up of a Crown Appointments and the Church Commission under the chairmanship of Lord Howick of Glendale. This recommended continuation of the existing system, but with the advisory role of the archbishops formalized and 'vacancy in see' committees formed to advise on the needs of dioceses whenever vacancies occurred. But, at a time when moves towards greater church unity were under discussion, there was no mention of what the implications might be for episcopal appointments. So there was disappointment in the general timidity of the report, and yet another commission, this time under the chairmanship of Professor Owen Chadwick, was appointed to dig deeper.

This reported in 1970, and, while emphasizing the importance of retaining the Church–State link, recommended that in matters concerning worship and doctrine the Church should, through its new General Synod, be entirely free to make its own decisions in matters of worship and doctrine. Furthermore, bishops should no longer be nominated by the Prime Minister but by a committee made up of representatives of the vacant diocese and the Church as a whole. The fact that only the Prime Minister could advise the Crown was overlooked, but it turned out that Prime Ministers, who were no longer much interested in episcopal appointments, were ready to receive two names from a committee, it being understood that he or she would normally submit the first.

After much debate and some legislation, these recommendations were accepted by the State as well as the Church and, with a few minor modifications, govern current practice. While not wishing to venture on to the territory of doctrinal change, the General Synod embarked on liturgical reform with a determination that exceeded that of Thomas Cranmer and other sixteenth- and seventeenth-century reformers. It was agreed, and Parliament insisted, that the Book of Common Prayer should be retained but for the rest a Liturgical Commission was free to produce for General Synod approval a wide variety of variations and entirely new services. At the end of 30 years of experiment, these filled a small library of worship books which the Rector of St Michael's, Cornhill, in the City of London said, with pardonable exaggeration, required a wheelbarrow for their transport into church. Uniformity had given way, as in many other aspects of the life of both Church and State, to pluriformity.

Authority over appointments to bishoprics and deaneries moved inexorably in the Church's direction, assisted by the fact that Prime Ministers no longer employed a 'head hunter', who toured the country gathering information about likely candidates. Instead, a Crown Nominations Committee consisting of the two archbishops, six elected members of the General Synod and four representatives of the vacant diocese, meet for a day and a night in order to produce two names for submission to the Prime Minister, it being clearly understood that the first is the preferred. Increasingly, the methods employed in recruitment to secular posts have come into use and, as predicted, particular interest groups in the Church seek, often with success, to promote their own candidates.

Current Church–State relations are unrecognizable from those that held sway before the First World War, and, although there is sometimes talk of total disestablishment, the bond is now so loose that this seems hardly worth the trouble that legal disentanglement would involve.

2

Towards Democracy – Slowly

During the early decades of the nineteenth century, the government's involvement in national life was, by modern standards, small and bore none of the lineaments of democracy. The senior posts in the Cabinet were for the most part in the hands of the aristocracy, and both Whigs and Tories were the great landowners.

Neither was personal and social freedom as widely experienced as democracy now demands. Hostility towards Roman Catholics was still widespread, and they continued to suffer political disabilities, partly because of their rejection of the Established Church and partly because it was believed by many that their primary allegiance to a foreign power, namely the Papacy, called into question their national loyalty. They were excluded from any public office.

Under the Test and Corporation Acts of 1661 and 1673, Protestant Dissenters suffered the same disabilities, but these had been mitigated by the passing of an annual Toleration Act, which allowed them to sit in Parliament and hold other public offices. On the whole, they were content with this and were not inclined to press for change lest this should provoke a call for Roman Catholic emancipation.

As the pace of economic change accelerated during the 1820s, however, there were those in the governing classes, mainly but not exclusively Whigs, who questioned whether political rights should be determined by religious beliefs, and in particular allegiance to the Established Church. In 1828, therefore, the Test and Corporation Acts were repealed, with little opposition from the Church of England, since it concerned Protestants only.

However, it did not prove possible to separate entirely this reform from the position of the Roman Catholic Church, whose members remained subject to the old Penal Laws. The government was driven to remedial action by the eruption of discontent in Ireland over the provisions of the Act of Union of 1800. This had provided for 100 MPs to be elected to the Westminster Parliament, but if any of these were Roman Catholics they would be unable to take their seats in the House of Commons. The Roman Catholic majority in Southern Ireland had put up with this for many years but were now in open rebellion and the British army commander sought reinforcements to deal with the violence. In these circumstances, the government decided that, in spite of widespread opposition in the country, the emancipation of Roman Catholics would be a lesser evil than civil war in Ireland.

The public debate that followed the publication of the necessary parliamentary Bill in 1828 was hardly edifying. The Church of England generally was opposed, the parish clergy solidly so. There was talk of the country being 'once again ruled by priests' – an opinion fuelled by the Archbishop of Armagh, Marcus Beresford, who forecast that Roman Catholic MPs 'would in effect be agents and commissioners of the Roman priesthood, sent thither to give utterance to the sentiments, and to manage the interests of that body; a body, it should be recollected, which has objects to gain and views to promote, irreconcilable with the general good of the empire'.

Most of the English bishops preferred, however, to concentrate on the constitutional aspects of the proposed emancipation. They were led by the Archbishop of Canterbury, William Howley. Born in 1776 at Ropley in Hampshire, where his father was the Vicar, Howley was the last Archbishop to wear a wig, and, although he lived until 1848, he remained essentially an eighteenth-century figure. After Winchester and New College, Oxford, he was ordained and worked for some years as a private tutor in Somerset before becoming Regius Professor of Divinity and a Canon of Christ Church, Oxford.

He owed this appointment to royal influence, though he was capable as well as likeable, even if somewhat shy. At his consecration as Bishop of London in 1813, Queen Charlotte, the consort of George III, was present, together with two of the royal princes. This was the time of the Regency, the King being too ill to reign, and Howley's loyalty to the Prince Regent as well as his opposition to Catholic Emancipation, led in 1828 to his translation to Canterbury. The Prime Minister, the Duke of Wellington, was strongly opposed to this but King George IV, as he had become, insisted.

On the Emancipation issue Howley took the line that change would be incompatible with the Constitution and even more with the Coronation Oath that required the Sovereign to uphold the Protestant religion. The King felt this no less strongly and refused to sanction the appointment to bishoprics of any priest who supported emancipation.

Some bishops nonetheless did, including the Whig Bishop of Norwich, Henry Bathurst, who said, 'For more than half a century I have been uniformly of the opinion that civil disabilities on account of religious tenets are inconsistent with true ideas of justice, of policy and of Christian charity.' Thomas Arnold, the liberally minded Headmaster of Rugby School, felt moved to publish a pamphlet entitled *The Christian Duty of Conceding the Roman Catholic Claims*. In this, he argued that natural justice required acceptance and that only lack of faith and unholy zeal could lead anyone to suppose that God might be served by injustice.

Other bishops, eschewing theological and ethical issues, were persuaded that the Bill might actually strengthen the Constitution by bringing within its embrace the three and a half million Roman Catholics (out of a total population of 14 million inhabitants of England and Wales). Thus, at its second and third readings in the House of Lords in 1829, ten bishops voted in favour, with 20, including Archbishop Howley, against. The many opponents of the Bill were, however, eventually won over by the insertion of several safeguards, designed to protect the Church of England and the Protestant inheritance more generally. The problem now was how to achieve this without giving Roman Catholics the impression that they had not after all been emancipated.

The existing law already excluded them from occupying the throne and under the new order they would also be excluded from the offices of Regent, Lord Chancellor, Lord Chancellor of Ireland, Lord Lieutenant of Ireland and High Commissioner to the Church of Scotland. There was some discussion as to whether or not the Prime Minister might be a Roman Catholic, the problem being that he would have to advise the Crown on many Church of England appointments. A proposal that Roman Catholics be excluded from this office did not find favour, but, on the suggestion of Bishop John Sumner of Chester and destined for Canterbury, it was somewhat reluctantly agreed that, should there ever be a Roman Catholic Prime Minister, ecclesiastical matters would be dealt with by a commission. Catholic Members of Parliament would be required to take a special oath:

> I do hereby disclaim, disavow, and solemnly abjure any intention to subvert the present church establishment as settled by law within this realm; and do solemnly swear that I will never exercise any privilege to which I am, or may become, entitled, to disturb or weaken the Protestant religion or Protestant government in this United Kingdom.

Other requirements included the prohibition of Catholic bishops from being given the geographical titles of existing Church of England sees, of bishops, priests and monks wearing ecclesiastical dress in public and of further recruitment to religious orders.

The bishops, along with most of the other opponents, now fell into line, and the Emancipation Act was passed. They were, however, virtually unanimous in their opposition to the proposed changes to the parliamentary electoral system that led to the 1832 Great Reform Act. This brought them immense unpopularity in the country and did considerable damage to the Church's reputation.

The system the bishops sought to uphold made no pretence to be democratic, only one in seven of the adult population having the franchise. Moreover, this could be exercised only within a chaotic ordering of constituencies that had not changed significantly since medieval times, when the country was first divided into counties and county boroughs. Power in the former was exercised by great landholders, while the mercantile and commercial classes were supposed to be most influential in the latter. In the allocation of seats in the House of Commons no account was taken, however, of the considerable population changes that had taken place by the beginning of the nineteenth century.

Thus one borough might now be no more than a hamlet, yet entitled to return two MPs, while another had grown into a large city but had only one. Buckingham with 149 electors had the same number of MPs as Leeds with 4,172 electors. Even worse, there were rarely elections in the small ('rotten') boroughs, since a single candidate was nominated by a local wealthy landholder, whose wishes went unchallenged. Bribery was common and those with enough money and land accumulated many votes and widespread patronage. The corrupt system was characteristically described and condemned by the clergyman wit, Sydney Smith – at the time Rector of Combe Florey in Somerset and a Canon of Bristol Cathedral: 'The country belongs to the Duke of Rutland, Lord Lonsdale, the Duke of Newcastle and about 20 other holders of boroughs. They are our masters.'

The need for political reform was talked about long before firm steps were taken to find a remedy, but revolution in France made governments unwilling to take steps that might produce instability in Westminster. Some believed, however, that reform was more urgently needed in order to prevent revolution, or at least to make it easier to maintain law and order, and this belief became more commonly held when widespread unemployment created unrest in the large towns and cities.

The fact that the Whigs were wealthy aristocratic landholders did not prevent them from leading the way to reform, and their modest proposals were incorporated into the Great Reform Bill which was passed easily in the House of Commons in 1831. It was, however, fiercely resisted in the House of Lords and lost by 41 votes. Many of the Tory peers abstained. Not so the bishops, all but one of whom had been appointed by the previous Tory administration. They turned up in force and, although only Archbishop Howley spoke in the debate, 20 voted against the Bill, two for it, these being the recently (Whig) appointed Bishop Maltby of Chichester and the ancient Bishop Bathurst of Norwich, a known liberal, who voted by proxy. There were six episcopal absentees.

Some historians have suggested that the bishops were not against reform as such but only against the terms in which the Bill was couched. Others have suggested that they were (with good reason, as it turned out) fearful that political reform would soon lead to demands for church reform. Archbishop Howley's position owed more to caution, as he made clear in a charge to his diocesan clergy. Having urged them to be vigilant in 'a season when the Church is assailed by many enemies', he went on:

> from the hour in which I was called to an office, at all times of most awful responsibility, and more especially in these days of rebuke and peril, my attention has been fixed on the subject, with an earnest desire for the correction of abuses, and the removal of blemishes . . . But that which at first sight offends is not always wrong. Parts, which singly considered are pronounced to be faulty, may be found on a larger survey to possess a relative excellence, and to contribute by their bearings on the whole of the system to a beneficial result. A system again, far short of theoretic perfection, may be exquisitely adapted to the combination of circumstances in this mixed state of things . . . I am unwilling to hazard its safety by rash innovation; nor could I venture to act without full consideration of the probable consequences of any given change.

The Bill's supporters were not impressed by this argument and during the next three months waged an unprecedented campaign of violent speech and action against the bishops. Other opposing peers were not excused, but the bishops' vote was regarded as the chief cause of the Bill's defeat.

A mob of 8,000 marched on Carlisle and burned an effigy of the Bishop in the market place. The Bishop of Lichfield and Coventry was advised that if he ventured into Coventry he would be thrown into a pond. Archbishop Howley, often described either as Herod or as Pontius Pilate, was heckled when he addressed a meeting in Croydon, and on his return to Lambeth Palace a dead cat was thrown into his carriage. His chaplain remarked that this was better than a live cat might have been. The carriage of the Bishop of Bath and Wells was stoned on his return from the consecration of a new church.

The worst violence was experienced, however, at Bristol and Exeter, where mobs set fire to the episcopal palaces. At Exeter, the coastguards were called in to defend the arch-conservative Bishop Henry Phillpots whose effigy, along with that of Guy Fawkes, was consigned to a bonfire.

Three men who were believed to have instigated the Exeter riot were subsequently hanged for their pains. Placards denouncing the bishops were displayed everywhere, the contrast between the luxury in which they lived and the plight of the poor was emphasized, and the desirability of their continuing to sit in the House of Lords was questioned.

More constructively, Sydney Smith became active in a campaign to get the House of Lords decision reversed. Born in 1771, he went from Winchester to New College, Oxford, where he gained a fellowship and then served as a curate. This was followed by a spell as tutor to a wealthy family, after which he used his writing skills as first editor of the *Edinburgh Review* – a journal of high literary merit and committed to political and social reform. Soon, however, he was drawn to London and, although not a Whig by birth, was co-opted into the coterie as a kind of Wit-in-Residence. In constant demand for dinner parties, Smith provided unique entertainment and also developed gourmet tastes:

Tory and Whig in turns
shall be my host;
I taste no politics
in boil'd and roast.

It was in fact in Whig circles that he moved almost exclusively, but their influence in church preferment was limited to getting him appointed in 1806 as Rector of the dull and neglected parish of Foston, about eight miles from York. His wife's substantial private income enabled him, however, to make frequent trips back to his old haunts in London to keep up his social and political contacts.

Some relief came in 1828 when a Tory Lord Chancellor, who chanced to be a personal friend, made him a Canon Residentiary of Bristol Cathedral, to which was soon attached the Somerset parish of Combe Florey. He eventually became a notable Canon of St Paul's. At the time of the Catholic Emancipation debate, a sermon in Bristol Cathedral on the virtues of tolerance (a favourite subject) greatly annoyed the protestant Mayor and Corporation, and he later went to a meeting at Taunton to make a telling short speech in favour of the Great Reform Bill:

As for the House of Lords preventing ere long a reform of Parliament, I hold it to be the most absurd notion that ever entered into the human imagination. I do not mean to be disrespectful, but the attempt of the Lords to stop the progress of reform reminds me very forcibly of the storm of Sidmouth, and of the conduct of the excellent Mrs Partington on that occasion. In the winter of 1824 there set in a great flood upon that town – the tide rose to an incredible height – the waves rushed in upon the houses and everything was threatened with destruction. In the midst of this sublime and terrible storm, Dame Partington, who lived upon the beach, was seen at the door of her house with mop and patterns, trundling her mop, squeezing out the sea water, and vigorously pushing away the Atlantic Ocean. The Atlantic was roused. Mrs Partington's spirit was up, but I need not tell you that the contest was unequal. The Atlantic Ocean beat Mrs Partington. She was excellent at a slop or a puddle, but she should not have meddled with a tempest. Gentlemen, be at your ease – be quiet and steady. You will beat Mrs Partington.

This contribution was much enjoyed and went the rounds, giving encouragement to reformers and great annoyance to the bishops and other backwoodsmen peers. Bishop Blomfield of London, who was not opposed to reform as his record in church matters would soon demonstrate, had thought it best to sit on the fence when the House of Lords voted. But the Prime Minister, Lord Grey, persuaded him to come off it and, in combination with the King, got sufficient other bishops to change their minds. Thus, when the Bill returned to the House of Lords in April 1832, 12 bishops voted in favour and 16, including Archbishop Howley, against. This time, however, there was sufficient overall support for it to be carried.

But the defeated peers did not give up and a month later moved an amendment designed to postpone the full implementation of the Bill. Howley and some other bishops supported this amendment and again provoked the wrath of reformers among the public. On his arrival at Canterbury for a Visitation of the diocese, Howley was greeted by a hostile crowd, which hurled various objects at his carriage and broke a window. The Archbishop of York, who was too decrepit to know what he had voted for, was burnt in effigy outside Bishopthorpe, the palace itself suffering a broken fence and a number of broken windows. Bishop Ryder of Chester attempted to preach a charity sermon before the Lord Mayor in St Bride's, Fleet Street, but his words were drowned by hissing and booing, fighting broke out, and he was obliged to flee in his carriage, followed by the mob.

In spite of the bishops, however, the Bill passed into law, leaving future generations to wonder why its modest achievements had created so much fuss. Voter registration was introduced and polling was restricted to two, rather than 40, days. Birmingham, Manchester, Bradford and 38 other large towns were given representation for the first time, but, although the Rotten Boroughs were abolished, the average size of the electorates of the reorganized, but unevenly distributed, boroughs (responsible for returning almost half of the 658 MPs) was still under 900. The Whig reformers had been unanimous in requiring that the franchise be restricted to those who were deemed sufficiently well educated and owners of property valued at no less than £10. Furthermore it was for the first time decreed, rather than simply accepted, that only males should be allowed to vote. A petition for women to be included in the new arrangements had been dismissed in the House of Commons as 'facetious'.

The size of the electorate was increased from about 400,000 to about 650,000, but 95 per cent of the population remained unfranchized. The improvement was no more than one in seven to one in six eligible to vote and the continuing dissatisfaction of the powerless soon led to the formation of the Chartist movement which pressed for more radical change.

The middle decades of the nineteenth century proved to be a time of political instability where further parliamentary reform, though increasingly urged, proved to be impossible. In 1866, however, the Liberal administration of the ageing Earl Russell, a former Whig, produced a number of proposals: the property qualification in the boroughs to be reduced from £10 to £7, the occupancy qualification in the counties from £50 to £14. Non-householders who lived in expensive lodgings (perhaps as many as 60,000) were to be given the vote, as also the thrifty who maintained a deposit of at least £50 in a savings bank. A modest redistribution of parliamentary seats was envisaged. Overall about a million more names would be added to the electoral register.

These could hardly be regarded as radical proposals, but they were sufficient to arouse fierce opposition and it needed a series of highly skilled political manoeuvres, in which Disraeli outwitted W. E. Gladstone, the new Liberal leader, to secure the passing in 1867 of what became known as the Second Reform Act. The consequences proved to be far more important than its specific proposals, inasmuch as the increase in the number of voters in the towns eventually created a different political climate in which parliamentary candidates needed the organized backing of supporters. The modern party system was born. Five years later the secret ballot was introduced.

Another significant change had taken place a little earlier when the bishops, heavily preoccupied with the effects of enforced church reform, attended the House of Lords much less frequently – some never. Only matters concerned with the life of the Church itself brought them from their dioceses to Westminster, and they took no part in the debates on the new Reform Bill.

They were, however, stirred to action in 1884 by Gladstone, now Prime Minister. There was still much to be done when, of the 652 MPs, 394 were nobles, baronets, landed gentry or their near relations. A Third Reform Bill proposed a further, more carefully drawn, redistribution of representation, some extension of the franchise, giving rural and urban voters equal rights, the capping of the amount of election expenses, and steps designed to eliminate corruption.

This provoked strong Conservative, and some Liberal, dissension, so when Gladstone calculated that the passage of the Bill in the House of Lords was threatened, he wrote to all the bishops seeking their support. The Archbishop of Canterbury, Edward White Benson, had already told him that he believed the proposals would lead 'fast into revolution', but agreed not to propagate this opinion. Gladstone's letter hinted that support for the Bill would indicate that the bishops were on the side of the people, and when the time for voting came, all but the Bishop of Gloucester, Charles Ellicott, decided not to risk a repeat of the 1832 events. The Bill passed and Queen Victoria expressed surprise that so many bishops whom she considered good were 'on the wrong side'.

The remaining years of the nineteenth century witnessed the rise of movements aiming to secure voting rights for women. Chief among these was the National Union of Women's Suffrage Societies (NUWSS) founded in 1872, but lack of achievement led to the foundation in 1905 of the more militant Women's Social and Political Union. Led by the militant, courageous Emmeline Pankhurst, the Suffragettes, as they came to be known, engaged in a campaign designed to compel politicians and the public generally to take notice of their claims – sometimes by resorting to violence.

The bishops frowned on their activities and made little effort to engage with their concerns. Not so Maude Royden – a remarkable Anglican who shared their concerns but objected to violence, and so joined a revived NUWSS, editing its weekly journal *Common Cause* and later joining its executive. Born in 1876 into the large family of Sir Thomas Royden, a wealthy Liverpool shipowner and highly regarded Lord Mayor of the city, she went from Cheltenham Ladies College to Lady Margaret Hall, Oxford, during the time when women were allowed to take the same university examinations as men but were not awarded degrees.

After a short spell of social work in Liverpool, Royden returned to Oxford, where she joined the university's Extension Delegacy and, after some hesitation by its leaders on account of her gender, became one of its most brilliant lecturers. Also lecturing for the Delegacy was Hudson Shaw, who was also Vicar of South Luffenham in Rutland. His wife being seriously ill with an emotional problem, he engaged Maude to assist him in the parish, and there developed a lifelong, chaste relationship akin to marriage.

An increasing amount of work for the NUWSS took her on speaking engagements, often to crowded meetings, all over the country, and in 1913 she organized a massive nationwide pilgrimage designed to highlight the suffrage issue in the context of women's rights more generally. At a service in St Paul's Cathedral, no woman was allowed to take part, so she spoke on 'The Pilgrim Spirit' to a crowded congregation in the Ethical Church nearby. A year later, she was one of the speakers when Suffragists, as the NUWSS members were called, joined forces with Labour Party members to pack London's Albert Hall.

In 1914, however, she parted company with the NUWSS because of its support for the war – she being a deeply committed pacifist – but all women's suffrage campaigning was suspended for the duration of hostilities. Nine years earlier she had also become the first chair of the Church League for Women's Suffrage (CLWS), of which the reformist Bishop of Lincoln, Edward Lee Hicks, was the chairman and her only episcopal supporter. The League had the uphill task of trying to persuade church people, particularly the clergy, that women should have the vote, but Maude soon came to believe that the issue could not be separated from the leadership of women in the Church at every level, including the priesthood.

The decision after the end of the war in 1918 to grant the vote to women over the age of 30 led her to concentrate her efforts on the Church and, although lacking ordination, she became an outstanding London preacher, first at the Congregational City Temple, then at The Guildhouse – a frontier-type church, created in collaboration with Canon Percy Dearmer, which for about a decade attracted large congregations to Kensington.

The women's suffrage movement had the support of some parish clergy, but, although the bishops were generally in favour of some women having the vote, only Bishop Edward Lee Hicks was active in promoting their cause. They were, however, stirred to condemn the suffragettes for their violent activities. The Archbishop of Canterbury, Randall Davidson, received a huge mail on the broader issue and usually replied that, while he had for years taken a keen interest in the subject and voted in favour of women's suffrage on the one opportunity he had been given to do so, his influence on legislative change was minimal. He called for prayer for guidance on the issue and an end to the violence.

This did not satisfy Dr Ethel Smyth, a suffragette leader, who roundly rebuked him for his 'inaction' and warned him that 'the interruption of church services is to be our policy'. Action quickly followed, and demonstrations were held in a large number of churches, including Westminster Abbey. St Paul's Cathedral was, however, the main target, and in the summer of 1913, 20 women stood up during the Litany and sang their own version, which began 'Save Emmeline Pankhurst'. When asked to leave, they refused and had to be ejected. Two months later they returned to chant prayers and clung to their chairs when attempts were made to eject them. In the ensuing scuffle, a verger was given a black eye. The protesters were carried off screaming.

The Bishop of London, the amiable Arthur Foley Winnington-Ingram, strongly favoured women's franchise but was not exempt from suffragette attention, as his chaplain, Guy Vernon Smith (later Bishop of Leicester) recorded:

The methods of the more militant women were disagreeable as well as exaggerated. Once we were in his study at about 9 pm. There were French windows – open all day in summer – but the long curtains had been drawn. Suddenly a suffagette sprang forth from behind the curtains. The Bishop rose instantly, saying 'Will you deal with this lady' as he left the room. I was obliged to carry her in my arms down the long passage and, after depositing her on the door-mat, to lock the door. Once the Dean's Verger at St Paul's rang up to say that a bomb had been found in the Bishop's throne. True, it was not much of a bomb by modern standards but it *was* a bomb. Once London House in St James's Square (where the Bishop lived in winter) was rushed by about thirty women while I was out for my evening walk in St James's Park. The news was given on my return by the butler, Mr Wilkin, looking unusually solemn and scared: 'They are all in the dining room and refuse to go until they have seen his Lordship.' The Bishop was about to start for an evening engagement. We tip-toed out of the house and off he went. Then I entered the dining room. After a short discussion they rose and departed. The Lay Secretary had told them it was most improper to invade an unmarried man's house, but that did not move them.

Herbert Hensley Henson, at the time Dean of Durham and later to become a notable bishop of that diocese, was in no doubt that women were singularly unfitted for any political role since they would introduce an emotional element into decision-making. While Maude Royden was addressing 2,000 men at a Church Congress in Southampton in 1913, Henson was chairing a meeting of the Anti-Female Suffrage Society held in another part of the town. Until the end of his life in September 1947, he was convinced that the giving of the vote to women was a serious mistake in the development of the British Constitution. But he did not vote against the legislation in 1928, when the qualifying age for women was reduced to 21, in line with that of men. The reduction to 18 for both came in 1969.

3

Socialism with a Christian Soul

The first Christian Socialists were a small group led by a prophet-theologian, a novelist-priest and a politician–barrister who, between 1848 and 1854, sought to declare and express in practical terms an alternative to the secular revolutionary ideas then aflame in Europe and to a lesser extent in the Chartist movement in Britain. But the term 'Christian Socialist', chosen by the prophet-theologian Frederick Denison Maurice, is not as helpful as a description of what they were about.

The programme of social action they had in mind bears hardly any resemblance to what came to be regarded as Socialism embracing wide state intervention in the national economy, public ownership of the means and distribution of many spheres of production, and a welfare state. No overthrow of the existing social order was envisaged, and the extension of the franchise to all adults was considered by Maurice and Charles Kingsley undesirable until the working classes were educated to a level at which they could be trusted to cast their votes responsibly. In any event, each class should recognize its established place in society and seek to live caringly and sacrificially.

There were, however, two social problems that required early attention, the first of these being wages. This was not simply a question of remedying the low rates paid to both skilled and unskilled workers but also, and mainly, a change in the relationship between employer and employee. The Christian Socialists saw the imbalance in this as contrary to the laws of God's Kingdom relating to sharing.

Steps were therefore taken to set up Associations, something akin to what would now be called Workers' Co-operatives or Profit-Sharing Partnerships. With the aid of capital provided by rich supporters, a few of these were established and functioned for a time, but human cupidity as well as lack of competitive edge ensured that their success was short-lived.

The other initiative – less difficult and more successful – was concerned with education, the improvement of which had to be extended to all classes of society if all were to be free and equipped to play their fullest part in a Kingdom-orientated society. A Working Men's College was established, with Maurice as its first Principal, in Red Lion Square in London in 1854. Designed by him to be a community of teachers and pupils sharing a common search for a wisdom and learning that would enable both to become more useful citizens, many notable teachers were recruited, including on the arts side Ruskin, Rossetti, Lowes Dickinson and Ford Maddox Brown, who all gave their services. The enterprise flourished and continues today as a College of Adult Education.

Charles Kingsley, born in 1819 and the son of a clergyman, was a Victorian clerical polymath who based his entire ministry on the rural parish of Eversley in North Hampshire. He was nonetheless one of the best known figures in England – a remarkable character and widely read author; two of his novels, *Westward Ho!* and *The Water Babies*, have never been out of print.

His membership of a small group of men who formed a pioneering, and short-lived, Christian Socialist movement in the 1850s was due to several influences. Witnessing, as a schoolboy, the Bristol riots that followed the House of Lords rejection of the First Great Reform Bill left him, as he put it, 'full of hatred and contempt for those dangerous classes I had for the first time discovered'. But Magdalene College, Cambridge, ordination and a long courtship with Fanny Grenville, a devout Tractarian, led to a different perspective through association with one of her family's friends, Sydney Osborne. He was Rector of Durwent in Dorset and wrote letters to *The Times* for 40 years on various aspects of social justice. After staying with him on several occasions, Kingsley was driven to assert, 'The refined man is he who cannot rest in peace with a coal mine or a factory, or a Dorsetshire peasant's house near him in the state they are.'

By this time, he had been curate of Eversley for two years and learned quite a lot about the lives of peasants, gypsies and deer-stalkers, and when he succeeded to the Rectory in 1844, their physical as well as their spiritual welfare became his primary concern. Although afflicted with a stammer, he was an electrifying preacher, and people came from far and wide to hear him speak of the love of God, the holiness of nature and Christ's compassion for the poor, the sick and the oppressed.

Another important influence was that of Frederick Denison Maurice, and after he, Kingsley and J. M. Ludlow had launched the Christian Socialist movement in 1848, he contributed a column to the weekly publication *Politics for People* under the pseudonym Parson Lot. In this, he made a special point of emphasizing that the Bible reveals a God who has a special concern for the poor – 'You say that the poor man has his rights as well as the rich – so says the Bible; and it says more: God inspires the poor with the desire of liberty and helps them to their rights.' This so alarmed King's College, London, that it withdrew the offer to him of a part-time teaching post.

In the same year, Kingsley's first novel, *Yeast*, began to appear in instalments in *Fraser's Magazine*. This expressed his sympathy for the rural poor and drew heavily on his own experience at Eversley, with material relating to injustice, inadequate sanitation and education, and the indifference of the wealthy. But this was not what the well-off subscribers to the magazine wanted to read, and the editor found himself facing a storm of protest. The novel had therefore to be brought to a too-early conclusion.

Undeterred, he changed publishers for his next novel, *Alton Locke* (1850). This was concerned with the plight of the urban poor and developed from his pamphlet *Cheap Clothes and Nasty*, which had exposed the iniquities of the rag trade's sweat shops. The language was fierce, sometimes vitriolic, and Thomas Carlyle told him, 'While welcoming a new explosion of red-hot shot against the Devil's Dung-heap, I must admit your book is definable as crude.'

These defects did not prevent the novel from being widely noticed and it was also used by Kingsley as an opportunity to answer the charge sometimes made, that the Christian Socialists were really the hated Chartists in disguise. He spoke frequently at public meetings and considerable controversy arose over a sermon on 'The Message of the Church to the Working Man', which he preached in St John's, Charlotte Street, in London's West End in June 1851.

Westward Ho! (1855) was a very different sort of novel, being about unsavoury sea-dogs and patriotism, but it became a best-seller, bringing its author fame and respectability and putting the newly founded Macmillan publishing house on its feet. Different again, and a runaway success, was *The Water Babies* (1863) which, in a roundabout way, dealt with the great social evil of chimney sweep boys. Queen Victoria liked it and read it to her own children, but it was perhaps just a coincidence that the employment of climbing boys was made illegal a year after the novel's publication.

In 1860, the Prime Minister, Palmerston, ill-advisedly appointed him Regius Professor of Modern History at Cambridge – a post that was far beyond his capacity as a scholar and proved to be an embarrassment – but a Canonry of Chester Cathedral, then for the final two years of his life of Westminster Abbey, were highly successful. With the aid of curates, he retained his link with Eversley.

As his fame grew and his responsibilities increased, it became more difficult to identify his views with anything that might be included in the description Socialism. He certainly retained his deep concern for the poor and the underprivileged, but his romantic ideal was of a feudal society in which the different social classes recognized responsibility for those beneath them, leaving no one uncared for and everyone with sufficient for their needs – limited though they might be deemed to be. Nonetheless, he recognized that there could be no return to such a society.

He continued, however, to plead for better sanitation and was a long way ahead of his time in recognizing the connection between sanitation and health. His funeral at Eversley attracted a congregation from far and wide, including a number of generals and colonial governors, together with a group of gypsies, who called him their 'Patrico-rai' – their Priest-King.

Frederick Denison Maurice, the son of a radical Unitarian minister, was born in 1805 and brought up in a family of mixed religious beliefs. As a Dissenter, he was unable to take a degree at Cambridge but went to Trinity College and Trinity Hall with a view to becoming a lawyer. This did not materialize, and he spent a few years in London writing and editing a not very successful magazine. After baptism as an Anglican, he went to Exeter College, Oxford, to study Theology.

This led to ordination and a curacy at Bubbenhall, in Warwickshire, before securing appointment as chaplain of Guy's Hospital in London. Located on the south side of London Bridge and in the midst of appalling slums, Maurice was there for ten years, ministering to the poorest of the poor and also writing. *The Kingdom of Christ* was published in 1828. Motivated in part by the challenge of constructing a Christian response to the plight of the poor, as an alternative to the violent demands of the Chartists, this was a substantial book of philosophical and historical theology that dug deep and, in spite of its somewhat opaque style, is now regarded as one of the seminal works of Anglican theology.

His study of the Bible had convinced him of the essential unity of the divine and the human orders – the interlocking of the natural and the supernatural as demonstrated in the life, death and resurrection of Jesus Christ. In this incarnation, God disclosed his benevolent kingly rule over the entire creation, and when Jesus spoke, as he so often did, about the Kingdom of God, he was not inaugurating a new order, but drawing attention to and affirming something that already existed. His challenge, therefore, was to individual men and women to order their lives and that of the societies around them in accordance with the laws of God's Kingdom, for only so can both flourish. This must inevitably involve opposition to all that denies the values of the Kingdom.

The character of the Kingdom, said Maurice, is to be seen and experienced in the life of the human family and also in the life of the Church – at least, potentially – for '[t]he Church is human society in its normal state; the world that same society irregular and abnormal'. Thus a close link between Church and State is essential, for both are under the sovereignty of God.

This profound theology was not of a sort to call the proletariat to the barricades. Nonetheless, the implications of it fully worked out and applied were alarming to some, since they would far exceed the demands of the contemporary European revolutionaries. The authorities at King's College, London, eventually dismissed him from the chair of Theology to which he had been appointed at the time of the book's publication, ostensibly for other beliefs that were believed to be heretical, but anxiety about his Socialism was a more likely explanation.

In 1848, the publication year of *The Communist Manifesto*, a young Lincoln's Inn barrister, John Malcolm Forbes Ludlow, went to visit his mother in Paris and witnessed some of the violence on the streets, then at its height. He wrote to Maurice, his chaplain, and told him that unless Socialism were Christianized, it would inevitably overwhelm Christianity.

On his return to London, he accepted an invitation from Maurice to call on him to discuss the implications of what he had experienced in Paris, and this led to a further meeting on 10 April 1848, attended by Charles Kingsley, at which the Christian Socialist movement was launched. The purpose, explained by Maurice in a letter to Ludlow, was

> to show that economy and politics must have a ground beneath themselves, that society is not to be made anew by arrangements of ours, but is to be regenerated by finding the law and ground of its order and harmony, the only secret of its existence in God.

Workers did not flock into membership, but a weekly publication, *Politics for the People*, sold for a penny, and achieved a circulation of 2,000 by July. Its contents, especially those contributed by Kingsley, were nothing if not radical, though the slogan of the French Revolution was changed significantly from 'Liberty, Equality, Fraternity' to 'Liberty, Fraternity, Unity'. The paper was sharply criticized from within the Church, and, although none of its contributors were paid, it ran out of money and, after 17 issues, folded.

A series of *Tracts on Socialism* took its place, and Maurice and his colleagues continued to expound their beliefs whenever and wherever they could. A number of younger men, including Tom Hughes, the famed author of *Tom Brown's Schooldays*, joined them, but by 1860 the movement had run out of steam, and the energies of its leaders were turned in other directions.

There is less to be written about Ludlow, but he was no less significant among the triumvirate who led the small and short-lived Christian Socialist movement. A layman, he was a barrister by training and a politician by instinct, and, although he was not without theological acumen, his approach was always concerned with practical outcomes. He was younger than either Maurice or Kingsley, and his long life was devoted, in one way or another, to the welfare of the underprivileged.

The son of an Indian army colonel, Ludlow was born in India in 1821, but his father died when he was only six months old, and his mother then moved with her children to Paris. His upbringing there was formative, and, although he was sent to Merchant Taylors' School in England, he had, by the time he reached Lincoln's Inn for training as a lawyer, seen much of the plight of the Parisian poor and the violence of their revolutionary activity on the streets.

A return to Paris to visit his mother in February 1848 coincided with the climax of the Revolution, and it was in Paris on this same visit that he wrote to Maurice with the warning of the need for Socialism to be Christianized, otherwise it would shake Christianity, because 'it appeals to the higher and not the lower instincts in man'.

It was this letter and the subsequent meetings with Maurice and Kingsley that led quickly to the formation of the Christian Socialists. His relationship with Maurice became close, close enough to survive sharp conflicts of opinion and wounding candour. As far as policy was concerned, Maurice always had the last word but, having witnessed with Kingsley the fiasco of a failed procession that spelt the end of the Chartists, he never ceased to press for action that would enable Christian Socialists to take their place. In this he was frustrated, as he was in his attempt to put universal suffrage on the agenda.

When, however, *Politics for People* failed for lack of money, Ludlow was entrusted with the founding and editing of the *Christian Socialist* newspaper, which flourished for a time, though its title was soon changed to *Journal of Associations*. This reflected its author's special interest in the setting up of worker co-operatives along the lines of the enterprises which had impressed him in Paris. He saw these as a means of undermining the existing economic system and ultimately changing the whole social order, whereas Maurice and Kingsley saw them simply as a form of economic protest and part of a wider movement of social transformation.

Earlier Ludlow had been unsuccessful in securing the support of Maurice for a proposed National Health League that would promote throughout Britain better sanitation systems, clear water and air, housing and the environment generally. But he was continuously engaged in social and mission work among London's poor, and at one time hoped to establish something akin to a women's deaconess order, of the sort he had admired in Paris. Again, however, Maurice did not approve, so he joined a secular Strangers' Friend Society working in the slums. In an article in *Fraser's Magazine* he outlined a vision for the Church of the future:

The care of the sick, the reformation of the prisoner, the government of the adult pauper, the training of the pauper child, are all work which I am fully convinced can never be adequately performed either by mere mercenary skill or by solitary self-devotion, but require both a special religious vocation to the individual and the support and comfort of an organized fellowship. We must have Orders of nurses, Orders of prison attendants, Orders of workhouse matrons, workhouse teachers, parish surgeons, bodies of men and women that show forth in its purity the essential communism of the Church and leaven the whole of society with a spirit of self-devoted industry.

However, marriage in 1869 to a cousin, for whom he had patiently waited 20 years, took him away from the front line. Two years earlier he had written, in collaboration with Lloyd Jones, *Progress of the Working Class 1832–67*, and from 1875 to 1891 was Chief Registrar of Friendly Societies, a task for which his experience of mutual and friendly societies and his legal expertise well equipped him. He was one of the first members, and subsequently President, of the Labour Co-Partnership Association.

By the time of his death in 1911, the Christian Socialists had become a small part of Victorian history. Theirs had been a bold, albeit brief, experiment doomed to failure because, as explained by G. D. H. Cole in his study of *A Century of Co-operation*: 'The Christian Socialists aspired to convert the working classes to an impossibly high moral code, and to a theological approach which most working men were quite unable to accept.' Nonetheless, they sowed in soil that had been barren for over two centuries the seeds of a Christian social doctrine that, later in the nineteenth century, would spring to life in different forms and ensure that the Church of England would never again easily neglect this element of its mission.

Another two decades passed before any organized form of Christian Socialism emerged, though there were priests, and some bishops, who exercised personal ministries expressive of deep social concern.

Chief among these was James Fraser, the 'Citizen Bishop of Manchester', who from 1870 to 1876 was one of the most remarkable nineteenth-century church leaders. His earlier ministry did not, however, suggest any likelihood of this. Born in 1818 in Gloucestershire, his father died when he was only 14, leaving a wife and seven children in poor straits. James was subsequently brought up by his grandfather in Shropshire, who sent him to Shrewsbury School.

After taking a First in Classics at Lincoln College, Oxford, struggling all the time to pay his bills, he was ordained to a Fellowship of Oriel College. This he held for seven years; then, after 12 constructive years in a

Wiltshire parish, settled in Ufton Nervet in Berkshire, where he was happily engaged in a pastoral ministry and farming his glebe.

That the Prime Minister, W. E. Gladstone, should have turned to such a priest to become the second bishop of one of the most important and most difficult of dioceses must seem incredible in the present era of application forms, shortlists and interviews. Manchester was throughout the nineteenth century at the heart of Britain's Industrial Revolution. Its population grew at a phenomenal rate, creating a multitude of new and seemingly intractable social and religious problems.

It is hardly surprising then that Fraser, who knew nothing of industrial England, accepted the offer with trepidation. He had earlier declined the Bishopric of Calcutta on the grounds that he was too old at 48. Gladstone in fact nominated him for Manchester because he needed his support in the House of Lords for certain education reforms, he being well known for his mastery of education. But, possessed of enormous energy, he threw himself into the Manchester challenge and maintained the momentum for 15 years.

By the time of his death in office in 1885, he was the most respected man in Lancashire, and on the day of his funeral many businesses in Manchester closed, the Cotton Exchange ceased trading for several hours, and many thousands of people lined the streets as MPs, mayors and magistrates from all parts of Lancashire went in procession from the town hall to the Cathedral. It was said that he had been 'the prince and leader in every movement of civic progress, civic elevation, civic righteousness, for whom Mayors and Corporations were not less interesting than Archdeacons and Rural Deans'. Later, a statue paid for by public subscription was erected in his memory in Albert Square.

In his first speech to the diocesan conference, Fraser said, 'Our Church must show that in her wide and tolerant bosom every legitimate form of Christianity must find a home.' He added that he would never occupy a position of neutrality on any subject on which a bishop might reasonably be expected to hold an opinion. Neither did he.

It took him only a few weeks to decide that if ever the Church was to fulfil its mission, it must engage much more closely with the working class and the poorest in society. He became involved in virtually every organization concerned with social work and the improvement of the human lot and was in constant demand for sermons and speeches, often as many as six or seven a day. Lunchtime addresses were given in factories, mills and railway works. Much time was spent with boatmen on canals, scavengers and night-soil men. 'What is wanted', he declared, 'is not so much to Christianize our Socialism as to Socialize our Christianity.'

At a Church Congress held in Leeds in 1872, he advocated support of the infant trade unions – 'A labourer has a legitimate right to combine for the purpose of improving his earthly conditions' – and two years later, when arbitrators failed to agree over a wages claim by painters, he was called in to act as umpire and made an award that both sides accepted. This led to his employment as an arbitrator in other disputes, but when striking cotton workers in north-east Lancashire called for his services in 1878, the employers refused to accept him.

A dispute involving agricultural workers in another part of the county led him to ask in a published letter:

> Are the farmers of England mad? Fair wages will have to be paid to the labourer. If farmers can't afford fair wages at present, rents must come down – an unpleasant thing no doubt for those who will spend the rent of a 300-acre farm on a single ball or a pair of high-stepping horses, but nevertheless inevitable.

This brought him a mountain of letters – some abusive, others grateful – as well as a public rebuke from his neighbour, the evangelical Bishop J. C. Ryle of Liverpool. Another special concern was the development of the Co-operative movement and he presided over the first day of the 1878 Co-operative Congress. None of this led to any neglect of the Church's own life, and during his episcopate 99 new churches were built and 109 new parishes created.

Stewart Headlam was a colourful priest who, combining the sacramentalism of the early Tractarian Movement with the theological insights of F. D. Maurice and the pastoral concerns of Charles Kingsley, created in the Guild of St Matthew what is often regarded as the first modern Socialist society in Britain. Unlike these predecessors, he had an acute political sense and understood that true Socialism involved radical social and economic change.

Born in 1847 into the wealthy evangelical family of a Liverpool underwriter, he went to Eton, thence to Cambridge, where he attended the lectures of F. D. Maurice and Charles Kingsley. Ordination led to constant conflict with the ecclesiastical authorities of his time, most notably successive bishops of London, and after several brief curacies, terminated because of his beliefs and actions, he abandoned the idea of a parish ministry. Instead, he devoted his time to propagating Socialism, not least through his membership of the early Fabian Society, and also serving on London County Council. His independence was facilitated by a substantial private income.

Socialism was not the only, or even the chief, cause of his problems with the Church's hierarchy. Although the evangelical Bishop John Jackson had admitted him to the diaconate in 1869, he refused to ordain him to the priesthood the following year, having examined some of the essays he had been required to submit. These showed every sign of the influence of F. D. Maurice, in particular the belief that the ungodly were not destined for eternal punishment after death.

Even worse, perhaps, Headlam had, during his short time as a curate of St John's, Drury Lane, established pastoral contact with members of the theatrical profession who inhabited the area in considerable numbers. Many were later enrolled into a Church and Stage Guild. After a delay of two years, Headlam was eventually ordained to the priesthood, but, because he had spent this time in constant argument with the Bishop, the Vicar of St John's, who was generally a supporter, felt obliged to require his resignation. Several months of searching led to a curacy at St Matthew's, Bethnal Green, where most of the population were living in dire poverty. He was given responsibility for that part of the parish where poverty was at its worst.

By this time he was in touch with a number of other London curates with radical views and in 1877 formed a parish Guild of St Matthew (GSM). This was essentially a communicants' guild designed to encourage regular attendance at Holy Communion and observance of a disciplined Christian life. But its aims were much wider and he added later some words of Charles Kingsley, 'to justify God to the people', by which was meant the promulgation of those elements in Christian social doctrine that would ameliorate the conditions of the poor through the creation of a just and equal society.

Membership of the Guild in the parish grew to about 40, but Headlam was soon dismissed after giving a lecture in praise of the theatre and music halls which concluded, 'Above all, don't let us speak with scorn of the ladies who dance on the stage.' Both the rector and the bishop were appalled.

He took the GSM with him to another parish, St Michael's, Shoreditch, where the objects were revised to include '[t]o promote the study of social and political questions in the light of the Incarnation', and from 1884 onwards there was a much stronger emphasis on political action. Open-air meetings were started in Trafalgar Square, and a monthly journal, *The Church Reformer*, contained social and political comment, together with reviews of the theatre and dance. It survived until 1995, but his stay at St Michael's was brief as the congregation objected strongly to his views.

Next came a trial curacy at St George's Botolph, in the City of London, which was quickly terminated after he had spoken at a rally and called for the abolition of the House of Lords. Bishop Jackson firmly refused his request for a licence to work more widely in the diocese, as did his successor, Bishop Frederick Temple, whose broad churchmanship was not without limits. His letter was brief – 'The Bishop regrets that Mr Stewart D. Headlam appears to be doing serious mischief and, in holding this opinion, the Bishop is not able to give Mr Headlam facilities for doing more mischief.'

Meanwhile the membership of the GSM continued to rise, eventually reaching a peak of 364, of which 99 were Anglican clergy. But its Warden, Headlam, was increasingly involved in politics and, having left the Liberal Party, joined the executive committee of the Fabian Society, thus identifying himself with the development of the Labour Party. In 1907 he published *The Socialist Church* and in the same year was elected in the Progressive Group interest to the Greater London Council.

Concern for the arts and human freedom had led him in 1897 to contribute half the bail money, £5,000, needed to secure the release on remand of Oscar Wilde, who was facing a criminal trial arising from a homosexual relationship. He did not know Wilde, neither did he approve of his actions, but he believed that he should not be detained before trial. In 1906, he launched an Anti-Puritan League which attracted a few members, including G. K. Chesterton, but this did not survive for long. He continued to work in politics until his death in 1924.

Altogether different in style and method from the GSM was the Christian Social Union, founded in 1889 by Henry Scott Holland, a Canon of St Paul's Cathedral, and led by a group of distinguished, mainly Oxford, dons. Although there was a slight overlap in membership during CSU's early years, there was little love lost between the two organizations. Even so, their aims were broadly the same and are now best regarded as complementary attempts to arouse the social consciousness of the Church of England.

The main difference between Holland and Headlam, however, was that Holland was a serious and, in his day, a significant theologian – important enough to be invited to contribute to the ground-breaking symposium *Lux Mundi*, described in its introduction as 'an attempt to put the Christian faith into its right relation to modern intellectual and moral problems'.

Born at Ledbury, in Wiltshire, in 1846, Holland also came from a wealthy family and also went to Eton. At Balliol College, Oxford, he came under the influence of the Senior Tutor, T. H. Green, a distinguished philosopher who set his mind working on the social implications of religious faith. A congratulatory First in Greats led to a Senior Studentship (a Fellowship) at Christ Church. There he proved to be a born teacher, with well-attended courses of lectures on Plato's *Republic* and John's Gospel, was ordained in 1874, played a part in university life as Senior Proctor, conducted an eye-opening mission at Hoxton in London's East End, and published a book of particularly fine sermons, *Logic and Life*, which undoubtedly led in 1884 to his appointment, at the early age of 38, to St Paul's. Several other books of sermons followed, and these were the chief expressions of his thought.

He believed that 'the role of the Anglican Church is to convince society that duty to God and duty to man are the same thing', and the foundation of the Christian Social Union in 1889 was intended to win wider recognition of this role. Its aims were outlined in a leaflet:

This Union consists of Churchmen who have the following objects at heart:
(i) To claim for the Christian Law the ultimate authority to rule social practice.
(ii) To study in common how to apply the moral truths and principles of Christianity to the social and economic difficulties of the present time.
(iii) To present Christ in practical life as the Living Master and King, the enemy of wrong and selfishness, the power of righteousness and love.

The essentially religious character of the enterprise was emphasized by the expectation that its members would pray for the well-being of the Union at Holy Communion, 'more particularly on or about the Feast of the Epiphany, the Feast of the Ascension, the Feast of St Michael and All Angels'. It was not to be confused with politically orientated Socialist bodies.

With Bishop Brooke Foss Westcott of Durham as President, and Bishop Charles Gore of Birmingham, then Oxford, closely involved, the Union had to be taken seriously, and its membership grew very rapidly, eventually reaching about 6,000. Regional meetings were held in Birmingham, Manchester and Newcastle-upon-Tyne, and there were many local branches, of which that at Oxford was the most important. A small-scale periodical, *Goodwill*, was replaced in 1896 by the more substantial *Commonwealth*, which prospered for many years under Holland's editorship and became the main outlet of his social thought. A long series of pamphlets suggested solutions to a variety of social problems, including a minimum wage and state benefits for the unemployed.

Headlam accused the CSU of being 'too facile and not concerned with action', and there was a joke about its approach: 'Here's a glaring evil, let's read a paper about it.' Westcott's response to Headlam was that he confused eternal moral principles with a temporary and expedient programme of politicians.

Holland was certain that something more radical than settlements in slums was needed and that 'the structures of society must be changed in accordance with the principles of doing justice and the human brotherhood which the Gospel proclaims'. He thus favoured State intervention in certain situations, though he insisted that reform must always be driven by inner conviction and not imposed from outside.

The Oxford branch of the CSU was not only a distinguished think-tank, but also the initiator of practical measures such as a 'white list' of 20 local businesses that paid trade union wage-rates and therefore deserved support. 'White lists' were also produced in London and Leeds, and in 1890 Holland helped to form the Consumers' League, which had similar objectives. There was also CSU involvement in groups agitating for better working conditions in hazardous occupations and for women. Lewis Donaldson, Vicar of St Mark's, Leicester, and a member of the executive committee, led a protest march of unemployed men from Leicester to London.

In 1911, however, Scott Holland returned to Oxford as Regius Professor of Divinity, having been afforded the luxury of choosing between this post and the Deanery of Christ Church. That he should have been offered either was in fact a mistake. Good theologian that he undoubtedly was, the expression of his learning had been from the pulpit of St Paul's, and he had been far too busy with the CSU and other concerns to pursue the scholarly work that a professorship at Oxford, or any other university, demands. So the final phase of his great ministry was in many ways a disappointment and, inhibited by war and ill health, he died in 1918. The CSU had also declined in size and activity and was wound up soon afterwards.

The fact that it had once had as many as 6,000 members, of whom 16 became bishops between 1889 and 1913, indicates clearly that it was never destined to overthrow very much in either the Church or society. But it had an important influence on the Church inasmuch as it secured a place for social doctrine and action on its official agenda. No longer was the Church of England able to stand aside from events in the fast-moving society to which it belonged. Others were needed to take the movement forward, and some distinguished churchmen, most notably William Temple, embraced the concepts of Christian Socialism without necessarily including its name. Several lay Christian Socialists, not many of them Anglicans, served in the Cabinets of the Labour governments that won power in 1945 and 1997.

4

The Rise and Fall of Religious Education

Before about 1830 there was no national educational system in England. The sons of the upper and middle classes were prepared for the few public schools by tuition at home or by clergymen who took pupils into their rectories. The eighteenth century had seen the inauguration of the Sunday School movement, pioneered by Robert Raikes, under which some parishes augmented for a few hours the routine teaching of the Catechism. Other schools were started by Hannah Moore, while the Society for Promoting Christian Knowledge sponsored about 3,000 parish schools with the same limited aim of teaching children to read so that they might read the Bible. By 1811, there were sufficient church day schools to warrant the formation of a National Society for the Promoting of the Education of the Poor in the Principles of the Established Church, and three years later a British and Foreign Schools Society was formed with similar aims, except that religious education was provided only for the children of Dissenters.

During the 1820s, there had been discussions about a possible national system, but these were frustrated by disagreement over the Church's involvement in such a system. Canon Law required all schoolmasters in the land to hold a Bishop's licence. A proposal that the parish schools be given assistance from the local rate came to nothing because the Archbishop of Canterbury, Charles Manners-Sutton, could not accept any involvement by the magistrates. There was also the not uncommon contention that education might lead to discontent among the poor.

Nonetheless, escalating social change caused by rapid industrialization, coupled with the increased survival rate of newborn children, soon led the governing classes to recognize the urgent need for wider educational facilities, partly to equip pupils for employment in non-rural occupations, and partly to train them to be good citizens who would meet the needs of a changing, and potentially unstable social order. There were even some who believed that education was a good thing in itself.

It was still generally accepted that the education of children was a task for religious bodies, in particular the Church of England, whose parish schools were in the hands of clergymen – often the only educated men in the community – who trained one or two parishioners to share the task with them. All was fully integrated into the life of the church, attendance at school was not compulsory and did not extend beyond the age of 12 – sometimes earlier if fields, factories and mines needed 'hands'. A General Society of Education formed in 1831 to persuade the government to establish and pay for a national system of education from which religious teaching was excluded attracted little support and soon folded.

Instead, the government started to make grants of £20,000 per annum (each worth about £500,000 in today's money) to assist the National Society and the British and Foreign Schools with their work. Since, however, the grants were apportioned according to the ability of the applicants to raise their own money, most went to the Church of England. In 1839, the grants were increased to £30,000, but with the proviso that money could be paid directly to Roman Catholic and other schools outside the system and that all schools be open to inspection. Protests came immediately from Bishop Blomfield of London and, predictably, from arch-conservative Bishop Phillpots of Exeter, who objected to money going outside the Church of England and also claimed that inspection of schools would inhibit the freedom of the parish clergy. The Archbishop of Canterbury, William Howley, persuaded the House of Lords to address Queen Victoria on the subject.

The Whig government was not, however, intimidated and, strongly opposed to church control of schools, raised the possibility of a national secular system of education 'to prevent the growth of inordinate ecclesiastical pretensions, to vindicate the rights of conscience, and to lay the foundation of a system of combined education in which the young might be brought up in charity with each other, rather than in hostile camps'. Archbishop Howley, unimpressed by what seemed an alien philosophy, naturally objected, while the Bishop of Norwich, Edward Stanley, was convinced that 'Christian education alone deserves the name of education; it is through Christian knowledge only that we can hope to see the social and political condition of countrymen purified and protected'.

Almost all the other bishops were equally opposed, though Blomfield of London told a public meeting that the Church had no objection to Dissenters educating their own children, and the ever-liberal Thirlwell of St David's and author of an eight-volume *History of Greece*, advocated a system based on non-denominational principles. The Vicar of Leeds, Walter Hook, said that only State provision would ever meet the national need. Thus, in 1840, the government was forced to compromise over inspection to the extent of allowing the Archbishop to veto the appointment of particular inspectors or demand their removal if the supervision was deemed unsatisfactory.

The next move came in 1843, when the return of a Tory government led to a Factories Bill which proposed that children aged 8 to 13 should work no more than six and a half hours a day in factories, then spend three hours in school. The schoolmaster must be a communicant member of the Church of England and approved by the bishop. The religious teaching must be from the Authorized Version of the Bible and no other book. Schools were to be managed by a board of seven trustees, these to include the clergyman and the two churchwardens. The clergyman was entrusted with determining the syllabus and books. Children were to be compelled to attend church on appropriate occasions, unless their parents objected, and on Sundays for no more than three hours to be instructed in the Prayer Book, including the Catechism. Roman Catholics might be exempted from religious instruction, and licensed ministers of any church might attend the school once a week to instruct the children of their flock.

A few High-Church bishops objected to the 'conscience clause', but the bishops generally were content with the proposal, not least because of the substantial State financial aid attached to it. The Dissenters were, however, correspondingly angry, believing that their contribution to education was to be regarded as no more than something to be tolerated, and that they were about to be sidelined further. Yet they could not manage without State aid. Such was the commotion that the educational provisions of the Bill were quickly dropped.

This represented a significant victory for the increasingly organized Dissenters and indicated, if only implicitly, that the Church of England would never again have exclusive control of education. Yet they felt that it still had too much power. So Archbishop Howley and the National Society were now compelled to concede that schools in receipt of State funds should have a permanent management committee, with the parish priest for the time being having only a single vote. He was, however, to retain control over religious matters, and members of the committee were still required to be Church of England communicants.

The Bishop of Bath and Wells, George Law, and his Somerset clergy did not like what they perceived to be surrender of church control and led wider protests. The Vicar of the Somerset parish of East Brent, George Denison, who chanced to be a brother of the Bishop of Salisbury, told an inspector that if he ever attempted to visit his school again he would find the door locked and the boys standing ready to throw him in the village pond. On the other hand, a State-sponsored training college for teachers at Kneller Hall recruited as its first Principal a Fellow of Balliol College, Oxford, Frederick Temple, who would one day become Archbishop of Canterbury.

In the event, and in spite of continuing controversy and a variety of practice, many more children were educated and the Church of England remained overwhelmingly responsible for them. But disagreement over whether or not Christian education required a church-based environment continued until the next century. The fact that by 1859 the Established Church was receiving two-thirds of the State grant for education also created a long-lasting conflict with the Dissenting churches.

A struggle had also been taking place to moderate the Church of England's controlling influence over the universities of Oxford and Cambridge. During the early part of the nineteenth century, both were still scandalously corrupt. Admission to Oxford was restricted to those willing to accept the 39 Articles of Religion. College Fellowships were confined to clergymen, as they were at Cambridge. Attendance at chapel was compulsory. At Cambridge, however, there was no religious test for admission but only those who declared themselves to be members of the Church of England were awarded degrees. In 1834, 63 professors and tutors of the university petitioned Parliament to remedy this, but were not successful.

The bishops, urged on by the conservative dons who had organized a much more strongly supported petition, led the opposition, their motives being candidly admitted by Bishop Monk of Gloucester, who said in a university sermon that those seeking to destroy the Church began by 'putting restraint and force on the universities'. The Duke of Wellington, who had recently been elected Chancellor of Oxford University, went further and averred that the union of Church and State, and possibly the future of Christianity itself, was at stake.

At Oxford, a more heavily fortified bastion of Anglicanism, there was less agitation for change than at Cambridge, but in 1834 the Heads of Houses decided by a majority of one to abolish subscription to the 39 Articles as a condition of entry and possibly replace this with a declaration of membership. Even the Duke of Wellington thought this advisable. The liberally minded R. D. Hampden, who was at the time Principal of St Mary's Hall and would later, amidst much controversy, become Bishop of Hereford, published a pamphlet, *Observations on Religious Dissent*, in which he argued for the abolition of all religious tests and went on to assert that, since all Christians were united in their basic beliefs, they should have no difficulty in worshipping together in college chapels. This was not the view of the entrenched Tractarians, and, as a result of the ensuing controversy, the proposal of the Heads of Houses was first rescinded and, having been resurrected a year later, was then heavily defeated.

It was not until the early 1850s that non-Anglicans were admitted to the two universities on more or less equal terms, as part of a general reform demanded by the government. Significantly, the Oxford commission responsible for making the reform proposals was chaired by the Bishop of Norwich, Samuel Childs, its secretary was Arthur Penrhyn Stanley, a future

Dean of Westminster, and among the members was Archibald Campbell Tait, then Dean of Carlisle but soon to become Bishop of London and finally Archbishop of Canterbury. When the consequent Bill reached the House of Lords, there was no opposition from any of the bishops; in fact, Bishop Samuel Wilberforce of Oxford supported it.

A landmark in English children's education came in 1870, when Parliament passed a Bill making education to the age of 12 compulsory for all children and creating what became known as the 'Dual System', under which the Church's 'voluntary' schools were augmented by secular Board Schools in which religious education was not compulsory. A subsequent 'conscience' clause gave parents freedom to exempt their children from religious education in both types of school.

The Bill was hotly opposed by many bishops and most of the parish clergy – the 'conscience' provision being the main bone of contention. But William Walsham How, who later became Bishop of Wakefield and was known as the 'Children's Bishop' because of his gift for relating to them, took a new line in pointing out that 'the Church is not the nation, and this is a national measure'. He thought that the Bill was on the whole a good deal for the Church and that the best should be made of it – a view shared by Archbishop Tait and Frederick Temple of Exeter, his successor. Some bishops, most notably Christopher Wordsworth of Lincoln, sought to thwart the opening of Board Schools by creating many more church schools, so that by 1890 there were no fewer than 14,479 of these, educating two million children. Earlier church anxiety had by this time proved to have been unnecessary inasmuch as virtually all the Board Schools offered religious education, and fewer than 3,000 children in church schools were withdrawn from it.

By the end of the century, however, it was clear that education needed further attention. The secondary sector was uneven in its provisions, and the dual system had created a gap between the two categories inasmuch as the partially funded church schools could not keep pace in quality with the fully funded Board schools. The church schools had also become a heavy financial burden on local congregations, whose members questioned why they should have to pay both for their own school and, through the rates, for a Board School.

In 1901 a Conservative government led by A. J. Balfour drafted a Bill designed to put all forms of education under a single authority. This would bring the church schools into the national system and provide full financial support for the payment of teachers and the maintenance of buildings. In return, one-third of the membership of church school management committees would be nominated by the Local Education Authority and the committees would control the nature of the religious education offered.

The publication of the Bill led to a ferocious and sustained opposition on the part of some Nonconformist leaders, who objected to Church of England schools being heavily subsidized by rate- and tax-payers. At this point, the aged Archbishop Temple being unable to do much, the Bishop of Winchester, Randall Davidson, stepped in and entered into close negotiations with the Prime Minister. A consummate behind-the-scenes operator, who knew how to be effective in the corridors of power, Davidson sought to protect the Church's considerable interests while at the same time suggesting modest concessions that would placate the opponents. Balfour was immensely grateful for this assistance, and in 1902 the Bill passed into law.

This was in spite of the intense opposition, and when a Liberal government returned to office in 1906, Nonconformist dissatisfaction became even more clamorous and found a receptive hearing. After some unsatisfactory discussions and a few false starts, a Bill was presented to Parliament. This aimed to end the 'dual' system and bring all State-funded schools under central control. Local councils could choose to take over church schools. In all schools, non-denominational religious education would be given. But, at the discretion of the authorities, and with the consent of parents, denominational teaching could be given twice a week by teachers imported from outside. Teacher appointments were not to be influenced by religious considerations.

The Bill was naturally seen as a direct assault on the Church's involvement in education and provoked a national controversy of crisis proportions extending over two years. King Edward VII eventually felt driven to intervene, insisting that an acceptable compromise be found. Davidson, now Archbishop of Canterbury, regarded the Bill as totally unacceptable, but he too believed the only way forward to be by way of amendment, rather than outright opposition. When the time came for George Bell to write his classic biography of Davidson, he found that the crisis had spawned 'a larger array of boxes and files with more memoranda of interviews and correspondence, than any other single subject (save the Prayer Book) during the whole of the Archbishop's life'.

More than a century later it is hard to conceive of a modern era in which an Archbishop of Canterbury was so deeply and extensively involved in the political process – not only on educational matters in which he had important responsibilities, but on a wide variety of national issues when he had ready and frequent access to Prime Ministers, Cabinet Ministers, senior civil servants and other men of influence. Regular attendance at the House of Lords provided opportunities for the public expression of his views, and the fact that these were never couched in provocative language may well have been the secret of his influence. Sir Michael Sadler, a leading educationist at the time of the crisis, later provided Bell with a sketch of Davidson's style:

Amid treacherous currents the Archbishop proved himself a wise and cautious pilot. No chemist could analyse a broth with more scrupulous rectitude than His Grace employed in disentangling the factors which were knotted together in the English educational problems. He was determined not to be deceived by presuppositions, however dearly cherished, or to accept without firm use of the probe generalizations which were part of the worn currency of debate. But he never leapt to a conclusion until he had made sure of his ground. He never allowed himself to speak without first measuring his words and judging their public repercussions. Heavy strain on his strength and temper never broke his self-command. He had an inexhaustible patience; a bridle on his tongue; courage and a noble tact in withholding assent to views which he thought exaggerated, impracticable or delusively logical. Through the dense brushwood which impeded his progress he saw shining the light towards which his course was set. But he had no formula to cover all he hoped to save or win. He moved forward with a firm hold on realities and with an unflinching faith in the truth which was to him the way of life.

Admirable though these qualities might be, the Church as a whole did not agree with Davidson's handling of the Education crisis. Nothing short of a robust rejection of the Bill *in toto* would meet the need. Bishop Knox of Manchester led the opposition in combative style. Bishop Charles Gore said that 'It would be nothing short of a most grave national disaster if the elementary schools of the church were secularized'. Three-quarters of a million people signed petitions urging rejection. On the other hand, Bishop Percival of Hereford argued that the amendments secured by Davidson had made the Bill acceptable, as did most of the other bishops when the subject was debated in the Representative Church Council. But large majorities of the parish clergy and laity voted against it. This changed the situation and a few days later the Prime Minister announced in the House of Commons that the Bill had been dropped.

There was little development in the educational field until 1944, by which time the wartime spirit of social reform was demanding the raising of standards, especially in the low-achieving secondary sector. The Minister of Education, R. A. Butler – a 'One Nation Tory' – responded with a landmark Education Act. This proposed the raising of the school leaving age to 15 (with the hope that it might one day be raised to 16) and a tripartite system of secondary schools – grammar, technical and secondary modern. This was widely welcomed at the time as a significant advance, but the number of grammar schools remained tiny, few technical schools were opened and the majority of children were consigned to schools of only moderate quality.

The Church, mainly in the person of Archbishop Temple, collaborated closely with Butler in the designing of the Act and he ensured that the interests of the other churches would not be overlooked. The bitterness attending previous disagreements became a thing of the past and Butler paid tribute to Temple's part both in this and in bringing the Church of England's still considerable number of schools into what was in effect a joint enterprise.

These schools were now divided into two categories – county and voluntary – the latter being almost exclusively church schools. These in turn were divided into 'aided' and 'controlled' status. In return for payment of half the cost of building repairs and improvements, the Church retained a large measure of authority over 'aided' schools through the appointment of two-thirds of the members of management committees, all the teaching staff and the content of religious instruction. In the case of 'controlled' schools, the county met all building costs and, in return, appointed two-thirds of the managers and all the teaching staff, and provided religious instruction in accordance with an agreed syllabus – a conscience clause permitting parents to opt for denominational instruction. All schools were to begin the day with an act of worship.

In the event, the majority of church schools became 'controlled', mainly for financial reasons, but among the bishops there were some who believed it best for the Church to exert its influence in the wider field of education, rather than within its own enclaves. In some dioceses, however, especially in London and Lancashire, most opted for 'aided' status and in the longer term this proved to be the best way of maintaining serious religious education in schools. Spencer Leeson, a former Headmaster of Repton and Winchester, became Bishop of Peterborough in 1949 and was given responsibility for guiding the Church of England's schools policy. To this task he brought expertise, but, during a period when virtually all the bishops had been public-school educated, it is perhaps not surprising that questions were never raised about the place of the privileged independent sector – a subject which had been of considerable concern to William Temple.

Later attempts to improve the general situation by the introduction of large all-ability comprehensive schools, replacing the grammar and secondary modern schools, have proved only partially successful. They are to be found at their best in middle-class catchment areas, where there is strong parental support, and at their worst in deprived areas, where size and multiple social problems militate against effective education.

By the late 1960s, the place of religious instruction in county schools and of the Church in the national education system was again in need of attention. This was partly because it was proving increasingly difficult to maintain daily acts of worship and good quality religious instruction in the county schools, and partly because there was pressure from secular sources to have the Church removed altogether from the national system.

With a new Education Act in prospect, the Church set up a powerful commission under the chairmanship of the Bishop of Durham, Ian Ramsey, which produced in 1970 a substantial report, *The Fourth R*. This received considerable publicity and, in effect, conceded a good deal of ground, recognizing that religious instruction and daily worship could no longer be allocated protected slots. Instead, under a new title of Religious Education, schools should be allowed, while still under statutory obligation, flexibility to deal with the subject as they thought best, unhampered by agreed syllabuses. Church schools should be maintained only if they provided overall education of the highest quality.

Successive governments remained committed to retaining 'aided' schools and increased grants to make this possible, insisting, however, that entry should not be confined to the children of churchgoing parents. By the beginning of the twenty-first century, when there were still about 5,000 church schools, the educational quality of many of these made them attractive to a wider constituency. But in May 2013 the Bishop of Oxford, chairman of the General Synod Board of Education, announced that changes in government policy meant that the 70-year-old relationship between church and government over schools was now dead. The place of religion in most state schools had by this time become problematic.

5

The Durham Miners and their Bishops

The response of the Church of England to the challenges presented by the Industrial Revolution was everywhere totally inadequate. In the diocese of Durham, it was unbelievably bad. The Church there was trapped by its unique history and a fatal combination of power and wealth.

Until 1882, the diocese extended from the Tees to the Scottish border. Within this huge territory County Durham constituted for almost eight centuries a Palatinate, which during the Middle Ages served as a kind of buffer state between warring England and Scotland. During this time, the bishops, starting with the Norman Walchere in 1071, governed as the Palatinate Counts Palatine with the delegated powers of viceroys, including a standing army, a mint, judicial authority and ownership of massive land-holdings that yielded great wealth. Their portraits display a pastoral staff in the left hand and a sword in the other.

Their powers were substantially reduced at the Reformation, but some remained until 1836. The Bishop was still the most important figure in public life and appointed the High Sheriff and the magistrates to maintain law and order. Most of his land-holdings remained intact, as did those of the Dean and Chapter of Durham Cathedral. The diocese was almost entirely rural. In 1800, there were just 86 parishes in the two counties.

The need for coal to fire the newly invented steam engines during the second half of the eighteenth century, then for gas for a new form of lighting at the beginning of the nineteenth, had, however, consequences for County Durham and the southern part of Northumberland unequalled by the Industrial Revolution in any other part of Britain. In 1810, the output of the Durham coalfield was about two million tons; a century later this had risen to 41.5 million tons. During the same period the population had risen from 165,000 to 1.5 million. In 1850, *The Times* described Durham as 'very little more than one huge colliery . . . . the cities, the villages, the clergy, the tradesmen, the labourers and the farmers all derive their wealth, their competence, from coal'.

Since the Church owned about half of the land on which the coal was being mined, it was inevitably the chief single beneficiary of this revolution. Less inevitably, it might have been hoped, the clergy, far from being preoccupied by their prayers and studies and concerned for the welfare of the people, were astute and often ruthless in capitalizing on their new money-making opportunities. After the nationalization of the coal industry on 1 January 1947, former names such as Dean and Chapter Colliery were retained.

Until well into the nineteenth century, the miners were mercilessly exploited. Very large numbers were recruited from Ireland, the Midlands and as far away as Cornwall, and for several decades women and children as well as men were employed in winning coal in appalling conditions underground. For ten or twelve hours a day, miners worked on their backs, sometimes on their sides, often nearly suffocated by foul air. Overall, the conditions of the miners were no better than those of serfs or slaves.

The Church's extraordinary increase in wealth derived from this great enterprise was therefore bought not only at the cost of conflict and unpopularity with the coal-owners, but also complete alienation from the miners, who recognized the Church as a party to their plight. At the same time, the Church of England failed to make provision for the pastoral care of the massively increased population of the diocese, and it was not until 1860 that a major mission was launched to create new parishes, build new churches and recruit many more clergy to serve them. By now, Methodism was firmly established in all the new mining communities, with one or more chapels occupying sites at their centres, and a good deal of social work as well as evangelism under way. It was too late for recovery.

The Honourable Shute Barrington, son of a Viscount and married to the daughter of a Duke, was translated to the Bishopric of Durham in 1791, having previously occupied the sees of Salisbury and Llandaff and been Dean of St Paul's and a Canon of Windsor. He was at Durham for 35 years, a critical period in the development of the coal industry. But, although a vigorous administrator, he was quite unable to meet the demands being made on him by the changes taking place on his doorstep, though he neglected no opportunity for making money. After a miners' strike in 1810, he made the extensive stables at Auckland Castle available for the temporary incarceration of about 300 men for whom there was no room in the prisons to which they had been sentenced – often by clerical magistrates. This would not be forgotten.

The next four bishops did little better. Edward Van Mildert (1826–36), a distinguished scholar, enjoyed an annual income of about £1.3 million in today's money, with little taxation, and he used some of this for the endowment of the new Durham University, insisting that it must be an Anglican foundation. Both he and the Dean and Chapter strongly opposed the distributive reforms proposed in the 1830s, but the tide was flowing against them, and Van Mildert, who died in 1836, was the last of the Prince Bishops.

His successor, Edward Maltby (1836–56), had a reduced income of £8,000 per annum, still a very large sum. His appointment was opposed by the Dean and Chapter on the grounds that he was a Whig and therefore likely to favour social reform. But they need not have worried since he confined his efforts to the building of some over-large vicarages and felt driven to warn the Home Secretary that the miners' leaders were stirring up trouble that threatened the stability of the community.

Thomas Longley's stay was brief (1856–60), ending with his translation to York and thence to Canterbury. When the Honourable Henry Montague Villiers, brother to an earl and brother-in-law of a cabinet minister, was translated from Carlisle in 1860, the *Church Times* said that his Protestant views had 'raised him to a position for which he was not fitted by capacity or character'. He died within a year of taking office, so this could not be tested.

In the same year a public meeting, chaired by Earl Grey, Lord Lieutenant of Northumberland, was held in Newcastle Town Hall. This was a consequence of a House of Lords committee report which, having enquired into the 'State of Spiritual Destitution in the Metropolis and in the Mining and Manufacturing Districts', concluded that Durham and Northumberland were 'the worse provided with church accommodation than any counties in England'. As a result of this meeting, a major mission was launched to recover lost ground in the two counties. A thorough investigation of every part of the territory led to the creation of new parishes, the building of churches and the recruitment of a large number of clergy to serve them.

No bishop could have led this effort better than Charles Baring, a member of the banking family, who was quickly appointed after the early death of Villiers. He was a belligerent, intolerant evangelical of boundless energy who set about the task with a will. Since the Church's once more than ample financial resources could no longer meet such a heavy demand, he was obliged to turn for help to the coal-owners, whose profits had continued to rise even though the miners now had stronger trade unions. It was a reversal of roles, and the emergence of a new breed of coal-owner patrons did nothing to bridge the gulf between the Church and the miners. Still, large numbers of churches went up, but this was several decades after Methodist chapels had occupied the best sites in the mining and other industrial communities.

The need for more clergy was met substantially by turning to a very different source of supply. Some came from the small number of miners who attended church, or from their sons. Others, soon to be known as 'mountain clergy', were brought down from tending sheep on the western fells. All were to be missionaries to dark places, and it was believed, or at least hoped, that their closer identification with those they were called to serve would yield good results.

It did not. It turned out that the working-class parishioners did not always appreciate the ministries of clergy drawn from their own milieu and often they were seen as having 'gone over to the other side'. The infant Durham University did its best with the training of the recruits and over the years some high calibre priests emerged, but the overall result of the experiment was to lower significantly the standard of clergy in the diocese, the effects of which were felt until well into the twentieth century.

The Enthronement of Joseph Barber Lightfoot in 1879 brought to Durham a bishop in a class of his own. One of the nineteenth century's greatest scholars, and about to become one of the Church of England's greatest bishops, he had an international reputation for his pioneering work in Patristic and Pauline studies. Born in 1828, the son of an accountant, he went from King Edward VI School in Birmingham to Trinity College, Cambridge, where he carried all before him and emerged as Senior Classic and a Mathematics Wrangler.

A Fellowship of Trinity College followed and seven years later he became Hulsean Professor of Divinity, moving in due course to the Regius chair. On the face of it, there seemed no sense in the appointment of such a man to the diocese of Durham in the midst of an intense reforming mission. He was himself doubtful as to the wisdom of the choice but was persuaded by friends to accept. And, besides his massive gifts of learning, he turned out to have strong administrative skill and considerable money-raising capacity. His broad churchmanship also helped to unite the diocese.

Although his academic work was inevitably curtailed, Lightfoot enjoyed his next ten years as a bishop. Little time was lost in implementing a scheme for creating a new diocese of Newcastle and this was quickly followed by the first meeting of a Diocesan Conference of clergy and laity. A new church building appeal was launched, and within four years £224,000 had been raised and spent on new churches, vicarages and schools. By the end of his episcopate, 45 more churches had been built, one of these, Saint Ignatius Sunderland, paid for out of the royalties on a recently completed two-volume study of Saint Ignatius and Saint Polycarp.

Never an eloquent preacher, Lightfoot did not have much to say to the miners, though they found him easy to talk to. He remedied the loneliness of life in Auckland Castle by inviting into residence a group of Oxbridge graduates to complete their ordination training under his supervision and then serve in Durham parishes. The Auckland Brotherhood, as it came to be known, continued throughout his episcopate and did much to offset the prevailing low standard of the clergy. In the space of ten years, he ordained 323 men, and eventually 60 per cent of the clergy in the diocese were graduates. He also ordained a number of women deaconesses. In the end, all this effort, unaided by a suffragan bishop, proved to be too much, and his health broke down with a serious heart condition. He died in office in December 1889. It had been a remarkable episcopate, but the gap between Church and miners remained unbridgeable.

Brooke Foss Westcott, a friend and Cambridge colleague of Lightfoot, albeit three years his senior and his one-time tutor, also became one of the greatest Anglican bishops. He succeeded Lightfoot at Durham in 1890, when he was 66, and stayed for 11 years. He was unique in combining the roles of a New Testament scholar of international repute with that of an ardent social reformer. There was also a mystical element in his make-up and his pastoral concern for Durham's parishes secured him a permanent place in the history of the diocese.

He became the founding President of the Christian Social Union shortly before moving to Durham, when he was still Regius Professor of Divinity at Cambridge. The basis of his own social thought derived from his understanding of the significance of the Incarnation, and in his first letter to the Durham clergy, circulated before his Enthronement, he undertook 'to face in the light of the Christian faith some of the gravest problems of our social and national life'.

The son of a Birmingham manufacturer, he was born in 1825 and as a schoolboy saw a demonstration in support of the 1832 Great Reform Bill and also attended a Chartist meeting. He said in his later years that his interest in social and political questions dated from these experiences. After a brilliant academic career at Trinity College, Cambridge, he was ordained in 1851 and in the following year became an assistant master at Harrow School. Although an indifferent teacher, he remained on the staff for 17 years exercising a remarkable personal influence throughout the school. He also pursued the vocation of a scholar.

In 1869, he became a Canon Residentiary of Peterborough Cathedral, and a year later was appointed Regius Professor of Divinity at Cambridge, combining the two posts until 1883, after which he changed his canonry to one at Westminster Abbey. At Cambridge his influence was remarkable – academic standards were raised, an Honours degree in Divinity instituted, a divinity school built and a training course for ordinands, which later developed into Westcott House, started. His New Testament commentaries were standard works for many years.

Appointment to Durham in 1890 was at the insistence of Queen Victoria and against the resistance of the Prime Minister, Lord Salisbury, who argued that his scholarly gifts would be wasted in a northern diocese. More probably, he did not like Westcott's broad churchmanship and social outlook. By the time of his Enthronement, most of the fund-raising and church building initiated by the 1860 mission campaign had been completed, but whatever

Christian commitment there was still found expression mainly in the older Methodist chapels.

Westcott recognized immediately the need to establish bonds of friendship with the Methodists and if possible learn from their real, even if limited, success. And he was the sort of bishop whom they could admire and respond to. A project to provide homes for aged miners, in which Westcott had a leading role, led to inter-church collaboration. Besides this he often urged the mine owners to provide better housing for their employees.

But more urgent was the need to get alongside the alienated miners and to win the confidence of the trade union leaders. The more radical among these could never be convinced, however, that Westcott's apparent Socialism and broad sympathies were anything more than a commitment to minor reform in order to avoid a major upheaval in the social and economic orders. Nonetheless he attracted some of them to regular discussions of their problems at Auckland Castle and established a warm friendship with John Wilson, the leader of the Durham miners, who was a frequent attender and said after Westcott's death, 'From the time of his coming to this county the Bishop sought on all occasions to make himself acquainted with our conditions.' He also had regular meetings with colliery owners and managers and those of his clergy whose concerns extended beyond the pastoral.

The number of these increased. Lightfoot's Auckland Brotherhood continued, and the students, having absorbed Westcott's social doctrine, became a cohort of able priests, dispatched to minister in some of the most difficult parishes in the diocese. They did not pack their churches with miners, but they established lively congregations with their families and above-ground workers, and kept in close touch with them in their homes and meeting places.

Much longer lasting was the involvement of the cathedral in the annual Miners' Gala Day. This major rally, strongly supported from all parts of the coalfield, involved miners with bands and banners marching through the streets of Durham City to the racecourse for open-air meetings addressed by their own leaders and prominent, often national, political figures. As a result of Westcott's friendship with John Wilson, however, a service was introduced and the crowded building was enlivened by bands and banners. Westcott himself was asked to preach on many occasions.

A stained-glass window in the cathedral now portrays what became an iconic event in Durham's mining history. In 1892, not long after Westcott's arrival, the Durham coal owners, seeking to safeguard their profits during a period of falling coal prices, proposed a reduction of 13.5 per cent in the already meagre wages of the miners. This was strongly resisted, and when the offer of the miners to take a 10 per cent reduction was refused, the entire coalfield went on strike. In the absence of strike pay and social security benefits, the consequences for the men and their families were disastrous.

Westcott stepped in and invited both sides to meet under his chairmanship at Auckland Castle. The meeting lasted the best part of a day until a settlement of 10 per cent was agreed, and its announcement, made to a large crowd of miners and their families gathered outside the Castle, was greeted with cheers of relief. Westcott had been impartial in the chair, but the settlement was the one he had urged on both sides when they had met privately and informally at Auckland Castle a few days earlier. It was the most important event in his episcopate, and its success enabled him to help the miners to form conciliation boards to deal with future disputes.

Following his death in 1901, the Darlington Independent Labour Party recorded 'the deep sense of loss the cause of social reform has sustained, and the highest appreciation of the earnestness and zeal with which he sought to improve the social conditions of the masses'.

After the remarkable episcopates of Lightfoot and Westcott, it was perhaps inevitable that the Crown should return to Cambridge in search of another distinguished scholar for the succession. They found one in the person of Handley Carr Glynn Moule, the Norrisian Professor of Divinity. He proved to be an evangelical saint but, in the words of his successor, 'too good a Christian to have made a good bishop'. Essentially unworldly, he seemed incapable of addressing the acute social problems that still affected his diocese, and much of what had been achieved by Westcott was undone.

Herbert Hensley Henson, who was at Durham from 1920 to 1939, had a totally different temperament. Small of stature and with somewhat alarming beetling eyebrows, he was naturally combative and spent the greater part of his life tilting at ecclesiastical and political windmills. He revelled in controversy and was aided in this by a mind like quicksilver.

Born in Broadstairs in 1863, he had an unhappy childhood, being the victim of a broken marriage but, thanks to a schoolmaster who recognized his talents, he went to Oxford as a non-collegiate undergraduate, there being no money available for college residence. Living frugally in lodgings and with little in the way of tuition, he not only secured a First in History but won one of Oxford's most coveted prizes – a Fellowship of All Souls.

After reading Theology, he was ordained by the Bishop of Oxford in 1889 and a month later became Head of Oxford House – a recently established centre of social work in London's East End. Soon, however, All Souls used its patronage to appoint him Vicar of Barking – now a large and expanding east London parish. He was there for six years and, assisted by a large team of curates, exercised a highly effective ministry, with 1,000 or more people of all sorts crowding the church to hear his striking sermons.

But the strain of the work affected his health, and from 1895 to 1900 he was chaplain of an almshouse in Ilford, combining this with study at All Souls. The Prime Minister, Lord Salisbury, next came to the rescue by appointing him Rector of St Margaret's, Westminster, this being attached to a Canonry of the Abbey. There he thrived and was disappointed not to be appointed to the Deanery, when this became vacant. He went instead to be Dean of Durham in 1912.

He was now well known nationally as a churchman who declared his agnosticism over the historicity of the Virgin Birth and the physical resurrection of Jesus, and when in 1917 the Prime Minister, Lloyd George, nominated him for the Bishopric of Hereford, this created a storm of controversy.

The fuss having died down, and Henson having proved to be a popular Bishop of Hereford, Lloyd George felt emboldened two years later to have him translated to Durham. The Archbishop of York, Cosmo Gordon Lang, protested, but Durham was ready to welcome a bishop who already knew the diocese. He was not in fact a liberal theologian, but those aware of his opinions on political and social matters must have been somewhat apprehensive.

In these matters, Henson was deeply conservative, though not in a party political sense. He is best described as a nineteenth-century Gladstonian Liberal, believing in individual economic freedom, within a competitive system, and only as many restraints on this as were absolutely necessary to social justice. Fierce opposition to what he believed to be the growing threat of Socialism and the increasing power of trade unions were natural consequences of this belief.

Within a year of his Enthronement he was faced with a county-wide miners' strike and chose the occasion of a meeting in West Hartlepool to accuse them of ca'canny (going slow), and of being 'shirkers'. The audience had, he believed, been impressed by 'the absence of the usual cant and compliment'. Not so the miners when they read newspaper reports of the meeting. Their response was uninhibited. He had not made a good start.

In 1924, Henson felt moved to deplore what he discerned to be 'a drift to Socialism in Church and State'. The mining crisis, followed by a General Strike in 1926, drove him to near-despair, as did the effect of his utterances on the mining community. Attempts at helpful intervention by some bishops had, he said, 'been only effective in prolonging the conflict, rescuing the trade union leaders from a hopeless impasse, providing them with a new plea, and placing the Government in a very difficult situation'. He was certain that 'the Government must win' and, when the strike caused a serious breakdown in public services, he offered whatever practical assistance might be useful, advising the diocesan secretary to do the same. Their offers were declined.

An incident during the strike entered into Durham's folk memory and remains as a powerful reminder of the relations then existing between the Church's leadership and the mining community. Shortly before the annual Miners' Gala Day, Henson had written an article for the London *Evening Standard* in which he defended the coal-owners and criticized the miners' leaders. The Dean of the Cathedral, Bishop Welldon, joined in with a speech critical of the miners to Bishop Auckland Rotary Club.

On the day of the Gala, Welldon was unwise enough to go to the race-course, on the banks of the River Wear, in order to address a fringe meeting on the subject of Temperance. There he was greeted by a crowd of angry miners, bearing placards 'To Hell with Bishops and Deans' and some crying 'Put him in the river. Duck him'. Welldon was swept by the crowd out of the enclosure. His top hat flew into the river, he was kicked and struck on the head. About to be pushed into the river, the police intervened, got him on to a passing boat and took him to safety, accompanied by jeers and boos. Later it was put about that the Dean had been mistaken for the Bishop, but this was improbable since Welldon was a huge man, all of 20 stone.

Throughout his episcopate, Henson's direct contact with miners was largely confined to chance encounters when, either on strike or unemployed, some of them were, as he put it, 'loafing about' in the large park attached to Auckland Castle. His relations with Lord Londonderry and the other major coal-owners were, not surprisingly, more close and cordial, but even they were not beyond criticism and were sometimes warned that their employment policies might well stir the miners to a violent reaction and thus become counterproductive as well as a threat to the stability of society.

Although he never came to terms with the miners or any of the other industrial workers in the diocese, he eventually won the loyalty of a large proportion of the clergy, who came to value, and sometimes enjoy, the leadership of a notoriously controversial bishop. When he retired in 1939, they thanked him for 'a great and generous episcopate'.

Alwyn Terrell Petre Williams, Henson's successor, was another former Fellow of All Souls. He had been a distinguished Headmaster of Winchester College and was now Dean of Christ Church, Oxford. A meticulous scholar, he became chairman of the committee responsible for translating the *New English Bible*.

Such a man would never have found it easy to translate his own expertise and experience into that of a mining community, and Williams was initially greatly hindered by the outbreak of war. A kind, albeit shy bishop, a major preoccupation was maintaining ministry in the parishes after their clergy had left to become chaplains to the forces, and in this he was effective. When ill-health intervened in 1951, he was translated to more congenial Winchester.

The all-out effort required for the production of essential coal during the war years left no time for conflict between miners and coal-owners, and the nationalization of the coal industry on 1 January 1947 was marked by the erection of signs 'This Colliery is managed by the National Coal Board on behalf of the People'. Things would never be the same again.

The pits were still difficult and dangerous places in which to work, but working hours were reduced, pay was increased, free coal was provided and a higher cheese ration allocated. A programme of constructing pit-head baths was started and overall the improvement was significant. But most miners vowed not to allow their sons to follow them into the pits.

This was just as well since, except in East Durham, and in particular those collieries that ran under the North Sea, this coalfield had entered into terminal decline. Most of the remaining seams of coal were too shallow for the exploitation to be economically viable. The former coal-owners had escaped in time and heavy government subsidy was needed to keep the majority of mines open. New industries and enterprises were entering the region and, although the mining villages remained tightly knit communities, there was now a degree of variety in their populations.

This was of some advantage to the Church of England. Although most of the diocese's churches had been built far too late, they had never been entirely devoid of congregations. Some miners did attend, though their numbers were too small to register significantly on the diocesan returns. But their wives and families attended in larger numbers, as did those in managerial and other surface posts. Not all shopkeepers and teachers were Methodists. And there were many parish clergy who exercised what, in the circumstances, were heroic ministries, not least on the all too frequent occasions of mining accidents, and when there were strikes and unemployment. Some had supported the miners against coal-owners in local strikes. It was a Rector of Jarrow who, back in 1815, had convinced the scientist Humphry Davy of the need for a safe miners' lamp. But a new era had now dawned.

The Crown now returned to Cambridge for a new bishop. Michael Ramsey had been Regius Professor of Divinity there for only two years, but he had previously held the Van Mildert chair and a cathedral canonry at Durham from 1940 to 1950. It was the first time a diocese had been informally consulted about the choice of its future bishop, and Ramsey's affectionate nature, combined with a high degree of eccentricity, had made him a popular figure in the diocese as well as a much respected scholar.

In the event, he stayed for only four years, being soon required for the Archbishopric of York, but his popularity in Durham increased further. His deep Anglo-Catholic spirituality made him, however, unsympathetic to developments in the Church's burgeoning reform movement. Yet, his high regard for Bishop Westcott as well as his own Incarnational theology made him critical of unjust social structures, and a strong friendship was established with the miners' leader, Jack Lawson.

On learning of the name of his successor, Ramsey remarked, with a twinkle in his eye, 'This is good, very good, but it must never happen again!' The translation of Maurice Henry Harland from Lincoln in 1956 seemed to represent a deliberate turning away from the scholar–bishop tradition. The Archbishop of Canterbury, Geoffrey Fisher, had a large hand in it, and he, being essentially a managerial man who did not see the need for scholar–bishops, evidently believed that the challenges facing the post-war Church in the industrial North required pastoral, rather than academic skills.

On receiving the Prime Minister's letter proposing his translation to Durham, Harland modestly pointed out that he was 'only a Lincolnshire hedge priest', with no industrial experience and little academic interest. In truth, his relations with the miners proved no less cordial than those of any of his predecessors, apart from Westcott, and, although singularly lacking in new ideas, he offered strong support, including finance, to those of his clergy who wished to experiment with new forms of mission. Of these, the Teesside Industrial Mission proved to be the most significant and enduring.

Durham was now very anxious to return to the scholar model and more than grateful for the Crown's response. In his address at Ian Ramsey's Memorial Service, held in St Margaret's, Westminster, in November 1972, Archbishop Michael Ramsey said, 'It will not be surprising if history comes to remember Brooke Foss Westcott and Ian Ramsey as the two bishops who made the biggest impact upon the Durham community.' Few Durham people would have disagreed with that assessment then, and 40 years on it still stands. Yet he was its bishop for a mere six years. Unable to say 'No' to any request, national or local, for his services and apparently incapable of determining priorities, he died, exhausted, when only 57.

His Enthronement sermon could not have indicated with greater clarity that Durham now had an unusual bishop, inasmuch as a long section of it was devoted to an evaluation of a recently published Northern Economic Planning Council report on *Challenge of the Changing North*. The next six years were devoted to leading the diocese's response to this challenge and nationally (he was in the House of Lords every Wednesday) commenting on its implications for individuals and communities.

He was born in a small terraced house in a Lancashire mill town in 1915 and, having won a scholarship to the local grammar school, went on, with the aid of two more scholarships to Christ's College, Cambridge, to read Mathematics. His studies were, however, interrupted by tuberculosis and during a long convalescence he felt drawn to ordination. Returning eventually to Cambridge, he took Firsts in Mathematics, Philosophy and Theology.

This was followed by preparation for Holy Orders at Ripon Hall, Oxford, and a wartime curacy, 1940–3, at Headington Quarry, near Oxford. He was, however, always going to be called to an academic career, and the next 23 years were spent teaching in Cambridge and Oxford and writing several books, the first of which, *Religious Language* (1957), was the most important and established his reputation as a philosopher of religion.

By 1966, he had already chaired several church committees on social questions such as suicide, abortion and euthanasia. He was also the active chairman of a hospital management committee, expanding its provisions for the mentally ill, and one of the founders of the Institute of Religion and Medicine. 'The theologian justifies himself', he said, 'only in terms of the issues and problems which the world raises.' He believed there would be a revival of theology only when its scholars sat down with those of other disciplines to confront specific issues.

When he arrived in Durham, Ramsey knew little about the social and economic problems of the North East and immediately appointed Margaret Kane, long experienced in industrial mission and work among miners, as an adviser, and a fruitful partnership resulted. He also established strong relationships with National Coal Board officials and the miners' leaders, as well as with those of the shipbuilding and other major industries of the diocese. On visits to mining parishes, he always sought opportunities to meet miners in their clubs and, without seeming to be in any way patronizing, could join with them in a game of dominoes. They liked him. Small of stature and with a broad Lancastrian accent, he was easy to talk to and did not seem like other bishops.

There had been almost two decades of unprecedented peace in the mining industry, but Ramsey was soon made aware of new problems and causes of discord. Not even the National Coal Board could be allowed by the government to sustain indefinitely the heavy losses being incurred by the uneconomic Durham coalfield. The national miners' strike in January 1972, the first since 1926, was only partly about pay since miners were now the best-paid industrial workers. Pit closures became inevitable, and once again unemployment was taking its toll. The younger, more enterprising miners moved to the still prosperous Nottinghamshire and Derbyshire coalfields, but there remained behind increasing numbers on the dole.

Ramsey, whose support for the miners was unflagging, recognized economic reality and spoke frequently of the government's responsibility to attract to the North East new industries to replace those now being made redundant and to initiate re-training schemes for ex-miners. A speech in the House of Lords on this subject was widely reported in Durham's newspapers and won him many plaudits.

In the parishes more generally he fizzed with new ideas, schemes and projects. Team Ministries, then still uncommon, were encouraged, more clergy were urged to acquire specialist skills to enable them to serve in non-parochial spheres, a distinguished commission was appointed to report on the future of the Church in Sunderland, and there was much else. It was as if the diocese had been hit by a spiritual whirlwind, the effects of which were too great for Ramsey and his staff to manage. It was this same whirlwind that, as Archbishop Ramsey also said in his Memorial Service address, all too soon swept a unique bishop into heaven.

No less clearly than his predecessor, John Stapylton Habgood, who was at Durham from 1973 until his translation to York in 1983, saw the imperative of relating theology to secular social problems. But in personality and style he could hardly have been more different. Trained initially as a scientist, he brought to everything he touched a cool, analytical mind, and it would have been quite impossible for him to be a campaigner or radical reformer.

This was useful in sorting out the chaos left by Ian Ramsey and in evaluating the merits or otherwise of the multitude of schemes and projects awaiting development. He described himself as a 'conservative liberal', and his ability to see value in all sides of an argument led to his placing high value on paradox, but it was not easy for so subtle a mind to operate in miners' clubs or in conversation with mining managers and trade union leaders.

Born in 1927, the son of a medical doctor, Habgood went from Eton to King's College, Cambridge, to read Physiology. A double first in the Natural Science tripos led to a university teaching post and a Fellowship of King's. An evangelical mission to Cambridge and conversion intervened, however, and eventually took him to Cuddesdon theological college to prepare for ordination. He was a curate at fashionable St Mary Abbots, Kensington, from 1954 to 1956, followed by six years as Vice-Principal of Westcott House, Cambridge, then five as Rector of Jedburgh in the Scottish border country.

In 1967 he was appointed Principal of Queen's College, Birmingham, where he carried through in a mere three years a scheme to make it the first ecumenical theological college in England and eventually a strong centre of theological education and research.

At Durham, he quickly set about the necessary reorganization of the diocese's structures and wisely delegated a good deal of work to others. He tried hard to get to know the miners and their leader, but was hampered in this by a shy and seemingly aloof personality. Certainly, he sympathized greatly with the victims of the ever-increasing number of pit closures and deplored the destruction of their tightly knit communities.

Shortly after moving to become Archbishop of York in 1983, this led to a brief but significant furore. With what became the historic 1983–4 national miners' strike under way, the leader of the Easington District Council, whom Habgood had known in Durham, asked him to support a campaign to save pits in his area. Although his characteristically restrained response was careful to balance the need for pit closures with that for creating alternative employment, this was widely publicized and led a North East Labour MP to put a question to the Prime Minister, Margaret Thatcher, in the House of Commons: 'Is the Prime Minister so conceited that she proposes to ignore the advice even of bishops?' She replied, 'I do not propose to tangle with his Grace the Archbishop of York. But unless coal is as cheap and competitive as it could be, many jobs will be lost in other industries.'

When a successor to Robert Runcie at Canterbury was needed in 1991, the Crown Appointments Commission was driven to conclude that there was no possibility of getting Habgood's name past the Prime Minister. At a time when no other equivalent talent was available, this proved to be a serious loss to the Church of England and the Anglican Communion more widely.

The left-wing views of David Edward Jenkins had not, however, hindered his appointment as Habgood's successor at Durham, and shortly before his Enthronement he had been branded a heretic by some who objected to his televised views on the Virgin Birth and the physical resurrection of Jesus. When, three days after his consecration in York Minster the building was seriously damaged by fire, they claimed this to be a sign of divine displeasure.

Jenkins made no reference to any of this in his Enthronement sermon, but his discussion of the disastrous national miners' strike then taking place proved to be hardly less controversial and aroused the wrath of politicians as well as the gratitude of journalists. A few days earlier, he had been visited by the presiding officer of the Northumberland miners and two of his colleagues, as well as by a number of miners' wives, who told him of a traumatic experience at the hands of the police during a demonstration.

In his sermon, Jenkins said:

> I suggest that there must be no victory in the miners' strike. There must be a speedy settlement which is a compromise pointing to community and the future. There must be no victory because the miner must not be defeated. They are desperate for their communities and this desperation forces them to action. A society which seeks economic progress for material ends must not indifferently exact such human suffering from some for the sake of the affluence of others.

He went on to discuss a possible way towards a settlement and the roles in this of the chairman of the National Coal Board and the national miners' leader. He suggested that it would assist if the hard-line chairman stepped down and the no less hard-line miners' leader was prepared to compromise and put people before ideology: 'Without withdrawal and climbing down it looks as if we are faced with several people determined to play God. And this gives us all hell.'

The sermon, which was loudly applauded at its ending, had made a valid and important point, though not everyone outside the cathedral thought so. The Bishop of Peterborough, Douglas Feaver, told the *Daily Mirror*, 'I thought the man had no sense of time or place.' There was a general outcry of protest in the press, and the Prime Minister described Jenkins as 'a cuckoo in the Establishment nest'. But he had won the hearts of the miners.

Born of Welsh parents in 1925, he had, when still at school, aged 12, a Christian conversion experience that lasted. By the time he was 18, he felt drawn to Holy Orders and, after serving in the wartime army, went to Queen's College, Oxford, where he read Greats and took a First in Theology. Ordination led to appointment as Succentor of Birmingham Cathedral and as a part-time lecturer at Queen's College, Birmingham.

He was soon back in Oxford, however, and from 1954 to 1969 was Fellow and Chaplain of Queen's College. Always a stimulating teacher, he was closely involved in the *Honest to God* debate in the 1960s, and from 1969 to 1971 he was in Geneva as Director of the World Council of Churches Humanum Studies, concerned with the theological evaluation of some of the Council's work in social and economic fields. Returning to England, he then spent eight years as Director of the William Temple Foundation in Manchester, relating the Christian faith to contemporary social issues. Appointment as Professor of Theology at Leeds came in 1979, and he was contemplating retirement from this post in 1984, when the invitation to move to Durham came.

During the following years, he was a popular bishop. A fast talker of somewhat convoluted style, his sermons were not always easy to follow, but his lectures, given at various centres in the diocese, attracted very large numbers. He remained a sympathetic friend of the miners during the accelerating run-down of the coal industry and the consequent destruction of communities and families. At the national level, he was never afraid to speak out, often controversially, in the House of Lords and the General Synod on social economic questions. But before long, Durham itself could no longer be described as a mining community. He retired in 1994.

6

Greater and Lesser Prophets

The number of Church of England bishops bent on social reform has never been large. There were, however, two outstanding examples of this genre, albeit of very different character, at the end of the Victorian era and the beginning of the turbulent twentieth century.

> I judge him to have been the most considerable English churchman of his time; not the most learned, not the most eloquent, but so learned, so eloquent, and so energetic that he touched the life of his generation at more points and more effectively than any of his contemporaries.

So wrote Hensley Henson on hearing of the death of Bishop Charles Gore in January 1932. William Temple said that Gore was one 'from whom I have learned more than from any other now living of the spirit of Christianity, and to whom more than any other (despite great differences) I owe my degree of apprehension of its truth'.

For almost four decades, Gore dominated the Anglican theological scene. Although a devout High Churchman and deeply committed to all that the Oxford Movement had given to the Church of England, he firmly believed that the traditional catholic faith had to be put in a right relation to modern intellectual problems. Evolution and biblical criticism were to be regarded not as enemies but as partners in the quest for truth. He was not alone in this, and in 1889 a volume of essays, written by himself and six theologian friends who had been meeting informally for the past 12 years, was published under the title *Lux Mundi*. This became one of the landmarks in Anglican theology.

The reaction was, however, widespread and feverish, with the greatest distress being expressed by Gore's Anglo-Catholic friends, who believed that his essay on 'The Holy Spirit and Inspiration' departed seriously from catholic truth and betrayed their cause. It was also marked distinctively by his insistence that true theological reflection could never be separated from its ethical and social implications. His fellow *Lux Mundi* essayists also believed this, but it was Gore and Henry Scott Holland who translated it into a critique of contemporary society and a statement of Christian social principles. Their foundation, with Westcott, of the Christian Social Union was in the same year as publication of *Lux Mundi*. Much later Gore began a speech by saying: 'I have constantly sat down bewildered before the blank, and as it seems to me, stupid refusal of the mass of church people to recognize their social duties, to educate themselves about social questions.'

Charles Gore was born in Wimbledon in 1853 and was of aristocratic background, his mother being the widow of an earl and his paternal and maternal grandfathers were also earls. His parents were relatively poor during his early years, but they managed to send him to Harrow, where he was deemed to be one of the most brilliant pupils in the school's history. There he was greatly influenced by Brooke Foss Westcott, who was on the teaching staff and later became a notable social reforming Bishop of Durham.

A double-first in Classics at Balliol College and a prize fellowship at Trinity College, Oxford, took Gore into university teaching of Philosophy, but he also devoted much time to studying the Apostolic Fathers and seeking to formulate a contemporary Catholicism which demonstrated continuity with the faith of the earliest Church. Following his ordination in 1876, he spent two university vacations as a curate in two Liverpool parishes, where work among the poorest of the poor confirmed his commitment to social justice.

From 1880 to 1884 he was Vice-Principal of Cuddesdon Theological College, then became the first Principal of Pusey House, Oxford, established to offer within the university an Anglo-Catholic witness through worship, scholarship and pastoral care. It was during his nine years there that the *Lux Mundi* controversy erupted, and he also began the process of founding a brotherhood of celibate priests who held all things in common. This expanded to become one of the Anglican Church's major religious orders – the Community of the Resurrection with its mother house at Mirfield, in Yorkshire, and much significant work in South Africa.

A Canonry of Westminster Abbey from 1892 to 1904 provided him with an important pulpit and large congregations to hear expositions of his ever-developing theological convictions and social concerns. The bearded, impassioned preacher resembled an Old Testament prophet, courageously denouncing the evils of his time in the cause of righteousness. And there was more than preaching. Following a meeting attended by MPs and clergymen in the Abbey's Jerusalem Chamber, he became chairman of a group that pressed the government for a Wages Board Bill that would provide a machinery for establishing minimum wages and settling disputes. His home in the Little Cloister became an important centre of religious influence in London.

Gore's approach to social questions derived from the example of the Old Testament prophets whose declarations of God's righteousness had ethical implications for the Jewish community. This he believed to have been taken up and continued by Jesus, who declared and embodied the Kingdom of God – a spiritual kingdom which nonetheless defined God's loving will and purpose for his people during their earthly existence and was designed to secure their well-being through fellowship expressed in mutual love, exemplified in the Sermon on the Mount.

Gore was in no doubt that the teaching of this Sermon 'is not a law for individual consciences only, but for a society . . . . a law which is to be applied in order to establish a new social order'. The Church, created in order to continue and extend the work of Jesus, must therefore embody the teaching of the Kingdom of God in its own life, and the sacraments of Baptism, Confirmation and Eucharist demonstrate that the Christian life is a life in community, not in isolation.

In his 1927 Halley Stewart Lectures, published as *Christ and Society*, Gore discussed five areas in which British society was, in spite of post-war hopes and promises, still falling short of the Christian ideal. The first concerned industry and, having deplored the fact that 'the contrasts between luxurious and idle wealth and ignominious poverty at the extremes of society are as startling as ever', went on to argue that workers should play a part in the management of industry so that they were no longer regarded as tools of financial schemes in which they had no part or interest but partners in social service for their own good and that of society. They needed to be given a reasonable sense of security in response to faithful service and, above all, to be given an incentive to do their best work. He believed there should be local Industrial Councils related to a national Industrial Parliament that would oversee the interests of both owners and workers and integrate these with those of the nation as a whole.

He described the current educational system as 'notoriously and lamentably wasteful, because it ends too soon and too abruptly'. He added that no one who had had a prolonged education 'could contemplate the opportunities of education enjoyed on the one hand by "the workers" and those on the other hand enjoyed by the middle and wealthier classes without recognizing that our present system altogether fails to represent a fair opportunity for a child born into our citizenship to make the best of himself or herself'.

Under the heading 'Law', Gore first pointed out that the legal system 'has notoriously been much more concerned to protect the supposed right of the propertied classes than that of the general public'. Disavowing any support for Socialist or Communist solutions, he nonetheless advocated legislation that would endow the largest number of individuals with property and the sense of property. All in the interests of healthy family life.

He added:

Nothing seems to me at this moment more alarming than the concentration of capital, and the vast power which capital gives, in a few hands. For instance, in the department of journalism, so important for the life of any nation, it appears to have almost destroyed the freedom of the press.

The ambition to become a very rich man, 'wielding the power that riches can always claim', was, he declared, 'in the deepest sense contrary to the teaching of Christ'. He had no doubt that the industrial, educational and legal arrangements of the country were a denial of the demands of justice.

They have been fashioned by the false philosophy which made the acquisition of material wealth the end of industry instead of the good of the industrial society, and thereby have ministered to the satisfaction of a small propertied class to the detriment and dissatisfaction of the great majority.

Gore did not find that turning from national to international concerns (his fourth point) offered any greater comfort. Although the Great War was to be a war to end wars and to make the world safe for democracy, it had proved to be quite otherwise. On the contrary, 'the terms of peace seem in fact to foster war' and he urged much stronger support for the infant League of Nations, warning that the horror of war engendered by the 1914–18 experience would not last for ever and that the advent of 'awful and unknown resources of science available for destruction' would make any future wars even more terrible.

His final point was concerned with the issue of race, particularly as this affected the British Empire and Britain's responsibility within it. The issue was not different from that which involved differences of class. All privileged classes and races and nations needed to recognize that, whereas in the past they had been able to exploit the weaker, and the weaker had been forced to submit in silence, this was no longer so. Hence the present discord among them.

Gore asserted that the fundamental idea of democracy – the spiritual equality of all men, which gives all men and races an equal right to a fair opportunity to make the best of themselves, for their own good and also the future good of the world – 'has so got hold of the consciences of almost all men of all colours and races that we must either set ourselves in serious earnest to correspond to its demands or fall under the divine judgement which works in the slow process of history, and occasionally breaks out in catastrophes and cataclysms'.

The expression of Gore's social concern was by no means confined to his important writing on the subject. At the end of the nineteenth century, he and Scott Holland publicly opposed the Anglo–Boer War. In 1912, when a Bill for the disestablishment of the Church in Wales was strongly opposed by Archbishop Davidson and most of the rest of the Church of England's leadership, Gore, by now Bishop of Oxford, in company with Hicks of Lincoln and Percival of Hereford, supported it. He also advocated the disestablishment of the Church of England in order to secure the Church's spiritual freedom.

In the same year, he proposed that Christians should use their investments to bring pressure to bear on companies that imposed unjust conditions on their employees. This was reiterating a point he had made strongly, 20 years earlier, in a lecture to the clergy of St Asaph diocese: 'To put one's money, or allow it to be put, into any "concern" without enquiry into the moral or social tendency of the concern, is to serve mammon at the expense of Christ.'

In 1917, Gore intervened on behalf of strikers in Reading, and two years later in a tram drivers' strike in Oxford, though this time on the side of the employers. When the 1926 coal miners' strike was called off, the dispute in the coal industry continued and the Industrial Christian Fellowship convened a committee in the hope of mediating between the opposed parties. Gore, William Temple and seven other bishops were recruited, and the formation of the committee aroused the hostility of many politicians and the press, but nothing was achieved.

In his St Asaph lecture, however, Gore had advocated the setting up by the Church of small consultative bodies 'of men who know exactly what life means, in workshops, in different business circles, among the employers of labour, among workmen to determine policies on industrial questions'. In this, as in so many other matters, he was a very long way ahead of his time. He died in 1932, and many thousands filed past his coffin when it lay in Holy Trinity Church, Chelsea, before burial at Mirfield.

Edward Lee Hicks, who was Bishop of Lincoln from 1910 to 1919, rarely wins more than a footnote in the history of the twentieth-century Church, yet he was one of the most forward-looking and outspoken church leaders of his time. He was past his 67th birthday when the Prime Minister, H. H. Asquith, acting against the wishes of the Archbishop of Canterbury, asked him to succeed the saintly Edward King in the large, almost entirely rural, diocese.

It was a bold choice inasmuch as Hicks had spent the previous 24 years ministering in the heart of industrial Manchester. But although Liberal Asquith's letter spoke of the need to continue King's great pastoral ministry and develop more cordial relations with Lincolnshire's large Methodist community, he must have been well aware that Hicks' radical views would be far from palatable in a county notorious for its conservative outlook. They were not.

In his farewell sermon in Manchester Cathedral, Hicks acknowledged that he had learned much from his time in the slum-ridden city and went on:

> If any class of men may seem more than any other to have kinship with Christ and his Gospel, it is those who have at heart the interest of Labour, who champion the claims of the unenfanchised, the unrepresented, the unemployed and the underprivileged.

Soon after his arrival in Lincoln, his fellow-passengers in a railway carriage were surprised to hear their bishop complain in a loud voice to his neighbour that the Church was dominated by the Tory Party and the Party by the brewers. Silence reigned for the remainder of the journey. Episcopal Visitation Charges, more common then than now, normally concentrated on the affairs of the diocese, but Hicks was not prepared to be so confined and in his Primary Charge startled the clergy by asking:

> How are we as Christians, as Churchmen, to feel and act in respect of the enfranchisement of women, the restriction and suppression of the liquor traffic, the prevention of the state regulation of vice, the peace movement and the other forms of social and moral agitation? In particular, seeing that liberty is no longer seriously menaced by the claims of the aristocracy of birth, how are we to prevent the domination of the plutocrat and the corrupting influence of the millionaire?

He went on to forecast that traditional Christianity would be open to serious criticism and experience tremendous shocks unless it could find practical answers to these questions. His episcopate was devoted to seeking the answers.

Hicks was born in Oxford in 1842 and, having taken a double-first in Classics at Brasenose College, was elected to a Fellowship at Corpus Christi College. There he became an authority on ancient Greek inscriptions, but during his years at Brasenose College he had become a friend of John Ruskin, who enthused him with a love of the arts and also a concern for social reform directed at improving the lot of the poor.

Two years after his ordination in 1870, he left Oxford to become Rector of Fenny Compton, a rural parish in Warwickshire. He remained there for 14 years and during this time not only engaged in diligent pastoral work and introduced new-style church organization, but also concerned himself with the plight of the many unemployed labourers – victims of an agricultural depression. 'Half-spade' allotments on his glebe land were made available to a number of them, and, when these proved successful, he tried in vain to persuade wealthy Christ Church, Oxford, to do the same with their extensive local landholdings.

In 1886, he became Principal of Hulme Hall in Manchester. This new venture provided a hall of residence for Church of England students at Owens College – the beginning of what was to become Manchester University. For a time he combined this post with that of Lecturer in Classical Archaeology, but witnessing the immense social problems created by fast-growing Manchester aroused his concern for the poor, and in 1892 he was appointed to a Residentiary Canonry of Manchester Cathedral.

This cathedral was not like any other inasmuch as it had recently been created from an ancient collegiate church served by an ordained warden and several fellows. As the city had grown around them to house a million and more people, they had steadfastly refused to provide a significant ministry to them, being content to wax fat on their substantial incomes. The scandal of this eventually led to a public outcry, the outcome of which was the foundation of a cathedral with a Dean and four Canons. In order to remove any temptation to idleness, the statutes of the new body went to the extreme of attaching to each canonry a very large inner-city parish, and one of these, St Philip's, Salford, which included some of the city's worst slums, was allocated to Hicks.

Although he had the assistance of curates, this was an impossible combination of posts, but for the next 18 years he met the challenge vigorously with a threefold policy incorporating evangelism, much training of children and young people, and a great deal of social work designed to improve the lot of the many parishioners who were living in dire poverty. Aware of the devastating effect on these of alcohol abuse, he came to believe that there would be no social progress until this evil had been overcome.

His preaching in the cathedral was acknowledged to be of a very high standard, though his political comment sometimes aroused a hostile reaction. The call to Lincoln was totally unexpected, but he accepted immediately, having been assured by the Prime Minister that the Bishop of Southwark, Edward Talbot, who had seemed a more obvious choice, did not feel it to be right to leave south London.

His involvement in the Peace Movement started during the Anglo–Boer War (1899–1902), and he was one of the few churchmen (Gore was among them) who spoke out against it. In January 1900, he preached in Manchester Cathedral on the text 'They that take the sword shall perish by the sword', and his sermon, which had been uncompromisingly outspoken, was published by the Manchester Transvaal Peace Committee under the title *The Mistakes of Militarism*. His opposition to the War aroused intense and widespread hostility, with a questioning of his patriotism.

In 1910, Hicks became President of the Church of England Peace League, a position he continued to occupy until his death nine years later. The membership of the League was never large, but was particularly active in the short period before the outbreak of war in 1914. Two days before war against Germany was declared in 1914, he warned in a sermon at Cleethorpes against British involvement in 'European complications', but soon came to acknowledge what seemed to be the inevitability of war. When one of his sons was killed in France he provided an epitaph for the gravestone, 'HE SOUGHT PEACE AND FOUND IT'. At the same time, he spoke out and wrote letters to *The Times* in support of conscientious objectors – another highly unpopular cause.

Another special concern was the Women's Suffrage movement. This began during his Oxford years, when he urged the educational as well as the political emancipation, but it was not until he became a bishop that he took a public lead. Maude Royden, the courageous advocate of women's rights in the Church, as well as in the State, recorded her own gratitude for his support:

The churches as a whole, and the Church of England in particular, have stood aloof from the Women's Movement, but there have always been some individuals who saw both its ethical and religious significance, and were not alarmed either by the bitterness of its opponents, or by the eccentricities of some of its supporters. The Bishop of Lincoln was, in the Church of England, the first and boldest of these. I well remember our – fairly faint! – hope that the Church League for Women's Suffrage might, when it was founded, secure a bishop for its president. We asked Dr Hicks and he consented. I doubt if there was another bishop on the bench who would have done so, though there were some who sympathized. They felt for the most part that they ought not to commit themselves officially to a highly controversial movement. One can understand their difficulty, without ceasing to wish that the representatives of so revolutionary religion as that of Jesus Christ might have overcome it: without ceasing either to feel passionate gratitude to Dr Hicks, who carried his accustomed boldness of spirit into so controversial a movement as ours.

His was no nominal presidency, for he chaired or spoke at many of the League's meetings and shared in the development of its strategy, but the conservative churchman in him led him to part company with the League when the ordination of women to the priesthood was added to its agenda.

Hicks' chief preoccupation outside his diocesan duties was with what was known at the time as the Temperance Movement. He belonged to the section of it that advocated total abstinence, rather than responsible consumption of alcohol, and in this he represented only a minority within the Church of England. He was converted to the cause by his experience at Fenny Stratford, where he found unemployed farm labourers who sought escape from their immediate problems by resorting to alcohol. In common with most other Victorian social reformers, he recognized that this not only worsened their situations but also stood in the way of providing them with constructive help. The scale of the problem was demonstrated later when the wartime Prime Minister, David Lloyd George, announced that a national enemy more serious than the Germans was 'drink'.

At Fenny Stratford, Hicks joined in the founding of a local Temperance Society, the initial aim of which was to persuade working men to abstain from alcohol for 12 months. He believed that this required him to set an example, so he 'took the pledge' – for life. And kept it.

Removal to an academic post in Manchester did not reduce his zeal. In the great city he found among the labouring class overwhelming evidence to support what had become for him a crusade, and sometimes led to his being described as a fanatic. He spoke at countless meetings, identified himself with the many, usually Nonconformist, organizations that were also campaigning, and became honorary secretary of the national United Kingdom Alliance for the Total Suppression of the Liquor Trade.

As in rural Fenny Stratford, the wide acres of Lincolnshire were no less vulnerable to alcohol abuse than were the slums of Manchester, and Hicks used every opportunity to make the Temperance case in sermons and speeches to both church and secular meetings throughout the county.

He was President of the diocesan branch of the Church of England Temperance Society, though his relationship with it was not always easy, since most of its members advocated moderation rather than total abstinence.

Hicks knew a very great deal about the licensing laws and regulations, which he used in many attempts to restrict the sale of alcohol. The brewers and distillers were a constant target of his wrath, and this created some problems in Lincolnshire, where a number of both were resident. He opposed the election of a brewer as mayor of a town.

Before he became Prime Minister in 1916, Lloyd George was Chancellor of the Exchequer, a position he held for several years, and it was in this capacity that he invited Hicks to the Treasury to discuss the 'drink problem' and certain proposals for securing its reduction. The chief of these was to reduce the national production of beer and spirits and to bring the breweries and public houses under state ownership. Lloyd George recognized that both would require compromise by Hicks, who informed him that, in the circumstances of the time, he would welcome any steps designed to deal with the problem, though he suspected that the brewers would respond by weakening the content of beer to maintain their profits, rather than reduce output. He recognized that American-style prohibition was impossible, but believed that local communities should have the right of veto over the granting of licences in their districts.

The output of beer and spirits was restricted for a time, the right of veto was sought and granted in a few places, and public houses in Carlisle were nationalized, but no substantial progress was made in dealing with the problem, and when the war ended, the attention of politicians turned to what seemed more urgent issues. Hicks died in 1919, leaving a serious problem that would not go away.

7

John Bull's Other Island – Irish Crises

Conflict between Britain and Ireland – never far from the forefront of politics in the two countries during the nineteenth and twentieth centuries – can be traced back almost 500 years to the time when King Henry VIII decided to bring the patrimony of Saint Patrick under more direct English control. From then onwards rival nationalisms were inextricably linked to rival expressions of the Christian faith, with disastrous consequences. The Irish always regarded the English as ruthless invaders and had the active support of the Roman Catholic Church, while English rulers used the Anglican Church as an instrument of oppression, usually with the implicit, and sometimes explicit, support of its leaders.

Between 1534 and 1697, Crown hegemony over Ireland was enforced by a series of military campaigns involving brutal repression that became particularly vicious during the Protectorate of Oliver Cromwell and also by the importing of some thousands of English and Scottish settlers. These Protestants were allocated lands, mainly but not exclusively in the north, known as plantations, from which their Roman Catholic Irish owners had been forcibly evicted. The long history of sectarian violence began.

The establishment of an Irish Parliament under the English Crown was intended to give the impression of co-operation and common purpose, but this ended in 1603 when the creation of numerous pocket boroughs, with tiny electorates, enabled the Protestant settlers to take power. Roman Catholics were eventually banned altogether from this Parliament, even though they comprised 80 per cent of the population. They, and now the dissenting Protestants, were subject to severe penal laws designed to facilitate the English ascendancy.

Following a serious rebellion in 1801, the Irish Parliament was abolished, and an Act of Union created a new United Kingdom of Great Britain and Ireland. The Crown was represented by a Lord Lieutenant and the Westminster government by a Chief Minister. One hundred Irish seats were provided in the House of Commons, but, as in the rest of the United Kingdom, these could be occupied only by Anglicans. In any case, only a small minority of the Irish were entitled to vote.

Robert Peel, appointed Chief Secretary in 1812 at the age of 24, reported to the Prime Minister, Lord Liverpool, that Ireland was at peace. He soon discovered, however, that just beneath the surface of public life, and all too often bubbling over into violence, was intense resentment and anger. Absentee English landowners imposed harsh conditions on their Irish tenants, and there was universal objection to the payment of tithes to the Protestant clergy. The demands for a return to Irish autonomy became persistent.

The strategic importance of Ireland, emphasized by a growing threat to Britain by France, ruled this out and a substantial military force was deployed to maintain order and discourage invasion. Much of this remained after the defeat of Napoleon at Waterloo in 1815 in order to deal with increasing sectarian violence. Roman Catholic emancipation from political disabilities now began to be debated, with important implications for the whole of Britain, but it was not until 1829 that the necessary legislation was enacted.

Even this did not solve the Irish problem. Indeed, its immediate effect was to provoke a great revival of the Catholic Church there, with a decade of much church building and many more vocations to the priesthood. Bishop Charles Sumner of Winchester told his diocese that he would not have voted for emancipation had he known this would be the result. The revival did little to promote a spirit of reconciliation.

In 1831, the Whig government decided that the Church of Ireland was in urgent need of reform. Its small membership was served by four archbishops and 18 other bishops overseeing 2,436 parishes and 900 priests. As in England, large episcopal incomes were enjoyed by often absentee bishops, and at one point only two of the bishops were permanently resident in Ireland. Pluralism and absenteeism among the other clergy were no less common, though there were devout, conscientious men among them, and the names of Bishop Jeremy Taylor and Dean Jonathan Swift are now recognized as part of the Anglican inheritance well beyond Ireland's coasts.

In 1833, a Church Temporalities (Ireland) Bill proposed the abolition of two of the archbishoprics and the amalgamation or suppression of eight other bishoprics. The considerable surplus of funds created by this move was to be used to augment poor livings, repair dilapidated churches and also pay the clergy of other churches, including the Roman Catholic Church. The Bill was passed by the House of Commons but the House of Lords removed the clause that would have allocated money to Roman Catholics. Nine bishops were among the Bill's opponents who were not only against the clause, but feared, with good reason, that the Church of England would be next to suffer imposed reform.

The rejection of the clause further embittered relations between Britain and Ireland and in 1845 a proposal by the British government to make a grant to facilitate the development of an eighteenth-century Catholic seminary at Maynooth caused considerable controversy. In the end, it was passed by Parliament and led to the emergence of a breed of militant firebrand priests who stoked the blaze of rebellion.

In the same year, Ireland's potato crop, which provided the main diet of the peasant population, was struck by a fungal disease, causing widespread famine and appalling distress. This lasted until 1851, by which time as many as a million people had died and another 1.4 million had emigrated. The unwillingness of the Westminster government to provide relief led, not surprisingly, to the belief that it had been content to witness a Holocaust, and even today there are Irish historians who equate it with the Nazi extermination of the Jews.

Rebellions in 1848 and 1867 were suppressed, but not before the Roman Catholic Bishop of Kerry had called down upon the British 'God's heaviest curse, his withering, blasting, blighting curse'. He added for good measure that eternity was not long enough for their punishment, 'nor hell long enough'. But from 1870 onwards, Irish nationalists adopted political tactics as well as violence and pressed for Home Rule, which had the support of W. E. Gladstone's Liberal government, who saw it as the only solution to the Irish problem. A Home Rule Bill was, however, defeated by a Unionist majority in the House of Commons in 1886, and, although a second Bill was passed in 1893, this was vetoed by the House of Lords. A third attempt succeeded in 1914 but was immediately suspended owing to the outbreak of war. A violent uprising in Dublin at Easter 1916 led to permanent suspension, and from 1919 to 1921 a guerrilla war was waged by an Irish Nationalist Army (IRA).

A year later, a Government of Ireland Act created an independent Irish Free State, comprising the 26 predominantly Catholic southern counties. While remaining in the British Empire, Home Rule was also granted to the six predominantly Protestant northern counties, which remained more closely attached to Britain. The South remained neutral during the Second World War, but its strategic importance again required close Royal Navy surveillance. In 1949, it became the Republic of Eire.

After 1922, peace and stability returned to the South, where the Protestant community, comprising no more than one-quarter of the population, was mainly Anglican and therefore tolerant, lacking the will and the means to create trouble. It was different in the North, where the Protestant majority included not only Anglicans but a significant number of Calvinist Presbyterians and other Dissenters. These had no love of Roman Catholics and felt threatened by their numbers in the South, believing, with good reason, that many of these longed for a united Ireland, free of Britain. Fearing the minority status that such a development would bring, and doubting whether the Anglicans would offer sufficient resistance, these Protestants became more radical and eventually constituted a significant political force. Religion and nationalism remained alive.

The peace in the North was uneasy. Protestants and Catholics tended to live in separated communities, the education system kept their children apart, the Orange Order and other societies maintained the memory of past conflicts, and there was substance to the charge that Catholics were seriously discriminated against in matters relating to employment and housing.

The Second World War brought full employment, German bombing of Belfast and a broad distraction from these issues, but by the early 1960s, threats of IRA violence and the response of a militant Unionist Protestantism made conflict inevitable. The next 40 years experienced much violence and bloodshed, which sometimes spread to the British mainland, required the return of substantial military forces, the internment of many terrorists, direct rule from Westminster and conditions of warfare in the main cities. It was not until 1998, by which time the men of violence were becoming exhausted and their political leaders were recognizing that a political solution was the only means of progress, that a so-called Good Friday Agreement brought the bloodshed to an end. This has been punctuated by sporadic outbursts from small, surviving dissident groups, but, although the situation generally is not tranquil, considerable political progress has been made. Visits by the Queen to Eire and to Northern Ireland, where she shook hands with a former IRA leader, suggests that a return to hostilities is no longer contemplated by either side.

The record of the Anglican Church in the history of Ireland has for the most part been lamentable, though its past failings have been redeemed, at least in part, by its recent contribution, under the leadership of Archbishop Robin Eames, to a Peace Process that brought open hostility and violence to an end in 1998. The close association of Church and State in England and the use of the Church by the State from the sixteenth century onwards in its attempts to dominate and control Ireland were bound to leave the Church's Christian witness fatally compromised. Four centuries of complicity in the oppression, accompanied at various times by the imposition of English bishops and other dignitaries, the seizure of land and revenue, attempts (unsuccessful) to enforce the use of the Book of Common Prayer, severe civic disabilities on Roman Catholics, and harsh penal laws: these combined to create, then reinforce, conflicting and ultimately destructive forms of religious nationalism. Even today, when the issues are essentially political, religious identity remains significant.

Although the Home Rule Bill eventually reached the Statute Book, albeit temporarily in 1914, its acceptance was preceded by a serious political crisis. The Unionists, both in Northern Ireland and the mainland, were hotly opposed to the proposals of Asquith's Liberal government, the survival of which required Irish Nationalist support in the House of Commons, and demanded that, since the Bill had vital Constitutional implications, it should be submitted to a national referendum or, alternatively, Parliament should be dissolved and the matter decided at a General Election. The latter course would require the consent of the King who would, in consequence, be drawn into the controversy.

In ways that have long been inconceivable, the Archbishop of Canterbury was closely involved in the crisis discussions. This did not surprise Randall Davidson, though he confessed to only limited knowledge of the Irish problem. Yet even then, when his involvement became public knowledge, some radical newspapers wondered what the crisis might have to do with an archbishop.

By the early part of 1914 the situation was getting desperate, and on 3 March Bonar Law, the leader of the Conservative Opposition and for several years the fervent leader of the Unionist cause, went at his own request to see the Archbishop. Their confidential conversation ranged over the entire situation, and Bonar Law told Davidson that he believed Asquith would, on the following Monday, offer a compromise in the form of a separate Home Rule for the Northern counties, but this subject to a Dublin Parliament. He and his fellow Unionists would, however, find such a proposal totally unacceptable (only the total exclusion of the North from any proposed arrangement could be supported), therefore they must continue to insist on either a referendum or dissolution.

Davidson appears to have been broadly sympathetic to this position and made suggestions as to how, in the event of Asquith continuing to reject any appeal to the country, the King might order dissolution without himself appearing to be partisan. Bonar Law said that this would be an unusual course for a King to take, but then it was an unusual situation and might well be acceptable on the grounds that the King had the duty to ascertain the wishes of his people.

On the day of the expected compromise announcement Davidson had a letter in *The Times* supporting it, albeit cautiously, and concluding, 'It is an hour for steady thought, for broad resolve, for expectant prayer.' In the event, Asquith proposed a number of concessions to the North, but discussion of these was overtaken by reports of a possible mutiny by army units there in the event of any government attempt to use them to enforce new legislation. Davidson kept in close touch with the situation and went to see Bonar Law and the Prime Minister, and put himself at Asquith's disposal for explaining the complexities of the issues to a puzzled public and helping to resolve the remaining difficulties.

Asquith responded by telling Davidson that, while he was not in a position to speak for his colleagues, he would be prepared to consider having a plebiscite in the North or, alternatively, exclude the North from the Bill and let these counties have a plebiscite at the end of x years. This would, however, have to be proposed by the Unionists, and he was far from certain if his own colleagues would accept either proposition. Davidson asked if he might convey this to Bonar Law, and Asquith agreed that he might, provided it was made quite clear that it did not constitute an offer, only a possible line upon which a solution could be found.

Bonar Law told Davidson that he thought the message from the Prime Minister was of great importance and asked him to inform Asquith that he believed the alternative suggestion might offer a way forward but the proposal must come from him. Before any announcement was made, however, he would first ascertain that his fellow Unionists would agree to take part in discussions. The King now sent for Davidson to give an account of what was taking place, and on the following day the Archbishop conveyed Bonar Law's message to the Prime Minister. In the end, nothing came of it, though when Asquith met Davidson in the Athenaeum, he thanked him for his services as a go-between and said that his efforts had not been fruitless.

The tragedy of the First World War did not, however, free Davidson from concern about Irish affairs – at least not entirely. Back in 1904, he had shared in a growing anxiety about the Belgian administration of its Congo colony, in which something akin to the slave trade was being carried out. He was particularly impressed by a report on the situation sent by a British Consul, Sir Roger Casement, who was also engaged in humanitarian relief work. And he came to know him when he was in London and admired him.

A few days before Easter 1916, however, Casement landed in Southern Ireland from Germany in order to lead an uprising against the British. As an Irishman, his experience in the Belgian Congo, as well as that of the Boer War, had made him both anti-imperialist and revolutionary in outlook. On the outbreak of war in 1914, he therefore entered into negotiations with the German government, promising, in return for the supply of arms to the Irish rebels, to provoke an uprising in Dublin that would distract the British from the Western Front. How seriously the Germans took this arrangement is not clear, but they conveyed Casement and 20,000 rifles to the Irish coast. On his arrival in Dublin, he was immediately arrested but the uprising took place, devastating central Dublin and killing 300 citizens, 70 insurgents and 130 British soldiers. Fifteen of the rebels were summarily tried and shot.

Casement was charged with treason, put on trial in London, found guilty and sentenced to death. His trial inevitably created great public interest, and after the death sentence some public figures pleaded for his reprieve. Among these was Archbishop Davidson, who first wrote to the Home Secretary, Herbert Samuel, explaining that, while he had refused to sign a petition for clemency, he was nonetheless aware of Casement's important work in the Congo and elsewhere and had been impressed by his capacity, enthusiasm and apparent straightforwardness. He was driven to believe that he had been 'mentally afflicted'.

Davidson went on to say that he knew of certain other charges made against Casement's moral character which, if proved, might be taken as further evidence of his having 'become mentally unstable'. The charges related to the discovery of Casement's so-called 'Black Diaries', which portrayed him as a promiscuous homosexual. Davidson had been allowed to see these, and it is widely believed that their circulation among a few influential people was designed to undermine any sympathy that might have been had for Casement. Davidson interpreted them differently.

He next saw the judge who had tried the case, as well as Casement's niece and secretary, and, after seeing the Lord Chancellor, wrote him a very long letter. In this, he emphasized again Casement's humanitarian record in Africa, and, turning to the question of his moral character, said that while the opinion of 'professional experts' as to his sanity must be respected, this should not exclude 'solid experience of actual facts which is possessed by some of us'. Most important of all, however, was the likelihood that 'even though Casement deserved to be hanged', his execution would cause anger and resentment in Ireland, America and other parts of the world sympathetic to the Irish rebels. In these circumstances, added Davidson, a more courageous course for the Home Secretary would be to grant a reprieve.

Casement was in the event hanged and when the Lord Chancellor next met the Archbishop in the House of Lords he explained that the decision had eventually been remitted to the Cabinet, who were supplied with a copy of his letter. He believed that his 'impressive' submission had, however, been outweighed by certain political considerations relating to German ill-treatment of loyal Irish prisoners of war.

After the separation of North and South in 1922, the uneasy peace in Ulster provoked no significant episcopal pronouncements, and the Church of Ireland's leaders did not feel moved to comment on the disabilities experienced and growingly resented by the Roman Catholic leaders. By the 1970s, however, the violence of IRA terrorists and the breakdown in community relations which this both expressed and exacerbated made it impossible for any church leader to ignore the tragic events surrounding them.

It was fortunate therefore that the Church of Ireland produced, just in time, one of the outstanding church leaders of the next half-century. From the time of his appointment in 1975 to the Bishopric of Derry and Raphoe at the unusually early age of 38, until his retirement from the Primacy of All Ireland in 2006, Robin Eames was in the thick of the quest for reconciliation and also in the promotion of better understanding between the North and the Irish Republic.

That he became a key figure in the long and tortuous peace process owed everything to the fact that he combined a deep religious faith with high intelligence, legal training, political skill, pastoral sensitivity and an unswerving sense of moral purpose. Added to this a warm, attractive personality, and he quickly won the trust of both sides in the conflict, thus enabling him to build bridges over many dangerous religious, political and social chasms.

Born in Larne on 27 April 1937, Robert Henry Alexander (he was always known as Robin) Eames is the son of a Protestant car dealer who was driven from Cork by Republican pressure and lived in Dublin for a time before returning to Larne as a Methodist minister. Later he moved to Belfast and became an Anglican. Young Robin originally hoped to become a doctor, but his sciences were weak and, after completing a PhD in History and Ecclesiastical Law at the Queen's University, Belfast, he started on a promising academic career. Following the death of his father, however, he decided to seek ordination in the Church of Ireland and in 1963 became a curate at Bangor, Co. Down.

Three years later he was appointed Rector of a new housing estate parish in East Belfast, where the population was almost exclusively Protestant, and for the first two years church life prospered. But then 'The Troubles' brought Protestant paramilitaries into the parish on recruitment campaigns, and the effects of sectarian conflict in other areas began to be felt. Eames responded by concentrating more on community work designed to promote confidence and a concern for reconciliation. Although this was successful up to a point, the external pressure was great, and he failed to persuade some of his parishioners not to burn down the house of a Roman Catholic family on the edge of the estate.

After eight years of this demanding ministry, he was appointed Rector of a large parish in East Belfast, but had hardly settled in before being elected Bishop of Derry and Raphoe in 1975 – a diocese straddling the frontier between North and South, with Derry comprising what was then Londonderry and its surrounding territory, and Raphoe the beautiful, peaceful County Donegal in the Irish Republic. Derry, with its sharply divided Unionist and Republican communities, was already boiling over with hatred and violence and it was fortunate that an equally young and capable Roman Catholic Bishop, Edward Daly, had been appointed at about the same time. A strong friendship and close collaboration followed.

Eames was, however, soon required for the diocese of Down and Dromore, which included the now seething cauldron of Belfast. On his arrival in 1980, he said that whereas he had five years earlier left the city a place of riots, now it was a city of atrocities. In his Enthronement sermon, he declared what was to be a constant theme of his preaching:

> We, the Church, must constantly remind Belfast that individuals matter. That in the new Belfast emerging around us what will really matter at the end of the day is the value we place on the quality of life of its people. Every other consideration must stem from this.

When the Archbishopric of Armagh and the Primacy of All Ireland fell vacant in 1986, Eames, though still only 48, was the automatic choice, though his removal from Belfast at that juncture was not an easy strategic decision. There were nonetheless serious problems of violence in Armagh as well as equal need for reconciliation, and in the longer term the building of bridges with the Irish Republic, over which he had Anglican jurisdiction, proved to be of vital importance to the peace process.

He continued to collaborate closely with the Roman Catholic and other church leaders, establishing personal friendships with most of them, even when they were on opposing sides of the political divide. Of special importance were his relationships with successive Prime Ministers of the United Kingdom and the Irish Republic, as well as with the Northern Ireland Secretaries of State.

These amounted to more than mere formalities. He was in constant touch with 10 Downing Street, offering opinion and advice, and Sir John Major said that during his time as Prime Minister,

> I saw him as an effective bridge-builder between the policy I wished to carry out and also the Unionist politicians, and more important the Unionist population. I felt that if I could frame policies that Robin Eames could accept, it was going a long way towards producing a policy that would be accepted by the Unionist population generally.

Major was fully aware that Eames was also collaborating closely with Albert Reynolds, the Irish Prime Minister, especially in the drafting of his contribution to what became known as the 1993 Downing Street Agreement. This Joint Declaration on Peace was designed among other things to allay Unionist fears about the Republic's intentions and included some of Eames' own words and phrases in Reynold's request that Unionists should

> look on the people of the Republic as friends, who share their grief and shame over all the suffering of the last quarter of a century, and who want to develop the best possible relationship with them in which trust and new understandings can flourish and grow.

This Joint Declaration led five years later to the Good Friday Agreement and the real, even if fragile, peace that developed from it.

Eames' efforts, which included secret meetings with the IRA and other paramilitary organizations, were not, however, always so fruitful, and of lasting regret to him was his inability to reconcile the opposing sides in what became known as the Duncree Standoff in July 1996. Serious rioting, involving many deaths and injuries, resulted from the determination of Protestant Orangemen in the heart of his own diocese to hold what had become a highly provocative parade to Duncree Church. Eames always described the events of that time as his 'Calvary'.

He went several times, usually in the company of other church leaders, to America to explain more carefully the true situation in Ireland and thus discourage moral and material support for the Republican cause. He was, however, no less concerned with the cost of the conflict to individuals and local communities. On some occasions he walked into Republican districts of extreme hostility, and in the homes of the people listened to their grievances and aspirations. He conducted innumerable funerals, often under media spotlight, consoling grieving relatives (sometimes after breaking bad news to them) and spent a great deal of time in parishes that felt under threat of terrorism.

Eames was awarded a peerage in 1995 in recognition of what he had already achieved and to enable him to do more, though Republicans regarded it as a sign of too close an attachment to the Westminster Establishment. Admission to the Order of Merit a year after his retirement in 1996 was widely applauded. Never again would church leaders in Ireland be free to ignore the claims of reconciliation and social justice.

8

The War that Did Not End Wars: 1914–18

The great act of human folly signalled by the outbreak of war on 4 August 1914 was, for all but a handful of people in Britain, totally unexpected. Eleven days before its declaration the Cabinet had met for the first time for a month to discuss foreign policy. On 9 July, the Chancellor of the Exchequer, David Lloyd George, informed a meeting of bankers: 'In the matter of external affairs the sky has never been more perfectly blue.' A fortnight later, he told the House of Commons that Britain's relations with Germany were 'very much better than they have been for a few years'.

Relations between the British and German churches were more than cordial and strengthening, even though the ecumenical movement had yet to be born. Large delegations from each country made fraternal visits to the other, and one of these encouraged the Archbishop of Canterbury, Randall Davidson, to speak of 'The eloquent expressions of the great Sovereign of the German Empire [Kaiser Wilhelm II] in favour of peace.'

In these circumstances, it might have been anticipated that the sudden outbreak of war would be greeted with horror and apprehension, deep concern for safety and (for some) anxiety as to their continuing prosperity. Nothing could have been further from the case. A sense of relief, almost exultation in a renewed sense of unity and common purpose; delight in the challenge now offered; euphoria mixed with jingoism; these gripped the nation. Men rushed to the colours in numbers sufficient to ensure that not until January 1916 would compulsory conscription be needed to replace the mounting casualties being sustained in France and Flanders. There was talk in both Britain and Germany of the war being 'over by Christmas'.

By the end of 1914, however, the Battles of Mons and The Marne, which virtually wiped out Britain's standing army, had administered a painful and unpleasant shock. Yet many still believed the war to be a divine judgement, inasmuch as the nation had become too comfortable and complacent and needed to endure a period of suffering to ensure its return to responsibility. Many young men, especially the products of public schools, were motivated by an almost romantic sense of honour that demanded sacrifice in the cause of duty.

With very few exceptions, the Church of England's leaders did nothing to discourage any of this, though Randall Davidson was not the sort to indulge in anything emotional. Few Archbishops of Canterbury before him, and certainly none since his day, were as close to the levers of power in Britain. Of the six Prime Ministers who served during his time at Lambeth, four were personal friends who enjoyed social as well as official encounters. Davidson's meetings with them and members of their governments, as well as other public figures including the military, were regular and serious, especially during the war years.

At the beginning of August 1918, he summarized his activities during the previous three months which, he said, 'have in some respects been the most important months in our common life, as regards things that have been happening'. He went on:

I have been in pretty close touch with prominent actors and thinkers who have been handling English affairs and policy . . . I have been in close and constant touch with Stamfordham [personal secretary successively to Queen Victoria, Kings Edward VII and George V], who has kept me abreast of many things, and prevented my ever being quite out of touch with any important things that were happening. I have also had my ears open in the House of Lords, where I have attended with great regularity, and in the House of Commons when important things were under debate. All this results in my finding myself abreast of conversations among public men, when I am present at such, and on a good many points I think I have perhaps a wider knowledge than many with whom I converse, even though they be officials with access to government information. And yet there is no outstanding controversial matter in which I find myself brimming or effervescing with thought, or controverting vehemently a current view.

His relationship with the King was also unusually close. Audiences were readily granted, and he was often summoned to Court to discuss a wide variety of current concerns.

Davidson was an archetypal Anglican – with a deep regard for tradition and a cautious attitude to innovation; a liberal mind that eschewed the niceties of theology in favour of pragmatic action; a strong belief that Church and State should be united in a common effort to create an inclusive society, not free of class divisions but one in which justice, freedom and responsibility reigned. So, although a natural courtier and a senior member of the Establishment, he was never a Tory and was prepared on some occasions (not many) to speak and vote against policies which he believed to be inimical to Christian moral values. It was perhaps the strength of these convictions that turned him into a workaholic, so that with the assistance of only

possible policies of retaliation. In a House of Lords debate on 15 March 1915, he said: 'If once we became infected with a lower spirit and adopted a lower ideal by imitating bad habits and bad ways of which we might hear elsewhere, it would be the worst misfortune that the War could bring upon us.' These fears were considerably reinforced when, on 6 May, he heard of a proposal to adopt poison gas in reply to the German use of it. A strongly worded letter went to Lord Stamfordhan pointing out that just a few weeks earlier it would have seemed 'altogether out of the question' that such a barbaric act would be carried out by English soldiers, and that 'our barbarian-like opponents have sunk to that level is no reason why we should sink with them'.

An equally strong and much longer letter then went to the Prime Minister, and, after a meeting with him, a milder version of the letter, together with Asquith's reply was published. But on 24 May, Davidson was informed that the British army had been authorized to make use of gases for urgent military reasons, the French having already decided to do so.

The issue of reprisals was one to which he returned several times as the clamour for them increased the longer the war went on, and the casualties reached horrendous totals. The generals felt driven to ever more desperate tactics, and Davidson's interventions were not always welcomed by them or by the general public, as he noted in October 1917:

> I am the recipient of a continuous shower of protests, denunciations, and often virulent abuse from every part of England, especially from London. I am said to be the cause of the air raids, to be in league with the Germans, and to be responsible for the deaths of those who suffered, and so on. Devout prayers are expressed that I and occasionally my wife, to whom they sometimes write, may be the next person to be blown to pieces.

Following the introduction of conscription in 1916, the position of conscientious objectors to military service also became a matter of concern to him. In general, he believed that their stance should be recognized and accepted, but only if they were prepared to undertake other, non-combatant work, incumbent upon them as citizens of a country in peril.

Before long, questions were being asked about the exemption of clergy from conscription. More than 3,000 Anglican priests were in fact serving as chaplains in the services, 88 of whom were eventually killed, and for most of the war Davidson argued that this and ministry in the parishes was the most effective contribution the clergy could make to the war effort. There was also the important point that Canon Law did not allow those in Holy Orders to carry arms. Not everyone in the country was prepared to accept this, and quite often clergy would be accosted in the streets by a woman, who may have lost her husband and one or more sons, and who told him 'Kitchener Needs You'.

In the early part of 1918, when the situation on the Western Front threatened a possible German victory, Davidson was driven to change his mind and supported in the House of Lords a government proposal that the age for conscription should be extended and that clergy be no longer exempt from its demands. It was expected, but not guaranteed, that any clergy so conscripted would be assigned to non-combatant duties. In the event the claim on them was quickly rescinded, partly because it was made clear that the Roman Church in Ireland would not allow its priests to be conscripted and partly because the numbers involved could hardly be significant.

Davidson was somewhat taken aback by this decision and explained to the House of Lords that it was not due to any desire on the part of the Church of England to escape from its obligations in an emergency. He and a number of other bishops, with varying degrees of enthusiasm, undertook to encourage their clergy to volunteer for military service, and some did, but it turned out that most of those remaining in the parishes were too old to be useful.

By September 1918, it was evident that America's entry into the war had tipped the scale decisively in the Allies' favour, and that the end could not long be delayed. President Wilson was thus prompted to make proposals for the formation of a League of Nations to ensure that the current struggle really would, as had always been hoped, be 'a war to end wars'. At the suggestion of Lord Robert Cecil, Davidson wrote to *The Times* on 28 September strongly supporting the idea and pointing out that eight months earlier the bishops had voted unanimously for just such an organization and desired this to be included in the conditions of the peace settlement when it came:

> The issues are worldwide. Our vision and our purpose must be worldwide too. Let Mr Wilson rest assured of the vivid and eager response which his appeal awakens in the minds of tens of thousands of the Christian men and women upon whose will, in the long run, the effective decision must turn. We give no mere lip-service to a great ideal. We mean that the thing shall come to pass.

The letter met with wide approval, and the next day he attended a meeting on the subject in the Central Hall, Westminster, where he moved a vote of thanks to the speaker, Lord Curzon, and renewed the Church's commitment to the President's proposals.

He was in the House of Commons on 11 November when the Prime Minister, Lloyd George, announced the armistice and gave an account of its terms. It having then been announced that both Houses of Parliament would adjourn to St Margaret's Church for prayer, he went to take part in the service and reflected later: 'I do not suppose there has ever been in our history a more significant recognition of the Divine Presence and aid than in this sudden attendance of the Houses at Divine service in lieu of a Commons debate.'

Three months earlier, on the fourth anniversary of the outbreak of the war, he had preached in St Margaret's to both Houses and to King George V, emphasizing once again the importance of not allowing 'a poisonous hatred of the enemy', which he had discerned here and there, to spread more widely. Reflecting on his sermon immediately afterwards, he summed up what had in fact been his understanding of his role from the war's beginning:

> I felt the occasion to be an important one, but it would I think have been an abuse of the pulpit had one tried to outline questions of policy, even in the largest way. It was not an easy sermon to preach, for the very reason that political questions in the controversial sense had to be avoided, and, on the other hand, one wished to avoid, and I think I did avoid, the comparatively easy and certainly popular course of beating the big drum, and simply belauding ourselves and our cause. I tried to say some things that are not politically controversial but which cut at the root of our religious attitude and temptation. I was listened to with unbroken attention. It remains to be seen whether I have so trodden on susceptible toes as to produce protest or attack. Whether my words do so or not, I am at present sure that I was right in saying them.

No such inhibitions would have been felt or such care taken had the pulpit been entrusted to the Bishop of London, Arthur Foley Winnington-Ingram. On Advent Sunday 1915, he had preached in Westminster Abbey, next door, what can confidently be described as the most unchristian sermon ever uttered in that great church. Taking as his text Isaiah 11.9, 'They shall not hurt nor destroy in all my holy mountain', he began by deploring Germany's assault on freedom and 'everything that is noblest in Europe', and went on:

> Everyone that loves freedom and honour, everyone that puts principle above ease, and life itself beyond mere living, are banded in a great crusade – we cannot deny it – to kill Germans; to kill them, not for the sake of killing, but to save the world; to kill the good as well as the bad, to kill the young men as well as the old, to kill those who have shown kindness to our wounded as well as those fiends who crucified

the Canadian sergeant, who superintended the Armenian massacres, who sank the *Lusitania*, and who turned the machine guns on the civilians of Aerschott and Louvain – and to kill them lest the civilization of the world itself should be killed.

He went on to explain to the congregation that he was not trying to stir up hatred of the German race – 'I do it to defend Christianity.'

As much as any twenty-first-century religious fanatic, Winnington-Ingram saw the First World War as a holy war. Shortly before its outbreak, he was in camp with the London Rifle Brigade, of which he had been chaplain since 1901, and, following the declaration of war he stayed with them for the next two months. As a territorial unit, it was expected initially that it would remain in south-east England to defend the home country, rather than embark for France. This was soon reversed, however, and on Sunday 9 August the General appealed to Winnington-Ingram to 'Put a little ginger into your sermon, as some of these men have not volunteered for foreign service.' At the end of the service, all those who had hesitated volunteered, as did the soldiers of another unit whom he exhorted the following day – 'We would all rather die, wouldn't we, than have England a German province?'

Even greater success attended a sermon addressed to 5,000 Territorials at Bulswater Camp on 31 August. Having reminded them of what the Germans had done to the women and children of Belgium, he assured them that the men of Agincourt, Crecy, Inkerman, Alma and Waterloo were with them. Duty to their country was part of their duty to God, so they must be ready to go overseas. Christ had said, 'If ye love me, keep my commandments'; therefore love demands obedience. In the end, 10,000 men volunteered for overseas service and Winnington-Ingram received a personal letter of thanks from Lord Kitchener, the Commander-in-Chief.

During the next four years, he constantly sought to emphasize what he believed to be the religious imperatives in the nation's struggle against evil, and he drew freely on the imagery of the crucifixion to equate the sacrifice of the men in the trenches with that of Christ on the cross.

The opportunities for doing this were greatly increased when in 1915 he spent Holy Week in France engaged in what he regarded as a mission to the fighting army. He gave an undertaking not to enter the front-line trenches but, clad in a uniform of the sort worn by senior officers, he went close to the action and carried out a remarkable schedule of over 50 services, including Holy Communions, Confirmations and very large outdoor parades, besides visits to hospitals and rest camps. He also distributed 10,000 prayer cards and wished he had taken twice that number.

A frequently used text was 'Endure hardship as a good soldier of Jesus Christ'. Wounded soldiers were told that their clean hospital sheets were a gift from God, and that time spent between them should be regarded as an opportunity to return to him.

Although some of the more thoughtful chaplains had serious reservations about the enterprise, Winnington-Ingram was generally received with great enthusiasm, and personal conversations with him were much valued. So much so, that he returned to England fully convinced that the fighting on the Western Front was bringing about a religious revival. This provided another theme for his wartime sermons, but in the event the opposite proved to be the case.

The son of a Worcestershire clergyman, Winnington-Ingram was born in 1858 and went from Marlborough College to Keble College, Oxford, where he distinguished himself in Classics. He was ordained without any kind of theological education, but as chaplain to the Bishop of Lichfield proved to be a successful conductor of parish missions. On the strength of this, he was appointed Head of the Oxford House Mission in Bethnal Green, where he began his love affair with London's East End. Adopting a Cockney accent, which he retained for the rest of his days, he threw himself into social and evangelistic work, again with great success, and after two years was made Bishop of Stepney, combining this with a Canonry of St Paul's. More than 3,000 people frequently packed the cathedral to hear sermons that were, in the opinion of W. R. Inge, who was Dean at the time, 'of almost childish simplicity'.

No one anticipated that he would ever become Bishop of London, and when the diocese fell vacant in 1901 it was initially offered to Randall Davidson, at that time Bishop of Winchester. He was, however, advised on health grounds to decline, and so the Prime Minister, Lord Salisbury, turned to Winnington-Ingram. A later Prime Minister, H. H. Asquith, would not have done so – 'He is so superlatively silly that he can do a great deal of harm. He was a good enough little curate in an East End parish; the biggest mistake ever made was to put him where he his.' Twenty years later, another Prime Minister, Stanley Baldwin, said, 'The best service I can render to the Church of England is to get Winnington-Ingram moved from London.' He failed in this, and it was not until 1939 that physical frailty ended the 38-year-long episcopate. For many years the administration of the diocese was in chaos, but he had been greatly loved by a multitude of Londoners.

His only rival in this was Dick Sheppard, a very different character, whose brief experience as a chaplain in France in 1914 drove him to embrace pacifism as the only Christian response. Born in 1881 and the son of a priest, who became Sub-Dean of the Chapel Royal, he went to

Marlborough College, though he stayed for only 18 months. In 1900, he volunteered for service in the Boer War, but while on the way to Waterloo Station one of the horses drawing his cab fell, causing a disabling injury to his leg.

An undistinguished academic career at Trinity College, Cambridge, was followed by a spell at Oxford House, Bethnal Green, but, although a Winnington-Ingram sermon in St Paul's on the subject, 'Why should I not be ordained?' made a great impact, he decided that he would best serve God as a layman. This he did for a short time as secretary to Cosmo Gordon Lang, who had succeeded Winnington-Ingram as Bishop of Stepney, but this ended with his decision to go to Cuddesdon Theological College to prepare for ordination in 1907.

He now returned to Oxford House, first as chaplain, then as Head, and remained deeply immersed in East End work until 1911, when he went with considerable reluctance to join the staff of St George's Hanover Square, in Mayfair. There he was put in charge of the smaller daughter church, St Mary's, then of the recently restored Grosvenor Chapel, both of which were soon filled to capacity.

During the summer of 1914 he was appointed Vicar of St Martin-in-the-Fields, in Trafalgar Square – a once fashionable church, but now completely run down, neglected and with a Sunday congregation of only seven at Matins and twelve at Evensong. He was not due to be instituted until November, so, against much advice and to the displeasure of King George V, a parishioner, he took the opportunity to enlist as a temporary chaplain to an Australian hospital in France.

This proved to be a devastating experience, for he identified himself closely with the casualties, and in October his own health broke down and he was sent home. Those few months influenced the remainder of his life and gave him a vision of what he was called to do at St Martin-in-the-Fields. There were 11 people present at his Institution one foggy day in November 1915, but, having first thrown the church open, 24 hours a day, to soldiers travelling through London on their way to and from the Front, he transformed it to become known worldwide as a church that ministered to people of every sort, especially the poor and the homeless. By the end of the war, the press were calling it London's Tabernacle of Peace, and it was at Sheppard's suggestion that an annual Festival of Remembrance be held in the Albert Hall on the eve of what was then called Armistice Day.

His personal experience of war and subsequent identification with many of its victims also led him to an utter detestation of war, and when in the 1930s rearmament started and conflict again threatened, he wrote a letter to the *Manchester Guardian* and some other papers inviting men to send him a postcard undertaking to renounce war. Within two days, 2,500 had responded, and at the end of three weeks this had risen to 30,000. This led to the formation of Dr H. R. L. Sheppard's Peace Movement, and in July 1935 he chaired a meeting in the Albert Hall attended by 7,000 of its adherents. Soon afterwards the name was changed to the Peace Pledge Union, which quickly grew to be 100,000 strong, with many prominent religious, literary and political figures among them.

White, rather than red, poppies were worn at Remembrancetide, the call for international disarmament became more frequent, and as Hitler and Mussolini displayed their aggressive intentions, the PPU became a popular mouthpiece for appeasement. Sheppard and his friends in the leadership were as horrified as anyone by the dictators' actions, but they believed that another European war would be worse. At first this pacifist position was very widely shared, but when Hitler's expansionist threat became a reality, the national mood changed, and the PPU was accused of displaying undue sympathy for the Nazis. They were denounced by some leading politicians, and when Sheppard addressed the Church Assembly on the subject in 1937, he was heard in silence and immediately opposed by his friend William Temple. Nonetheless, the PPU survived and continues its witness today.

Cosmo Gordon Lang, another close friend of Sheppard, became Archbishop of York in 1908, and, although he expressed from the pulpit of York Minster on the Sunday following the outbreak of war in 1914 his detestation of war, he was an unequivocal supporter of the war effort. Without ever approaching the extremes of Winnington-Ingram, he joined enthusiastically in the recruiting drive, and in November 1915 felt moved to declare, 'The country calls for the service of its sons. I envy the man who is able to meet the call: I pity the man who at such a time makes the great refusal.'

In this, he was expressing no more, or less, than almost universally held public opinion, but a few months earlier he added an indiscretion that had a traumatic effect on him. Since the time of Queen Victoria, he had been closer than any other churchman to the Royal Family, and when attending a highly charged meeting in 1915, at which there was much angry denunciation of all things German, he tried to cool things by recalling one of his royal experiences.

He was Vicar of Portsea at the time of Queen Victoria's death and conducted a service on the Royal Yacht that conveyed her body from the Isle of Wight to Portsmouth, and he told the meeting how moved he had been to see the new King and the German Kaiser, her son-in-law, kneeling side by side at the bier. This was, he said, 'a sacred memory'. Far from cooling the situation, this only added fuel to the flames, and for some time afterwards he was subjected to much public denunciation and abuse.

Outwardly he seemed unperturbed, but he was a lonely man and sensitive to the opinion of others, not least to King George V and Queen Mary, who were for a time less friendly. In 1916, he suddenly lost all his dark hair, leaving only a small white fringe above his ears. This transformed his appearance so that he became unrecognizable, even to many of his friends. It would not be the last time that he failed to judge public opinion in a matter relating to Royalty.

9

Living and Talking in
Hope – Three Conferences

Although the Christian Social Union, with its once large membership, had run out of steam during the First World War, there was no possibility of social reform leaving the Church's agenda while Charles Gore and William Temple were still alive. In any case, the war had not only been described as 'a war to end wars', it had also led to a determination to create a 'country fit for heroes to live in'. This could only involve considerable social change in which a collectivist approach played an important part.

The 1920 Lambeth Conference of Anglican bishops, representing a worldwide constituency, resolved:

An outstanding and pressing duty of the Church is to convince its members of the necessity of nothing less than a fundamental change and working of our economic life. This change can only be effected by accepting as the basis of industrial relations the principle of co-operation in the service of the common good in place of unrestricted competition for private or sectional advantage. All Christian people ought to take an active part in bringing about this change.

An industrial dispute in the following year provoked even the cautious Archbishop Davidson to issue a statement in which he affirmed 'the fundamental principle that the remuneration of labour is the first charge upon any industry must require the proper maintenance of the labourer'. The much less cautious Bishop Kempthorne of Lichfield told the bishops in the Convocation that the railway and coal industries should be nationalized and went on to condemn 'the wasteful, vulgar and extravagant luxury shown by a considerable part of the community' at a time when workers were being asked to accept lower wages.

The then Bishop of Manchester, William Temple, needed no convincing of this, and the success of the Life and Liberty Movement in its campaign to reform the Church of England's government left him free to resume his activities in a wider field. Appointed to Manchester at the early age of 40, he had boundless energy as well as outstanding ability, and, through his involvement in the developing ecumenical movement, much experience of meetings and conferences. He believed in these as a means of sharing insights, stimulating enthusiasm and encouraging action. Moreover, he was a genius at synthesizing facts and opinions and therefore a superb chairman. All of which were brought into action in a major ecumenical Conference of Politics, Economics and Citizenship (COPEC) held in Birmingham in the spring of 1924.

It is hard to believe that any conference could ever have been better prepared for. The idea was first mooted in 1919 (Temple traced its origin back to a Student Christian Movement conference held in Matlock in 1909) and launched as an International Conference of Social Service Unions, of which Gore was the president. In the following year, however, this became a COPEC Council of 350 members, with Temple in the chair. Twelve commissions were formed and 200,000 questionnaires were distributed to discover interests, skills and opinions. These were dealt with at 75 centres, and the whole of 1923 was spent by the commissions analysing the responses and producing book-length reports for the conference.

The purpose of the conference was declared to be 'the establishing of a norm of Christian thought and action for the further working out of a Christian order'. Temple himself was in no doubt that an adequate social order could be built only on Christian foundations, and he was therefore anxious to reaffirm the concept of Church and State working in close partnership.

About 1,500 delegates attended, 80 of these from outside the British Isles. Messages were received from the King, the Prime Minister, Ramsey MacDonald, and two former Prime Ministers – Stanley Baldwin and Herbert Asquith. The Archbishop of Canterbury, Randall Davidson, regretted his absence, he being on holiday in Italy. The subjects, provided by the commission reports, with appropriate resolutions for amendment if necessary in the light of debate, were The Nature of God and his Purpose for the World, the Social Function of the Church, Education, Relation of the Sexes, Treatment of Crime, International Relations, Industry and Property, the Home – far too much for serious discussion in one week and on such a scale.

In his opening address, Temple emphasized the essentially spiritual character of the enterprise:

With the steadily growing sense that Machiavellian statecraft is bankrupt there is an increasing readiness to give a heed to the claim of Jesus Christ that He is the Way, the Truth and the Life. We represent here today the consequences of a spiritual movement in the Church prompted by loyalty and hope, and a spiritual movement in the world prompted by disillusion and despair. Our opportunity is overwhelmingly great; so also is our responsibility . . . Our aim is to hear God speak . . . Those who speak will speak in God's presence; those who listen will listen in dependence on God.

It is not clear what evidence informed Temple's analysis, but it was certainly inspiring stuff. Yet the need to relate social action to religious faith was given little attention. The report of the commission on the Nature of God and his Purpose for the World was presented but not discussed. Delegates were anxious to get their teeth into more immediate practical issues and some of the discussion was certainly thoughtful and constructive; but as always on these occasions, a lot of hot air poured forth, and only Temple's firm chairmanship prevented voting on resolutions concerning capitalist cartels, imperialism, international warmongers and the like.

A high point in the conference was the appearance of the Bishop of Birmingham, Charles Gore. He was greeted with a sustained ovation and made just one contribution – a lecture in which the seasoned warrior warned:

This conference will be judged by its practical work, and for that I tremble. We need tremendous courage to ask ourselves frankly whether we are really prepared to accept these fundamental principles and to apply them whatever the effect upon our party politics.

How influential was this warning? The answer must be 'Not very' – at least not in the short term. There was some follow-up in the form of regional conferences and continuation committees, but the short-lived Labour government, in the background of the conference, went out of office, thus eliminating the possibility of significant social reform. The 1926 coal miners' strike, leading to a General Strike, found all the churches powerless to intervene constructively. COPEC had spoken of the need for more collaborative industrial relations without so much as a hint as to how this might be achieved – a fatal weakness in much Christian thinking.

Another, related comment on the conference, made by a sympathetic and astute participant, Maurice Reckitt, was that it represented the climax of a phase of social idealism rather than the initiation of a new phase of Christian realism. Hensley Henson, entirely unsympathetic to the enterprise, described it as 'Christian Socialism in its latest phase'.

Yet COPEC was not without significance. It picked up and reinforced the achievement of the Christian Social Union in establishing that concern for the welfare of one's neighbour involves, inescapably, social and political action. The scale of the conference, and the publicity surrounding it, placed this truth permanently on the Church's agenda. It was not to be expected that the Church of England's bishops would be unanimous in their acceptance of the diagnosis and the prescription. They were not. But COPEC set most episcopal thinking in the direction of greater state intervention in social matters and towards what would come to be known as the Welfare State. Inseparable from this, it established William Temple as a coming, outstanding leader of the Church of England, and the World Church, whose reputation lay primarily in the fields of Christian unity and social ethics.

Much smaller than COPEC and different in method and style was a conference on Church, Community and State held in Oxford for a fortnight in 1937 and now seen as one of the landmarks in the development of the ecumenical movement. It was organized by a pioneering Life and Work Institute which, together with a similar Faith and Order body, became a constituent part of the soon-to-be-founded World Council of Churches. The atmosphere in which the delegates gathered was sombre. The Great Depression cast a shadow over the economic and social life of the Western world. Communist Russia was at war with its churches and denying basic freedoms to all its people. Nazi Germany was an ever-growing threat to European peace, and aggressive militarism in Spain and Italy compounded the anxiety. How might the churches respond?

Although the conference was billed as international and ecumenical, and ground-breaking at the time, its membership of 300 was chiefly North American and European. The German churches were forbidden by Hitler to send a delegation, and of the 30 who came from the developing world, most were European missionaries. Just 17 women were present. The calibre of the delegates was, however, high. Reinhold Niebuhr led the Americans and made a considerable impact. John Foster Dulles, the future Secretary of State, was among their laymen. Karl Barth and Paul Tillich were there, together with other leading European theologians. In the absence of William Temple, Bishop George Bell of Chichester led the Church of England delegation, which included some distinguished laymen – T. S. Eliot, R. H. Tawney, Walter Moberly, Ernest Barker and John Maud. Another Anglican layman, J. H. Oldham, handled the careful preparations for the conference, which introduced the term 'middle axioms' into economic discussions, and he also edited the report, *The Churches Survey Their Task*.

The possibility of another European war was met head-on with a statement that war always involves compulsory enmity, diabolic outrage against human personality and wanton distortion of the truth. 'It is a particular demonstration of the power of sin in the world and a defiance of the righteousness of God as revealed in Jesus Christ and him crucified.' The conference recognized, however, that in some situations the maintenance of the international order might require a just war, though it also acknowledged that pacifism was a valid Christian choice and one that ought to be accepted as such by the churches.

Its verdict on the role of the State was no less forthright: 'The State is not the ultimate source of law, rather its guarantor. The State is not the lord but the servant of justice. For the Christian the ultimate authority is God.' The delegates had been urged not to take sides in the differing witness of Christians in Germany, but in the end firmly supported that of the Confessing Church in its opposition to Hitler. The recent theological work of Karl Barth re-emphasizing the priority of God and the gospel was now influential, and the development of the ecumenical movement was based on an understanding of the Church as a universal institution transcending national and racial boundaries. Hence the call of the conference – 'Let the Church be the Church' – echoing another call from Oxford almost exactly a century earlier.

When it turned to the grim economic situation of the time, the conference was critical of both capitalism and Communism and said that the rise of Communism was due to the Church's neglect of social problems. It was necessary to be aware of the corporate, as well as the personal nature of sin, and the Church must assert constantly that to make the acquisition of wealth the chief criterion of success is as fatal in its moral consequences as any other form of idolatry.

The influence of the conference was largely international and ecumenical, but Leslie Hunter, the future Bishop of Sheffield, and the other British delegates were stimulated and encouraged by it and took new insights into the national debate. The work of COPEC was, however, carried forward and developed mainly by the Christendom Group, whose membership included some of the Christian intelligentsia, the likes of T. S. Eliot, Dorothy L. Sayers, V. A. Demant, W. G. Peck and Maurice Reckitt.

There was nothing at all superficial about any of their discussions and studies, which were shared with a wider public at an annual Summer School of Sociology. The description 'Christian Sociology' was used to categorize their interests, but bore no resemblance to the much later professional study of the Sociology of Religion. Its theological basis was Anglo-Catholic, and a serious weakness of its work was the belief that a Christian society required a society of Christians such as existed in medieval times.

This inevitably coloured the papers, and some of its most learned members were asked to provide papers for discussion at a national Anglican conference on church and society held at Malvern in January 1941. The idea for this had come from Prebendary P. T. R. Kirk, the General Director of the Industrial Christian Fellowship, and been eagerly taken up by William Temple, who was now Archbishop of York and would soon be called to succeed Cosmo Gordon Lang at Canterbury.

That such a conference should have been convened at such a time can, in retrospect, be regarded only as extraordinary. The Soviet Union had not yet been drawn into the Second World War on the Allied side. A sea-channel of no more than 21 miles stood between Britain and a ruthless German enemy. A mere three months had passed since the Battle of Britain prevented an imminent invasion. London and other major cities were being subjected to nightly bombing. The future of Christian civilization was in the balance.

In this desperate situation, 240 bishops, other clergy and laity gathered for three days in a boys' public school, in the heart of quintessentially English countryside to think out (in the words of William Temple): 'the general implications of fundamental Christian principles in relation to contemporary needs, so supplying what among the ancients were called "middle axioms" – maxims which mediate between fundamental principles and the tangle of particular problems'. It never became clear how these might have influenced the Prime Minister, Winston Churchill, who had only recently declared that the nation would fight Hitler on the beaches and in the hedgerows, but the conference was lacking the high optimism which had characterized COPEC. The memory of the 1926 General Strike and the mass unemployment and social deterioration of the 1930s was also still fresh enough to discourage belief that Christians held easy answers.

Many of those who went to Malvern came away feeling that the conference had been a failure. Certainly it had not been well prepared, and it was rushed. The material offered for consideration consisted mainly of Christendom Group papers which, besides their medieval presuppositions, made few concessions to those unacquainted with their concepts or their technical language. Thus they were not so much affirmed or disagreed with as not really comprehended. When taxed with this, the Christendom members responded that they had understood it to be a serious conference and that those who failed to understand them had no right to be there.

William Temple was not among these and once again his chairmanship was remarkable. With consummate skill he drew together a veritable ragbag of opinion, disagreement, hopes and fears that led to *The Life of the Church and the Order of Society*. Soon after the conference the ICF distributed 200,000 copies of a brief summary of its conclusions, and this was followed by a 16-page pamphlet drafted by Temple, *Malvern and After*, of which 38,000 copies had been sold by the end of the following February. Its impact was therefore far from negligible and the issues it raised were discussed in many parishes.

Cyril Garbett, at that time Bishop of Winchester and soon to succeed Temple at York, was driven to lament that Malvern had been 'a gathering of the Left-wing intelligentsia who intended to commit the Church to an economic programme'. Hensley Henson, now retired, went further and described the participants as those whose 'feelings and passions are strong in proportion to the narrowness of their experience, the smallness of their knowledge, and the strength of their prejudices'.

Temple said afterwards that the conference had 'fulfilled my own hopes in a very high degree', and, contrasting it usefully with COPEC, which he had presided over 17 years earlier, he outlined what he believed to have been its main achievement:

1. Malvern was far more theological. There was a more pervasive belief that the evils in society arise from our desertion of an ascertainable order for society which springs from and coheres with Christian faith in God as Creator, Redeemer and Sanctifier.
2. Malvern was more concerned than such conferences have usually been with the function of the Church itself and the need for drastic reform in the financial and administrative system of the Church of England if its voice is to be heard in connection with social and economic questions.
3. The main problem now is not concerned with the conditions of employed labour but with security of employment or at least of status. Our discussion led us to suggest that the remedy must be sought in a new appreciation of the true relations between finance, production and consumption and adjustments of our economic system in the light of this; we further considered that a reform of the monetary system might be indispensable, and that the rights of labour as compared with those of capital called for redress.

This third point he would return to frequently, and a good deal of Malvern was expressed in his landmark *Christianity and Social Order* (1942), but it remains scarcely credible that so detached an approach to national life could have been taken by a conference meeting at so critically dangerous a moment in its history.

10

Responding to the Dictators

With the benefit of hindsight it seems obvious that the unsatisfactory conclusion of the First World War was bound to lead, sooner or later, to the
rise of a dictatorship in Germany. The military, economic and psychological
consequences of the Treaty of Versailles led to the total demoralization of
a once great nation and a series of weak governments created a dangerous
vacuum in its public life. The Communist Party was gaining ground rapidly.
Equally obvious now is the fact that installation in the Chancellorship on
30 January 1933 of a man of the stamp of Adolf Hitler was certain to bring
catastrophe to Germany and the rest of Europe if not quickly checked.

It did not seem so at the time, except to a very small number of
informed observers. Few people had read, or were even aware of, Hitler's
Mein Kampf, and the news from Germany initially caused the Church of
England's leaders no great concern. Even Bishop George Bell of Chichester,
of otherwise impeccable, indeed heroic, record, felt moved to express 'profound sympathy for the great awakening of the German people'.

Bishop Arthur Cayley Headlam of Gloucester went much further in a letter to *The Times* in which he praised the Nazis and denounced their Jewish
critics as 'clever, malicious and untruthful'. The letter was reprinted widely
in the German press. Within a year he was driven by events to change his
opinions, but until the outbreak of war in 1939 he was prominent among
the overwhelming majority of British people who believed, or at least hoped,
that accommodation with Hitler offered the best prospect of continuing
peace in Europe.

Headlam, born into an old County Durham family in 1862, inherited both
its wealth and its intellectual tradition. Winchester, New College, Oxford,
and a Fellowship of All Souls led to ordination and seven years as Rector
of Welwyn in Hertfordshire. Then came appointment as Principal of King's
College, London, where his combination of intellectual and administrative
gifts, allied to unbounded energy, saved the college from what seemed a
likely demise. He was a formidable character of overbearing manner, little small talk and a reputation for rudeness. His friend Hensley Henson
described him as 'Like a brazil nut: repulsively hard in the shell and admirable in the kernel.'

two chaplains and a secretary he achieved an almost unbelievable amount of important work.

Despite his sources of information and proximity to the decision-makers, Davidson seems to have been as surprised as anyone when war came. As recently as 17 July he had received from the Kaiser's senior court chaplain, Dr Ernst Dreyander, a courteous letter enquiring whether the Anglican Church would welcome an invitation to take part in celebrations marking the 400th anniversary of the Reformation in 1917. With equal courtesy, Davidson explained that this would not be possible since the Anglican Church embraced the Catholic as well as the Protestant tradition and could not therefore emphasize the one against the other. His letter was prefaced, however, by an ominous paragraph expressing anxiety about the international situation and the importance of daily prayer that 'the possibility of conflict may be removed from us. War between two great Christian nations of kindred race and sympathies is, or ought to be, unthinkable.'

On 30 July he was asked to sign a memorial to the Prime Minister, H. H. Asquith, prepared by a House of Commons committee and calling for Britain's non-intervention in a possible war. He replied that he objected to much of its phraseology and that in any case he could not sign it 'without an assurance that it was on lines which the government would find helpful'. When he saw Asquith the following day, he was told that for the next few days at least a memorial of this sort would be 'actively harmful'.

On Sunday 2 August, he preached at 10 a.m. before the King at Buckingham Palace, conducted a wedding at noon and preached in Westminster Abbey at 3 p.m. on the text 'Our Father'. As he started, however, there were cries of 'Votes for women' from Suffragettes who had chained themselves to transept seats. He waited until they had departed, then began again: 'What is happening is fearful beyond all words, both in actual fact and in the thought of what may be to come . . . This thing which is now astir in Europe is not the work of God but the work of the devil.'

The first words of his speech in the House of Lords on the day following the outbreak of hostilities were an appeal to the nation to abstain from acts of individual selfishness and gain, which made it harder for others to meet the difficulties 'which we should all try to face as well as may be, standing shoulder to shoulder'. On 17 October, and at the suggestion of the head of the army, Lord Kitchener, who wished to discourage excessive drinking by his troops, he addressed a letter to *The Times* in which he urged as many citizens as possible to abstain from drinking for the duration of the war in order to 'strengthen the hands of those soldiers – the large majority – who are manfully resisting such temptation'.

As the war intensified and public opinion became increasingly belligerent because of German atrocities, Davidson was especially concerned with

Headlam's attitude to events in Germany was determined by two factors. The first was opposition to Socialism in all its forms, Communism in this case. He believed it to be inimical to individual freedom, inefficient in its ordering of society and ultimately a threat to Christian values. The second factor, more subtle, was a burning desire for Christian unity. After leaving King's College, London, in 1928, he spent five years as Regius Professor of Divinity in Oxford and during this time delivered the Bampton Lectures, published as *The Doctrine of the Church and Christian Reunion* (1920). Appearing early in the twentieth-century quest for church unity, this had a considerable influence on the Church of England's approach to the subject, and after Headlam became Bishop of Gloucester in 1922, he became its chief representative in international discussions on the theological issues at stake. This also equipped him uniquely for the chairmanship of its Council on Foreign Relations, established in 1933.

Although his knowledge of the German churches was limited, he was immediately sympathetic to Hitler's decision that the Protestant churches, organized on a regional basis, should be unified to form a single national Church. Hitler explained, disingenuously, that this would enable the Church to get closer to the people and thus fulfil its mission more effectively. What he really meant was that it would make it easier to bring the Church under his control – a fact quickly realized when he stepped in to replace an elected Reichsbischof with a more compliant Nazi church leader. The promulgation of a law forbidding Jews to hold any public office, and effectively become non-citizens, also required the Church to dismiss all its pastors who were of Jewish background.

Headlam now found himself on shaky ground and sought more information about what was happening in Germany, but relied far too much on views expressed by those church leaders who had fallen into line with Hitler's demands. The German Church was now becoming divided between those, the great majority, who were compliant and known as German Christians, and others whose loyalty to the gospel rather than to the Church took them to membership of a soon to be outlawed Confessing Church.

As the situation for all Christians in Germany became ever more perilous, Headlam's communications with the church leaders became increasingly critical, but he was unwilling to abandon his policy of appeasement, and as late as 1937 prepared a report on the subject for publication in a Council on Foreign Relations journal. In this, he said he believed Hitler had no desire to destroy the Church but wished there to be a united Church. Naturally, he expected all people to accept the National Socialist policy. But even if he was intent on destroying the Church, it would not be wise diplomatically to treat a person in Hitler's position as if he were a criminal. Much better to ascribe to him good intentions which on some occasions he seemed to have had. Headlam went on to say that he was sure it would be better for the Confessing Church to join with the orthodox Lutherans and not to stand out since this would be playing into the hands of those who were trying to induce Hitler to take extreme steps.

The Council was not prepared, however, to accept this report for publication, and asked another of its members, the Dean of Chichester, A. S. Duncan-Jones, who was very knowledgeable on German affairs, to produce something less tendentious. Nonetheless, Headlam insisted on expressing his views in a preface to the survey and, when presenting it to the Church Assembly, made matters worse by declaring that National Socialism was not anti-Christian and that the Confessing Church was much smaller than most people imagined and was getting weaker. 'The majority of German pastors are living quietly in their own parishes and doing good work, faithful alike to the Christian religion and to the German state.'

All of which provoked widespread criticism, and the Archbishop of Canterbury said that Headlam's views were no more than personal and were not to be regarded as those of the Church Assembly or of the Church of England as a whole. In the following year, Bishop Bell placed before the House of Bishops in the Convocation of Canterbury a resolution expressing grave concern over the sufferings of Christians in Germany. Headlam objected and moved the Previous Question, but this earned a rebuke from the Archbishop, and when there was no seconder to the motion it fell to the ground.

Undeterred, he returned to *The Times* in July 1938 (shortly before the dismemberment of Czechoslovakia) with a deplorable letter restating his views and concluding that it would be 'better to abstain from the pleasing task of continuously scolding other nations and attempt to understand them. It would be wise to be courteous even to dictators.' Until the outbreak of war in the following year, Headlam remained hopeful that Hitler's intentions were not fundamentally evil and that if the German Church refrained from political statements it could expect to continue its worship and pastoral work without hindrance.

By this time, he was just past his 77th birthday, but it was not until 1945 that he resigned from the Gloucester Bishopric and the chairmanship of the Council on Foreign Relations, where he unfailingly sent messages of comfort and support to churches enduring repression and the cruel consequences of war. He died in 1947 in Whorlton Hall. He had been an effective diocesan bishop and one of considerable influence for good in the central councils of the Church of England during the inter-war years, but failure to discern unmitigated evil in the rise of Nazism in Germany was a fatal blemish.

The same blemish could not be discerned in Herbert Hensley Henson, whose reading of history had led him to detest all forms of tyranny and who, while lacking any first-hand knowledge of Germany, felt instinctively that Hitler was a threat not only to the well-being of his own country but, if left unchecked, to the peace and stability of the rest of Europe.

At first, he expressed his misgivings only privately, and had not intended to speak in a Church Assembly debate in November 1935, when Bishop Bell proposed a fairly carefully worded motion expressing sympathy with the Jewish people in Germany and warning Hitler that if he continued his policy towards them this would be an obstacle to good relations between Germany and the rest of the world. An English layman, who was the German consul in Plymouth, immediately proposed that the motion 'be not put', since, as he said, the Church Assembly was no place for politics and interfering in the affairs of other countries.

Henson was outraged and delivered a devastating response in terms rarely heard in any Church of England gathering. He said that civilization is not the property of this nation or that, but is a common possession and carries with it obligations. The Germans, he believed, were hypnotized by a fiction about race that had no foundation – 'When I read the news from Germany I feel a kind of blind rage within me that it is not possible to draw the sword and go to the help of the low against the mighty.' When his speech ended, he was given loud and continuous applause and was widely praised in the press on the following day.

The British Jewish community obtained his permission to translate the speech into German and have it distributed as a pamphlet among the afflicted Jews in Germany. Thus he became something of a hero to them, but not to the Nazi regime, which thereafter regarded him as an enemy and a warmonger.

In February of the following year, he intervened in a public discussion as to whether or not British universities should send representatives to the 550th anniversary of Heidelberg University, from which all Jewish professors had been ejected and to which Jews could not be admitted as undergraduates. In a letter to *The Times*, Henson declared, 'It cannot be right that the universities of Great Britain, which we treasure as citadels of sound learning, because they are the vigilant guardians of intellectual freedom, should openly fraternize with the avowed and shameful enemies of both.' A Dutch society distributed 1,000 copies of the letter among the universities of Holland. Soon afterwards this issue arose again on his own doorstep when Durham University accepted an invitation to send representatives to the bicentenary celebrations of Göttingen University, which had actually suffered even more than Heidelberg from Nazi intervention. In his capacity as Visitor of Durham University, he wrote to the Vice-Chancellor and told him that if the visit were to go ahead he would be in the unhappy situation of having publicly to make known his personal disapprobation. The university withdrew its acceptance.

About this time, and following the assassination of the Japanese Prime Minister and a member of his cabinet by army generals, there was some discussion as to whether such actions could ever be morally justified. Henson was in no doubt about this.

> Who could deny the morality of a patriotic Italian who, for public reasons, killed Mussolini? Or who would not applaud the German who, in the interest of elementary morals, killed Hitler? I should give them Christian burial without hesitation.

Sentiments of this sort were uncommon in an Anglican bishop, and shortly before the cruel invasion of Abyssinia in 1935 he wrote to *The Times* arguing that justice was more important than peace and that Britain, being still a great power in the Mediterranean, had the force to intervene. The failure to intervene and the appalling consequences for the Abyssinian people, allied to the silence of the Pope, caused great anger in Henson, some of which he expressed in a 24-page pamphlet, a copy of which he sent to every MP – again without effect.

He nonetheless continued to deplore Britain's involvement in what he saw as a failure by the League of Nations and returned to the issue with force in 1938, when, in an attempt to win Mussolini's support in resistance to Hitler's ever-increasing aggression, the British and French governments agreed to recognize Italy's suzerainty over Abyssinia. Following a letter of protest at this to *The Times*, Henson decided that he must take part in a forthcoming debate on the subject in the House of Lords, even though many peers would resent the intervention of a bishop in a matter of foreign policy.

A proposed censure of the government was opposed by Archbishop Lang who, while deeply regretting Mussolini's action and the plight of its victims, believed that it was necessary to face the facts and turn to the building of bridges before Europe was fatally divided into two camps. Henson would have none of this. Having denounced a speech by the Foreign Secretary, Lord Halifax, at the League of Nations as 'marked by the cold sophistry of a cynical opportunism', he went on to describe Britain's part as shameful:

> What you can do, by conceding now this point and now that point, is to put off the immediate conflict, but you are only making sure that when the inevitable strife does at last occur you have conceded the strategic points to your adversaries and made it as certain as you can that you and your civilization will be destroyed. My Lords, really, as practical

people looking coldly at the world and weighing facts calmly in the scales of reason, is it reasonable to trust the word of these dictators?

This question was given added urgency a few months later when Hitler's threats to Czechoslovakia prompted the Prime Minister, Neville Chamberlain, to fly to Munich to negotiate a better outcome. Henson was in two minds about the proposed meeting but in the dire circumstances thought it probably wise for Chamberlain to make one more attempt to avoid a European war. Yet, he said, 'I dread even more, and with deeper loathing, another effort to avert war by dishonour.'

When, however, his fears on this count were fully realized, he remained uncharacteristically silent, and, to the regret of many, did not attend the House of Lords when the Munich Agreement was debated. The Church's leaders, including William Temple and George Bell, were in fact unanimous in applauding Chamberlain's achievement. In a radio broadcast, Archbishop Lang went so far as to thank God and the Prime Minister and quoted with approval an MP who had told him, 'This is the hand of God.' It was left to the knowledgeable Dean Duncan-Jones to denounce the agreement with Hitler as 'the most shameful betrayal in English history'.

Father St John Groser, a legendary London East End priest, declared, 'Blackmail has succeeded . . . that the Archbishop of Canterbury should say this is an answer to prayer is beyond endurance.' The reason for Henson's reticence is not at all clear, but he may have felt that amid the widespread euphoria over the avoidance of war the voice of a dissenting bishop would not be heard, and that in any case it was too late to change the national course. A few weeks later, having reached the age of 75, he announced his retirement and for his final Diocesan Conference invited Bishop George Bell to speak about the persecution of the Church in Germany.

He could not have chosen better, for although Bell was a notoriously poor public speaker, no one in Britain had a better knowledge of the subject. The son of a clergyman, he was born in 1881, and, after Westminster School and Christ Church, Oxford, spent three years as one of a large team of curates at Leeds Parish Church – then the most notable parish in the north of England. Although by no means a scholar of the first rank, he then returned to Christ Church as a tutor and lecturer, but left after four years to become chaplain to the Archbishop of Canterbury, Randall Davidson, who treated him as a confidant and adviser.

In 1924, he became Dean of Canterbury, and, in company with Frank Bennett at Chester, proved to be one of the most far-seeing, reforming cathedral Deans of the first half of that century. The commissioning of T. S. Eliot's play, *Murder in the Cathedral*, was just one of his many enterprises. Appointment to a diocesan bishopric in 1929 was not unexpected, and the next 29 years at Chichester were to be notably historic both for that conservative, comparatively wealthy diocese and the whole Church of England.

Bell's concern for events in Germany following the rise of Hitler came from his involvement in the developing international ecumenical movement. But whereas Headlam, because of his scholarly gifts, was drawn into the doctrinal discussions of a Faith and Order Council, Bell found a place, as chairman, of a separate Life and Work Council, concerned with ethical, social and political matters.

It was at meetings of this council that Bell received early warnings of Hitler's dangerous policies and felt it to be his duty to make the facts known widely in the Church of England and wherever else in the world justice, freedom and peace were valued. In marked contrast to the style of Henson, he was never strident and his approach was that of the shy, gentle reconciler, a man of peace and hater of conflict, though uncompromising in his opposition to crude nationalism and the subjugation of individuals. Moreover, he was a rather poor public speaker with an unfortunate capacity to make explosive material seem rather boring. Besides which his friendship with the German people gave him empathy with the appalling predicament in which they found themselves. Sensitivity to matters of life and death were needed, and the quest for peaceful solutions was never to be abandoned. This required a different kind of courage in a church leader.

None of which was lacking in Bell. In a letter to *The Times* on 14 June 1933, he drew attention to the danger facing the German Church following Hitler's demand that its recently elected Reichsbischof should be replaced by a Nazi sympathizer. Four months later he wrote to its leader, Dr Müller, on behalf of Life and Work, in which he referred to two developments of the German Church which were 'gravely disturbing to the Christian conscience'. The first of these concerned the adoption of the State's Aryan policy of excluding Jews from public office, including some who had become Lutheran pastors. The second was the suppression of freedom of speech within the Church – 'It ought not to be, that in denial of brotherly love the Church of Jesus Christ should, through the domination of force, be made a kingdom of this world.' This letter was made public and appeared in the press soon afterwards.

Of critical importance was Bell's encounter with Dietrich Bonhoeffer. He first met the brilliant young theologian briefly at an ecumenical meeting in Geneva, but they did not really get to know each other until Bonhoeffer came to England to be pastor of two German congregations in south London. The purpose of this move was to enable him, now a leading figure in the Confessing Church, to make more widely known the significance of what was happening in Germany.

Within three weeks of his arrival, Bell had invited him to Chichester, and there began not only a close collaboration in a common cause but also a deep personal friendship. Thereafter, Bonhoeffer was the chief influence on Bell, expressed in many letters to *The Times* and reflected in the authority with which he was able to speak at ecumenical meetings on the central issue of the time.

As the situation became worse and efforts to change Hitler's attitude were even more strongly resisted, Bell turned his attention to the plight of the Jewish refugees who were fleeing from persecution in increasing numbers. By January 1936 this had reached 80,000, and after the annexation of Sudetenland and Austria in 1938 it rose to more than 200,000, not all of them Jewish. Bell became chairman of an International Christian Council for Refugees and went to Berlin in January 1937 to discuss the situation with the leaders of the Evangelical Church, many of whose pastors had been forced to leave.

In spite of his efforts, however, the response in Britain to the growing crisis was shockingly poor. An early speech on the subject to the Church Assembly was sympathetically received, but a 1936 appeal for £25,000 did not reach even £10,000, and the work of the International Christian Council was in the end deemed to be a 'spectacular failure'. Neither was it simply a question of money. Bell came up against a stubborn resistance to the admission of many refugees to Britain, and in his maiden speech in the House of Lords in July 1938, he pleaded with the government to make a more vigorous response and also to press the countries of the Empire to open their doors more widely. The result was minimal, but he persisted, and, following the outbreak of war in 1939, turned his attention to the welfare of the refugees who were interned as enemy aliens.

Meanwhile, at Birmingham Bishop Barnes was maintaining uncompromisingly the pacifist position he had espoused in August 1914, when, as he explained later, he had tried to give an address at a service of a military character and 'I realised at once that for myself war could not be combined with the religion of Christ. Since that time I have never been at a military function.' Instead, he worked closely with Dick Sheppard and his Peace Pledge Union.

Soon after Hitler came to power in 1933, Barnes deplored his treatment of Jews and helped to organize a Christian protest meeting in Birmingham. At the same time, he continued to exercise a long-standing sympathy with the German people in their resentment of the Versailles Treaty. A few months later, in a sermon to a National Peace Congress, he called for universal disarmament and said that if this could not be achieved internationally, Britain should set an example – 'Any alternative policy will lead ultimately to large-scale war.'

In 1935, when it was evident that neither Britain nor any other country was willing to embrace such a policy, he took the opportunity of a General Election to advocate the abandonment of bombing as a military weapon. This led to the accusation that he was using his cathedral for political ends, though the Secretary of State for War, Duff Cooper, was content to describe the sermon as an 'episcopal error'.

More acceptable, perhaps, was his description on another occasion of Hitler as 'a public house politician' and Mussolini as 'a doss house dreamer'. But there was an alarming moment for even his friends and admirers when, reflecting something of his long-standing interest in eugenics, he went so far as to say that German legislation on 'race hygiene' was on the right lines, as it provided for voluntary sterilization.

As the European crisis deepened, his warnings about the increasing danger of war became more insistent, but for him pacifism and disarmament offered the only answer, and he was a strong supporter of the Prime Minister, Neville Chamberlain, in his policy of appeasement. A university sermon at Oxford in 1936 called for the abandoning of rearmament and the renewal of the League of Nations at Geneva by placing Britain's Crown colonies under its jurisdiction. Duff Cooper said that Barnes' views would have 'disgraced a street-corner orator', while his suggestions about the colonies were impracticable and ludicrous.

After Munich, however, he adopted a policy of silence, explaining to a friend that to speak of the horrors of war would now increase national tension and 'bring nearer the war which would be the supreme evil'. But in July 1939, on the eve of war, he reiterated his belief that war was incompatible with Christianity, called for generosity to conscientious objectors and urged these objectors to help protect women and children, the sick and the old, if war should come.

11

The Catastrophic War: 1939–45

The outbreak of war on 3 September 1939 was not attended by any of the euphoria and jingoism that had been so prominent in 1914. The experience of that war, combined with knowledge of the destructive potential of modern weaponry, witnessed cruelly in Abyssinia and Spain, was sufficient to ensure sobriety. The building of air-raid shelters, the sandbagging of public buildings and the issuing of gas-masks was also a clear indication that the entire nation, not just the military, was bound to be involved.

Yet, apart from those with pacifist convictions, there was remarkable unanimity that the right decision had been taken and that the forthcoming struggle would be not only against a particular country and its aggressive rulers, but against powerful forces that were fundamentally evil. The British churches were part of this consensus.

Cosmo Gordon Lang, who had been Archbishop of Canterbury since 1928, was not destined to play a significant part in the leadership of the nation during the years of crisis that were to come. He had been badly bruised by his attempts at leadership in 1914–18, his gifts were not of the prophetic sort required by the times, he was now 75, and, as it turned out, two years from resignation.

During these years he was diligent in visiting and caring for the parishes of Canterbury diocese, which were soon in the front line of defence against bombing and threatened invasion. He was in Lambeth Palace when it was bombed, arranged National Days of Prayer, argued for the legitimacy of praying for victory, conducted services for the armed forces and generally offered words of encouragement and hope to his compatriots, while being aware that he lacked what he called 'pushful ardour'.

He spoke little in the House of Lords but made two speeches there on 23 October 1941 – the first declaring that, in spite of Russia's past excesses and persecutions, against which he had often spoken, it must now be regarded as an ally against a common enemy, and the second in support of a plea that some of the now scarce materials and labour should still be made available for the production of books 'to sustain the spirit of the people'. This was still the time when Prime Ministers and other government ministers felt the need to consult the Archbishop over some matters of policy. During the darkest period of the war, Winston Churchill continued the tradition of inviting the Archbishop to lunch to discuss appointments to vacant bishoprics, though he spent most of the time discussing war issues. At a meeting with Anthony Eden, the Foreign Secretary, Lang complained about a law that church bells could not be rung except as a warning of invasion.

By this time the Archbishop of York, William Temple, was widely regarded as the spokesman not only for the Church of England but for the Christian conscience of the nation. Intellectually, morally and spiritually he was born for the hour, and no church leader, before or since, has exercised so critical a role in the nation's life. Allied to unusual gifts as a speaker – on the radio as well as in the pulpit and at great meetings – he had the capacity to apply deep religious and moral insights into the great issues of the day in a way that compelled serious attention.

On the eve of the war, Sunday 27 August, it was Temple to whom the BBC turned for the address at a special evening service. He began by asserting that it was a time of crisis for the churches as well as for the Western world inasmuch as they had failed to create a worldwide Christian fellowship that would have made war impossible. There was still time, however, for war to be averted, and this must be the fervent prayer of every person of faith. But if war came, Christians, apart from those with pacifist convictions, could not refuse to take part in it. He added:

> No positive good can be done by force; that is true. But evil can be checked and held back by force, and it is precisely for this that we may be called upon to use it. If it be so, let us do it in calm but unshakable resolution, trying, in spite of all the agony, to bear no ill-will to those whom we must resist, seeking to inflict no more suffering than is inevitably involved in the resistance we must offer, bearing with patient courage the suffering that comes to ourselves. But our hope is set on the time when we and our enemies may together serve their God and ours by promoting together the welfare of all His people.

At the beginning of October, he was back at the microphone with an address on 'The Spirit and Aims of Britain in the War'. He said that when the suffering of war became more acute it would be harder to maintain 'the lofty mood of sober resolution which is almost universal today'. It was therefore important now to 'register our high purpose and consider what is needed for its achievement'. No terms could be made with Hitler or members of his government, since they had proved to be utterly untrustworthy. Equally, conditions for justice and peace for all the European nations involved in the struggle could not be imposed (as had been attempted at Versailles) but would only succeed if they were negotiated by a Congress of European Nations.

The themes of war aims and peace aims were ones to which he often returned in broadcasts, letters to *The Times* and articles in newspapers and periodicals. In company with other British church leaders, he endorsed and elaborated on a Five-Point Peace Plan proposed by the Pope, and there were many addresses and articles on specifically religious and theological aspects of the war.

As the war situation became grave, however, and Britain's own freedom and independence became seriously threatened, there was, as Temple had himself foreseen, a reduced concern for high ideals and moral objectives, though what he had said during the early stages was regarded as important enough to warrant a Macmillan hardback collection of his addresses and articles in 1940.

Increasingly, Temple became concerned with the plight of the war's victims, particularly the European Jews now caught up in a Holocaust that would eventually claim six million lives. On 23 March 1943 he initiated a debate and made a very remarkable speech on this subject in the House of Lords. He pleaded for the admission to Britain and Palestine (then under British mandated rule) of more Jewish refugees, dismissing the commonly made objections that Britain lacked sufficient food and that more Jews in the country would only exacerbate antisemitism. He concluded:

> We cannot rest so long as there is any sense among us that we are not doing all that might be done. We have discussed the matter on the footing that we are not responsible for this great evil, that the burden lies on others, but it is always true that the obligations of decent men are decided for them by contingencies which they did not create and very largely by the actions of wicked men. The priest and the Levite in the parable were not in the least responsible for the traveller's wounds as he lay there by the roadside and no doubt they had many other pressing things to attend to, but they stand as the picture of those who are condemned for neglecting the opportunity of showing mercy. We at this moment have upon us a tremendous responsibility. We stand at the bar of history, humanity and of God.

With a few notable exceptions, this did not discourage the British from joining the company of the priest and the Levite. But Temple's efforts made him a hero of the Jewish communities in Britain and other parts of Europe.

Bishop George Bell's wartime leadership proved to be more extensive and far more controversial. After the German invasion of Holland,

Belgium and France in May 1940, the British government ordered the interning of all men and some women of alien origin, including even those who were refugees from Nazi persecution. In the desperate circumstances of the time this was a reasonable action that could not afford to distinguish between friend and foe.

Bell was, however, outraged by the failure to distinguish and said so in a House of Lords speech in which he pleaded for an improvement in the conditions at the internment camps at Huyton, near Liverpool (where a number of refugee pastors were being held) and the Isle of Man. He subsequently visited these camps, where he made a great impression, and in company with a number of politicians continued to agitate until the government began to release the friendly aliens. Throughout the war, he continued to explain that many Germans were no less victims of Hitler than the citizens of other countries he had attacked, and he believed the released refugees would help to make this plain.

There was a dramatic development in 1942 when Bell flew to Sweden in company with T. S. Eliot and Kenneth Clark, the art historian, on a government-sponsored three-week visit designed to maintain contact with influential Swedish people and secure whatever support they could for Britain's war effort. By this time, Dietrich Bonhoeffer was heavily involved in an underground movement that planned to overthrow Hitler and his Nazi regime and substitute a civilized government that would negotiate peace.

He was at a church meeting in Geneva when informed that Bell was in Sweden, and, having immediately flown back to Berlin, secured permission to go to Sweden, ostensibly on church business. His arrival in Stockholm caused Bell both astonishment and joy, and the two friends, in company with another German pastor who was also in Sweden, discussed a document, the gist of which was that if the German plotters were to gain numerical strength and also risk their lives in an assault on Hitler and his henchmen, it would be necessary for the Allies to abandon their requirement of unconditional surrender.

Bell was entirely sympathetic to this approach and on his return to London immediately reported on the meeting to Anthony Eden, at the Foreign Office. Eden had, early in May, stated publicly that if the German people really wanted to return to a German state based on the rule of law and the rights of the individual, they must understand that no one would believe them until they had rid themselves of the Nazi regime. He maintained this line when responding to Bell and added that a more positive response would require the agreement of Britain's American and Russian allies, which was hardly likely to be forthcoming. When Churchill heard about the affair, he simply dismissed it, adding 'the highest personalities in the German Reich are murdering one another'. Thus Bell and Bonhoeffer were deeply disappointed and the incident provides one of the 'What ifs?' of European history. The war still had a long way to run.

Meanwhile, Bell was becoming increasingly concerned at the effects of Allied bombing policy on the German civilian population. During the early months of the war, it had been the intention to bomb only military and other war-related targets. This soon proved to be impossible because the RAF lacked the equipment necessary for precision bombing, and the German defences were strong enough to protect industrial targets.

The appointment of Air Chief Marshal Sir Arthur Harris to be head of Bomber Command led, with the support of Churchill and the Defence Chiefs, to a radical change of policy, which involved the carpet bombing, with increasingly heavy bombs, of the main German towns and cities. The purpose was still to destroy armaments factories, but also to hinder the activities of those who worked in them, and eventually to weaken German morale so that the war could not continue. In the end, whole cities were devastated and some millions of civilians killed. The effectiveness and morality of this policy are still debated.

But Bell had no doubt that it was entirely wrong (a view not shared by Temple), and in his diocesan gazette in September 1943, on the fourth anniversary of the outbreak of war, he warned, 'I see signs in some quarters of giving way to the spirit that caused the war and I beg you to do your best to resist such a spirit wherever it may appear.' He went on to illustrate this: 'To bomb cities as cities, deliberately to attack civilians, quite irrespective of whether or not they are actively contributing to the war effort is a wrong deed, whether done by the Nazis or by ourselves.' This was widely reported and received a hostile reception. The Dean of his own cathedral, A. S. Duncan-Jones, asked him to withdraw from a forthcoming Battle of Britain service at which he was due to preach. On 9 February 1944 he raised the matter again in the House of Lords, in a speech of extraordinary courage – 'Why is there this blindness to the psychological side? Why is there this inability to reckon with the moral and spiritual facts? Why is there this forgetfulness of the ideals by which our cause is inspired?' The speech was even more widely reported and greeted with even greater hostility. The King and Queen were said to be annoyed. A cartoon in the *Daily Mail* portrayed two bishops carrying placards with the words, 'Let's not be nasty to the Germans' and 'Let's not bomb them any more'. The *Daily Telegraph* reported mounting indignation in the RAF and called on Sir Arthur Harris to denounce Bell's speech. On the other hand, some of the serious papers and magazines, while not agreeing with it, defended his right to make it.

Bell's disquiet at the use of atomic weapons to end the war against Japan in 1945 was, predictably, forthright. He then pleaded for the generous rehabilitation of the German people and an end to the war-crimes trials.

When William Temple died unexpectedly and inopportunely in 1944, it was, and still is, believed by many that, although George Bell was his obvious successor, Winston Churchill refused to appoint him because of his anti-bombing speeches, coupled with his desire in 1942 for a negotiated peace. This may well be true but it does not necessarily mean that he would have made a good Archbishop of Canterbury. Yet to have had a man of Bell's vision, compassion and courage at the helm of the post-war Church of England would have been worth this risk.

Never within remotest reach of such preferment and, in the views of some unfit, because of his beliefs, to hold even the Bishopric of Birmingham, Ernest William Barnes continued on his pacifist way throughout the war. He still steadfastly refused to attend any church services, of which there were many, at which there was any sort of military presence. He urged his clergy not to cast doubt in their sermons on the sincerity of the country's aspirations, but at the same time they should not speak as if national policy had always been good. He concluded:

> Preach as little as possible; pray as much as you can. Before beginning to prepare a sermon, put down your newspaper, turn off the wireless. During and for at least a quarter of an hour read slowly the New Testament which reveals the mind of Christ. You are his minister.

His own reading of the New Testament led him in January 1940 to move in the Convocation of Canterbury a motion calling on the government 'to allow the free importation of foodstuffs into Germany in accordance with the precept "If your enemy hunger, feed him"'. His fellow bishops, however, interpreted this differently, and there was no seconder for the motion. It was nonetheless sufficient to provoke a headline in the next day's *Daily Express* – 'Bishop wants food for the Nazis'. Later that year he warned: 'With war a new barbarism begins to spread over Europe: civilized progress will return when we begin to love our enemies and to do good to them that despitefully use us.'

Barnes' failure to secure a seconder for his Convocation motion stands as a sign of his isolation from all his episcopal colleagues apart from George Bell throughout the war. In retrospect, however, it may seem important that at least one bishop should have courageously reminded the Church of the huge compromises required of Christians whenever they go to war. No less than Bell, though not now remembered, he spoke against the bombing of civilian targets in Germany, and after the first 1,000-bomber raid on Cologne in 1942 urged his diocesan conference not to join in the general exultation. In 1944, he deplored in the House of Lords the destruction of 'little houses' in Germany.

Towards the end of 1940, Barnes had accused the Cement Makers' Federation of being a ring of monopolists who were holding back supplies of concrete required for the building of air-raid shelters in order to maximize their profits. This led to a High Court action for libel, which he lost, but his friends raised the £1,600 required for the damages and legal costs. He later repeated his allegation in the House of Lords, where he was beyond reach of the laws of defamation. The context of the accusation was the lack of sufficient air-raid shelters in Birmingham. During four days of bombing, 19–22 November, the city suffered 800 killed and over 2,000 injured and the inadequacy of protection for the citizens of a major centre of aircraft production was widely recognized. But there was an additional item on Barnes' agenda inasmuch as he believed, as a Socialist, that key industries and public services should all be under state control.

In 1943, Barnes said that after the war there should be a united Europe with a single currency and no tariffs. When peace came in 1945, he spoke against the division of Germany and advocated the rapid release of German prisoners of war as well as the ending of conscription in Britain. Although critical of some aspects of Communism, he described Lenin as primarily a social reformer and Communism as 'a politico-social movement for the welfare of the common man'. When the learned Bishop of Derby, A. E. J. Rawlinson, described him as 'the Stormy Petrel of the English episcopate', few were inclined to disagree.

12

Founding the Welfare State

The Welfare State, planned in wartime and maintained unchallenged by a long peacetime political consensus, owed a good deal to the influence of Archbishop William Temple – one of the greatest Archbishops of Canterbury. His father, Frederick, was at the time of his birth in 1881 Bishop of Exeter and himself destined for the Primacy – the only time father and son occupied this great office.

Each was, however, called to exercise it in very different circumstances. Frederick had to deal with tiresome church problems, but always against an apparently secure background in which the Church of England remained a firm pillar of the country's established order and its leaders generally accorded high regard and sometimes honour.

By the time William reached Balliol College, Oxford, in 1900, however, this situation, in common with much else in Britain, was changing rapidly. The Roman Catholic and Free Churches had for some time been using their hard-won freedom to express opinions, usually in furtherance of their denominational interests, and although comparatively few people had been captivated by the debates about biblical criticism and other belief issues, doubts were being expressed about aspects of orthodox church teaching.

Even more significantly, it could no longer be overlooked that a large proportion of the Church's nominal membership was either completely alienated from its life or in touch with it only on key family occasions. Preoccupation with church affairs meant that bishops no longer attended the House of Lords in large numbers, thus weakening the Church's contribution to national government.

Oxford at the turn of the century quickly acquainted Temple with these challenging facts and, having himself hesitated about some aspects of traditional doctrine before going forward to ordination in 1909, he saw the need for a reformulation of the Christian faith to make it more intelligible and also the development of a social doctrine that would equip the Church to contribute usefully to decision-making in a rapidly changing world. Attendance in 1910 at an epoch-making World Missionary Conference in Edinburgh drew him to the developing ecumenical movement, and he eventually became its foremost leader.

At Balliol, Temple absorbed the Idealist philosophy then in vogue and this found expression in a series of addresses to students published as *Christian Faith and Modern Thought* (1910) and, in one way or another, in his subsequent voluminous writings. His optimism remained unbounded, though experience of the ways of the world sometimes caused this to be tempered. Burning social concerns took him into membership of the Workers' Educational Association, of which he was president from 1908 to 1924, and the first conference of the Student Christian Movement he chaired in 1909 was on 'Christianity and Social Problems'.

A year earlier, he had addressed a Pan-Anglican Congress and given a foretaste of the message he would declare during the remainder of his life:

If Christianity is to be applied to the economic system, an organization that rests primarily on the principle of competition must give way to one which rests primarily on co-operation. The question of the competitive principle is driven down into the Labour market, so that men compete against each other for the right to work which is the right to live. Go and see it at work in the London docks. If one man is to secure the means of feeding himself and his family, he must be depriving another. Is that an exhibition of brotherhood? Such a system embodies no principle but selfishness and mutual antagonism. As citizens we are guilty of a whole system of oppression: it is there: we tolerate it, and so become responsible for its results. There is nothing inevitable in it: it is the result of human choices. I do not mean that anyone deliberately put it there; it is the greatest fluke in creation. But it is the net result of innumerable choices, and by human choices it can be modified. Here lies our duty – and our guilt.

He never ceased to be influenced by the thinking of R. H. Tawney, a Professor of Economic History at the London School of Economics, who had been a close friend since their schooldays at Rugby.

In 1910, aged 28, he became the only member of the Labour Party ever to be appointed Headmaster of Repton School, but this was not his forte and after four years he moved to be Rector of St James's, Piccadilly. There he exercised an influential wartime ministry, extended more widely by the publication of some addresses as *Readings in St. John's Gospel* and editorship of *Challenge* – a journal devoted to church and social reform. In 1917, however, he was drawn into the full-time leadership of the Life and Liberty Movement, campaigning for church reform, then held, briefly, a Canonry of Westminster before appointment as Bishop of Manchester in 1921.

Chairmanship of a ground-breaking ecumenical Conference on Politics, Economics and Citizenship held in Birmingham in 1924 established him as the forthcoming leader of the Anglican Church, and in 1932 he was duly translated to the Archbishopric of York. Two years later he had a notable clash with the Chancellor of the Exchequer, Neville Chamberlain, when he suggested that any budget surplus should go to relieve the unemployed, rather than to cut taxes.

The York years were remarkable for Temple's output of books and articles, involvement in the developments that led to the formation of the World Council of Churches in 1939, with himself as its provisional chairman, and much research and writing on social and economic questions. A senior episcopal colleague said that what took him two or three mornings to prepare was accomplished by Temple in 20 minutes and was better. His succession to Archbishop Lang in 1942 was inevitable, though it was initially resisted by the Prime Minister, Winston Churchill, who did not like his views.

A mere five months had passed since his Enthronement at Canterbury, and the war was in its darkest phase, with victory by no means assured, when on 26 September 1942 Temple made one of his most controversial utterances on economic and social questions. The occasion was a mass meeting organized by the Industrial Christian Fellowship in London's Albert Hall. The subject was 'The Church Looks Forward', and with him on the platform were the Archbishop of York, who had made himself an expert on housing, the Bishop of Bristol, an education specialist, Sir Stafford Cripps, a prominent member of the coalition government, and Miss Knight Bruce, a youth worker. This was the first in a series of similar meetings he addressed in major cities during the next 12 months, each attracting very large audiences.

Having asserted that, since land and water were human necessities they needed to be brought under a greater measure of public control, so that the rights of the public might be asserted over the rights of private owners, he then turned to the banks:

> In my judgement at least – I don't claim that it is worth much, but I offer it to you – it should now be regarded as improper for any private person or corporation to offer new credit; as it was in the Middle Ages for any private person or corporation to mint actual money, for the two are equivalent. And so I should like, I confess, to see the banks limited in their lending power to sums equivalent to that which depositors have entrusted to them, and all new credit to be issued by public authority.

The reaction of the City of London and many other spheres of economic activity was immediate and sustained. It was evident, they said (and with some reason) that the Archbishop simply did not understand how the modern banking system worked nor the vital place of credit in a developing economy. This was not the Middle Ages, and what he proposed was absolutely impracticable. Sixty years later, however, the banking crisis of 2008, caused in large measure by a failure to observe the right relationship between credit and capital, might suggest that the 'experts' were hardly better informed on the subject. The emergence of multinational banks, exercising greater power than governments, also had disastrous consequences which would not have surprised Temple.

The controversy provoked by Temple's speech led to renewed criticism of his intervention in political and economic matters, and what became a famous newspaper cartoon depicted a leading banker standing by a church font, baptizing a baby. 'What does the Archbishop think of this?' asked the caption, and many believed it to have made a fair point.

The Guild of Bank Officers next invited Temple to address a meeting in Central Hall, Westminster, on 4 February 1943. Undeterred by the widespread criticism of his Albert Hall speech, he chose as his subject 'A Christian View of the Right Relationship between Finance, Production and Consumption'. Professional economists would doubtless have baulked at the possibility of dealing with so huge a subject in less than an hour, but Temple paid his audience the compliment of delivering a lecture of considerable intellectual weight.

He began, as always, by stating the case for Christian involvement in social questions. The Faith was concerned with the welfare of human beings, both as individuals and in community, and in every aspect of their lives. He then devoted some time to tracing the Church's involvement from its earliest days, throughout the Middle Ages, pausing to consider, with some approval, its attitude to usury and 'the just price', moving through the Reformation and the rise of capitalism, deploring the complacency of the eighteenth and much of the nineteenth centuries, and expressing satisfaction at the revival of Christian social doctrine in more recent times.

He now turned to his main theme. Production exists for the sake of consumption and must therefore be organized to meet human need. But, noted Temple, advertising is invariably employed to adjust human demand to the interests of producers. Or, again, the development of new products is sometimes checked in order to maintain the monopoly prices of existing items. Moreover, the treatment of workers primarily as instruments of production is immoral. Turning to finance, he said this must obviously be used to facilitate production and not to create barren wealth, but in the present situation those who lend money may sometimes dictate how a borrowing company develops its business or even determine its survival.

He ended by saying that he did not see the smallest prospect of the principles he had been stating being applied unless there were to be a large body of people who found the inspiration for their application in something

much more than the hope of a terrestrial Utopia. 'Self-interest must be coun-
teracted by a Power other than the mere exercise of human volition – the
power of the Spirit of God in the hearts of those who are open to it.'

Christianity and Social Order, which had been written in 1941 while he
was still at York and published shortly before his translation to Canterbury
in 1942, added nothing new to his social thinking and to some extent simply
expressed again what Temple had always believed and taught. Nonetheless
it was a landmark publication inasmuch as it encapsulated in 90 attractively
written pages the main body of his thinking, included some highly controversial proposals for reform, and by means of a cheap Penguin Special,
which sold over 140,000 copies, reached a wide public.

It started on now-familiar ground with the assertion that the Church's
duty was to advance principles, not policies, and that no political programme
could claim unqualified Christian approval. Moreover, the implementation
of Christian moral principles required men and women imbued with the
Christian spirit and aware of the all-pervading power of Original Sin.

The first chapter dealt with the frequently raised question, 'What right
has the Church to interfere?' Four reasons were offered, starting with the
sympathy that Christians are bound to have for the suffering victims of
the existing social evils. Unemployment and bad housing were offered as
examples of this. Next, the educational influence of the social and economic
order by which people live. If an economic system is fiercely competitive and
based on self-interest, this is bound to have an adverse effect on individual
character and the quality of community life. Third, the issue of justice. Why
should some of God's children (all of whom are equal in his sight) have full
opportunity to develop their capacities in freely chosen occupations, while
others are confined to a stunted form of existence, enslaved to types of
labour which represent no personal choice but the sole opportunity offered?
'The Church is bound to "interfere" because it is by vocation the agent of
God's purpose, outside the scope of which no human interest or activity
can fall.'

The next chapter tackled the question, 'How should the Church interfere?' After pointing out that nine-tenths of the Church's work in the
world is done by lay Christians fulfilling responsibilities and carrying out
tasks which in themselves are not part of the official system of the Church
at all, Temple said that the most important task of the Church in the face
of social problems is to make good Christian men and women. But this on
its own is not enough.

The Church's members are called as citizens to play a part in shaping
political decisions that shape the nation's life and destiny, some to hold
political office. In a democratic society, Christians may legitimately have
different views as to how particular policies are to be pursued or problems

solved. The Church cannot therefore ever align itself with particular party policies and programmes, though it may in situations of crisis attempt to lift the parties to a level of thought at which the problem disappears. 'The Church may tell the politician what ends the social order should promote, but it must leave to the politician the devising of the precise means to those ends.' So the chief task of the Church is to supply its members with a systematic statement of principles that will assist them in the discharging of their moral responsibilities and the exercising of their civic duties in a Christian spirit.

Temple then provided a brief historical survey of how the Church has intervened in social and economic matters in the past, pointing out that the questioning of its right and duty to do so is a comparatively recent development. Silence during the eighteenth century was of the Church's own choosing and an aberration.

Now came the heart of the book: a statement of Christian social principles. These were divided into Primary and Derivative, the first being theological – an affirmation of God and his purpose and a recognition of man: his dignity and destiny – and the second being three basic values (sometimes known as 'middle axioms') arising from the wide perspective. These were Freedom, Social Fellowship and Service.

'Freedom is the goal of politics. To establish and secure true freedom is the primary object of all right political action. For it is in and through his freedom that a man makes fully real his personality – the quality of one made in the image of God.' He goes on to explain that freedom must be *for* something as well as *from* something. This requires self-control, self-determination, self-direction: thus 'to train citizens in the capacity for freedom and to give them scope for free action is the supreme end of all true politics'.

Under the heading 'Social Fellowship' Temple begins by asserting that 'Man is incurably social . . . he needs not only what his neighbours contribute to the equipment of his life but their actual selves as the complement of his own.' This finds expression first in family, then, later, in school, college, trade union, professional association, city, county, nation, Church. It is, he says, in the smaller 'intermediate' bodies, rather than in the organs of the State, that individuals enjoy their freedom. Thus: 'The State which would serve and guard Liberty will foster all such groupings, giving them freedom to guide their own activities provided these fall within the general order of communal life and do not injure the freedom of other similar associations.' They will also provide protection against an overbearing State – something very much in Temple's mind in 1941, when dictatorships were rampant in Europe. Moreover, 'the claim to obey God rather than men is a source both of moral strength, for it inspires devotion to duty, and of political stability, for such freedom may only be used in the service of the whole fellowship.'

'The combination of Freedom and Fellowship as principles of social life issues in the obligation of Service.' This service is rendered by individuals in their daily work and in voluntary service of the community – of which the churches should be offering much more. Temple recognized that this is often easier said than done. Many, probably most, people have work of routine drudgery in which the spirit of service is not easily recognizable. For them service has to be seen in terms of self-sacrifice. Again, the service of institutions and groupings in which Christian values are not recognized imposes limitations on the Christian believer, who is in no position to impose his views on others. In such situations, he must do as much as he can to serve and always seek opportunities to move the organization in the direction of service.

Love and Justice, argued Temple, cannot be used as principles of social life since they are too diffuse to provide direct guidance, but they can and should be used in the application of Freedom, Social Fellowship and Service. Recognizing that this application sometimes involves conflicting priorities, he offered Natural Law as the best solution. This involves an appeal to the laws that evidently govern the working of the universe, for example, collaboration is more constructive than conflict, production exists for consumption, economic life exists not for itself but the welfare of man. Inasmuch as these are incontrovertible they can be regarded as laws of God, and, although they may often offer unattainable ideals, they require every activity to be considered in the context of the whole economy of life.

So to 'The Task Before Us'. Although Temple was writing during the darkest period of the war, when its victorious outcome was a long way from assured, it did not occur to him or to anyone else in Britain that their future might be spent under the Nazi yoke. On the contrary, there was the determination that, because the First World War had not led to the creation of 'a land fit for heroes to live in', something very different must emerge from the current conflict. The Beveridge Report on Social Security and the Butler Report on Education were two other outstanding examples of confidence in ultimate victory and freedom to flourish.

Temple advanced as a priority 'The Family as the Primary Social Unit'. This would require much greater concern for good housing, and, since private enterprise had failed to deliver this in sufficient quantity before the war, 'it must be laid upon the government as a primary obligation to see that the housing necessary to healthy family life is available for all citizens'. Adequate leisure was equally necessary and this required more sensitive attention to working hours and shift systems, to enable families to enjoy leisure activities together, and wages high enough to make such activities possible. 'Real extravagance is always wrong. But to splash around a little on holiday is thoroughly right. It is not only permissible, it is a duty.'

Concern for 'The Sanctity of Personality' led him to assert that while 'the worst horrors of the early factories have been abolished, the wage earners are not yet fully recognized as persons. For the supreme mark of a person is that he orders his life by his own deliberate choice; and the workers usually have no voice in the control of the industry whose requirements determine so large a part of their lives.' He believed that, in some form, labour needed to share with capital in the control of industry.

On the related subject of education, Temple was even more forthright: 'Our whole educational system comes under condemnation as defective and inadequate.' Smaller class sizes were essential and the school-leaving age needed to be raised to equip young people to play a greater part in community life. There needed also to be a greater variety in forms of education, including the provision of strong technical and vocational education for non-academic children. He did not, however, regard the Public Schools as contributing to such a variety:

The so-called Public Schools, which have held the corporate tradition throughout their long history, have been inaccessible to the poorer children. This was probably inevitable when education as a whole had become a perquisite of the wealthier section of society. It is on the way to being a shocking anomaly as education is made available to the whole community. That what is generally felt to be the best form of education should be reserved to those whose parents are able to pay expensive fees, or expensive preparatory school education with a view to the winning of scholarships, makes a cleavage in the educational and social life of the community as a whole, which is itself destructive of the best fellowship. The time is ripe for a development in which it would be possible for children from every kind of home to come in to any kind of school provided that they are qualified by physical, mental and personal talents. The test must not be purely intellectual. We have overstressed the intellectual in recent educational developments, and the competitive examination system has tended to favour many who have been most industrious and have capable brains, but sacrificed to the development of many other gifts and aptitudes.

Seventy years on he would have been disappointed to find that, far from his views being heeded by Labour and Conservative governments, the Public Schools system remains alive and open largely only to the children of the very wealthiest parents.

'The worst evil facing the working class,' Temple asserted, 'is insecurity; they live under the terrible menace of unemployment. And in our own time a new and horrible evil has appeared – long-term unemployment on a

considerable scale. Unemployment is corrosive poison. It saps both physical and moral strength . . . it does most harm to the young man who never
forms regular habits of work at all.' Here he was looking back to the 1920s
and 1930s, since there was no unemployment of any significance in wartime Britain. But the long years of peace that followed brought no lasting
remedy to unemployment's corrosive poison.

Temple ended this chapter by reaffirming that, while Christians as such
could not draw up plans for a reformed society, they had a duty to proclaim Christian principles and denounce the evil that contravenes them.
They must also judge how far particular evils are symptoms of a disease
deeper than themselves, and if that seems to be so, to ask how far the
whole existing order is contrary to the Natural Order.

He was thus emboldened to declare that Christians were entitled to call
upon the government to set before itself the following objectives and pursue them as steadily and rapidly as opportunity permits:

1. Every child should find itself a member of a family housed with
   decency and dignity, so that it may grow up as a member of that basic
   community in a happy fellowship unspoilt by underfeeding or overcrowding or dirty and drab surroundings or mechanical monotony of
   environment.
2. Every child should have the opportunity of an education till years of
   maturity, so planned as to allow for his particular aptitudes and make
   possible their full development. This education should throughout
   be inspired by faith in God and find its focus in worship.
3. Every citizen should be secure in possession of such income as will
   maintain him to maintain a home and bring up children in such conditions as are described in paragraph 1 above.
4. Every citizen should have a voice in the conduct of the business or
   industry which is carried on by means of his labour, and the satisfaction of knowing that his labour is directed to the wellbeing of the
   community.
5. Every citizen should have sufficient leisure, with two days of rest in
   seven, and, if an employee, an annual holiday with pay, to enable him
   to enjoy a full personal life with such interests and activities as his
   tasks and talents may direct.
6. Every citizen should have assured liberty in the forms of freedom
   of worship, of speech, of assembly, and of association for special
   purposes.

He added as a background to these six points the need to insist on a principle laid down by the four religious leaders in their Foundations for Peace

in a letter to *The Times* in December 1940, namely, 'The resources of the earth should be used as God's gift to the whole human race, and used with due consideration for the needs of the present and future generations.'

Finally, a question: Utopian? Answer: Only in the sense that we cannot have it all tomorrow. But we can set ourselves steadily to advance towards that six-fold objective. It can be summed up in a phrase: *The aim of a Christian social order is the fullest possible development of individual personality in the widest and deepest possible fellowship.* There was, in fact, nothing distinctively Christian about his six points, which could be, and were, endorsed by a wide range of thoughtful people, including some of no religious belief at all. But for many Christians they were an important expression of their faith.

An Appendix was deliberately so designated in the hope of indicating that 'A Suggested Programme' represented no more than his own personal opinions. But he should have known that an Archbishop of Canterbury cannot be separated from any opinions he might publicly express. He made a number of proposals for advancing towards the six-fold Christian objective. First, however, he dealt with the possible charge that he was advocating Socialism. 'The question now is not – Shall we be Socialists or shall we be individualists? But – how Socialist and how individualist shall we be?' And he went on to offer what might be regarded as a classic Christian definition of the role of the State – 'The art of Government is not to devise what would be the best system for saints to work, but to secure that the lower motives actually found among men prompt that conduct which the higher motives demand.'

A number of his proposals were radical, some revolutionary. These included the nationalization of the banks and all urban land. Regional Commissioners should determine the use of land for housing. The school-leaving age should gradually be raised to 18, free milk and school meals be universal. Limited liability companies should have an employee on the board, as should the State, if public interest is involved. The government should always have three large public works projects available to absorb the long-term unemployed. Family allowances should be paid to mothers after the birth of the second child; wages earned should be raised to and maintained at a level sufficient for a family of four – father, mother and two children. His other proposals required no less State intervention, though he saw such intervention in terms of liberating individuals from existing constraints.

Striking though Temple's views now seem, not least because of their association with an Archbishop of Canterbury, they were at the time of their expression contributing to a broad tide of opinion flowing in the same direction. This led to the landslide victory of the Labour Party in the General

Election, overwhelming even Winston Churchill, the acknowledged war hero, and inaugurating what became known as the Welfare State. This made, in return for compulsory weekly contributions from the employed and employers, provisions 'From the cradle to the grave' that included maternity allowances, free education for all, better sickness and unemployment benefits, a National Health Service, better pensions and death grants.

All had been talked about for some time, more so following the publication in 1942 of a report by Sir William Beveridge, and there is general agreement that Temple's contribution to this social transformation was significant. A political consensus that maintained the new order went virtually unchallenged for more than 30 years. A new edition of *Christianity and Social Order*, published in 1976, contained an appreciative foreword by a Conservative Prime Minister, Edward Heath.

Had Temple not died unexpectedly in October 1944, when still only 63, there would have been much in the transformation of the social order of which he would have approved, though doubtless he would have been disappointed by some of its timidity. He would perhaps have been surprised to discover that State intervention does not always produce the desired economic and social results. And had his life extended into the late 1950s, he would have experienced the unanticipated beginning of what turned out to be a quarter of a century of remarkable economic boom – a Golden Age of, for most people in Britain, a period of growing prosperity on an unprecedented scale. This would naturally have required a serious review of his proposals, but not of the Christian social principles on which he based them. Unfortunately, there was no church leader equipped to take his work forward.

This work, though pointing to a new and hoped-for better Britain, can now be seen as marking the end of a period of highly creative Christian thinking that began with the COPEC conference in 1925. There has been nothing remotely like it since.

13

The Cold War

The international scene for virtually the entire second half of the twentieth century was dominated by the Cold War – a soubriquet given to a dangerous conflict of interest between the superpowers of the Soviet empire and the American-led North Atlantic Treaty Organization. This was an unforeseen but perhaps inevitable consequence of the Second World War, when the heavily damaged Soviet Union demanded, and was given by the Warsaw Pact (1945), military, economic and, as it turned out, political control of all the other countries of Eastern Europe.

Although this was primarily a self-protective measure, it was widely seen by the West as aggressive in intention, and the Soviet Union's possession of nuclear weapons helped to create a climate of fear that led to the building up by both sides of nuclear arsenals which threatened the future of civilization and possibly human life itself. The co-existence made possible by the existence of a 'balance of terror' did little to diminish the fear or the often destructive policies it encouraged, and, although there is no substantial evidence that the Soviet Union ever had designs on Western Europe, it was not until its collapse in 1989 that the Cold War was deemed to have ended and some relaxation of East–West relations made possible.

The Church of England, in common with all the other Western churches, was inevitably caught up in the consequences of this long conflict. Initially, and to some extent for the entire period, the Soviet Union was seen as every much a threat to national security as Nazi Germany had been in the 1930s. This had an obvious military aspect but there was an ideological factor inasmuch as the Soviet Communist order itself was incompatible with Western-style democracy and, if allowed to spread, could only destroy a precious inheritance.

The churches supported their national governments, as they had done between 1939 and 1945. This time the enemy was no longer at the gates, but the threat to Christianity by Communism was perceived to be in some ways a more insidious danger inasmuch as it could cross frontiers without military assistance. Resistance to Communism became a primary objective – more so in America than in Britain but important enough to keep some of the

Church of England's leaders preoccupied with its threat. With the passage of the years, their attitude tended to harden, and with few exceptions there was no suggestion from churchmen that the issues between East and West might not be quite so clear cut as they were generally presented. Opinion was undoubtedly influenced by an awareness that the churches of Eastern Europe were being subjected to serious persecution, though the scale of it was known to only a few, and reports from Romania that the Church there had only an underground existence were grossly misleading.

Foremost among the Cold Warriors was the Archbishop of York, Cyril Garbett, who was in many ways a tyrant to his clergy but nonetheless one of the most highly regarded churchmen of his time. He was an excellent communicator and had a particular rapport with the laity, to whom his sermons, speeches and writings seemed sanctified common sense.

Born in 1875 in what was then the Surrey village of Tongham, where his father was the Vicar, he displayed no special promise at Farnham and Portsmouth Grammar Schools. But he managed to get a closed scholarship to Keble College by reason of lineal descent from the Marquess of Lothian. There he flourished, took a prominent part in the affairs of the Oxford Union, of which he became President, and emerged with a respectable Second in Modern History.

He prepared for ordination at Cuddesdon, and in 1899 became a curate at St Mary's, Portsea – then the largest parish in England, with numerous mission churches, ministering to much of the great naval port. He remained there for 20 years, having become Vicar in 1909, and during this time made his reputation as an outstanding parish priest who knew at first hand the challenges facing the Church in working-class communities.

That he should have been assisted by 15 curates seems barely credible a century later, and these shared in an austere and highly disciplined regime in the large vicarage. Pastoral and social work on the streets was the priority, accompanied by well-ordered worship in the churches, and this yielded what now seem remarkable results in church attendance and community involvement. The experience of these years was formative for Garbett, who retained for the remainder of his long life the outlook of a parish priest.

The Bishopric of inner-city Southwark, which he occupied from 1919 to 1932, and that of largely rural Winchester, where he remained until he succeeded William Temple as Archbishop of York in 1942, could hardly have offered more contrasting challenges. In the end, he was reluctant to leave Winchester, where he had often complained that there was little to do and petrol rationing during the war years had restricted his movements in the diocese. Soon after his arrival there, however, he had published a pamphlet, *The Challenge of the Slums*, in which he reflected on his Southwark experience and concluded that in many places inadequate housing was a more serious problem than unemployment. He believed, however, that the creation of a strong and informed Christian conscience on the matter would make housing improvement irresistible. Possessed of considerable expertise in housing matters, he thereafter often spoke on the subject in the House of Lords and public platforms and was listened to with respect.

As Archbishop of York, Garbett proved to be a good partner to William Temple during his all too brief wartime years as Archbishop of Canterbury. Their political outlook was quite different, Garbett being a compassionate High Tory, though he supported Labour in 1945. They were, however, agreed on the need for social and church reform and offered complementary visions of a changed post-war Britain. But Garbett's chief interests and considerable reputation eventually lay in the field of international relations.

Germany's breach of an alliance and invasion of Russia in June 1941 eventually changed the entire course of the war but at the time raised difficult problems for the British government. It was obviously in the national interest to offer Russia maximum moral and material support since national survival would depend on Russian victory. Yet close collaboration and weakened opposition to Communism would inevitably affect adversely Anglo–American relations and raise concern in other parts of the world.

The dangerous situation created by the German invasion of Russia in 1941 and the need for national unity led, however, to significant changes in Soviet policy, including concessions to the Russian Orthodox Church in which national identity was still powerfully enshrined. An early sign of this came in September 1941, when Metropolitan Nicholai of Kiev, Administrator of the vacant Patriarchate of Moscow (which had been suppressed since the time of the Revolution), presented British diplomats with a copy of the State document containing the new concessions. He also suggested an interchange of visits between representatives of the Orthodox Church and the Church of England. That the Soviet authorities were for their own good reasons involved in this overture no one doubted.

In London, the Foreign Office was initially sceptical but, as contemporary documents made available long after the end of the war indicate, it was decided, following discussion with the Americans, that it might be in Britain's interests to accept the Russian suggestion. For one thing, there were many in Britain who, quite unaware of the precarious position of their country in 1941, were far from enthusiastic about an alliance with a Communist power which had hitherto been regarded as an enemy. If these could be reassured about the place of Christianity in Russia, their doubts might be reduced and overall morale improved.

Applied more widely, there were those in other parts of the world, including America, who accepted the German claim that they alone were opposing godless Communism. The welcoming of Church of England dignitaries to Russia would, if properly handled, indicate that Christianity remained a significant presence there, while the freedom of their Orthodox counterparts to visit Britain would suggest a degree of tolerance by the Soviet authorities. The interests of wartime propaganda were not thought to require strict adherence to the truth.

Liberally minded Archbishop Temple, unaware of government motives, had no difficulty in responding positively to the Russian proposal, and when steps were taken to form a delegation, Garbett immediately offered to lead it. The Foreign Office welcomed such an enhancement of the project and undertook to finance the arrangements, which involved a hazardous wartime flight to Moscow, via the Middle East.

In the event, the delegation consisted only of Garbett and two chaplains – Francis House, of the BBC's Religious Broadcasting Department, and Herbert Waddams, an Eastern European specialist on the staff of the Ministry of Information. The visit was, in its own terms, a great success. Stalin had allowed a Patriarch to be elected a few days before Garbett's arrival, the welcome could not have been warmer, the hospitality was lavish, visits were made to crowded churches, devout greetings were exchanged, and the Archbishop and his chaplains aroused much public interest as, clad in their cassocks, they walked freely in Moscow's streets and squares.

This was all reported in the British and American press, enabling the visit to capture the public imagination. On his return, Garbett was entertained by the King and Queen as well as the Prime Minister, gave a broadcast on his experience as well as many press interviews, and addressed meetings the length and breadth of the country. He was now a national hero and to some extent an international figure, there being no awareness that he had gone to Russia primarily as an agent of the Foreign Office rather than for religious interests, though the latter had doubtless also been served.

There was in fact a marked difference between Garbett's report to the Foreign Office and his public utterances, which painted a rosy picture of the religious situation in Russia. He spoke of freedom, the ending of persecution because Stalin, 'a great statesman', realized that he could now rely on the loyalty of the Orthodox Church. It was considered unfortunate therefore when a Roman Catholic priest, John Carmel Heenan, who would later become Archbishop of Westminster, reported otherwise on his own recent visit to Russia. He had no hesitation in announcing that Garbett had allowed himself to be totally misled by his hosts. The Moscow churches might well have been crowded but only a handful of them were open, many hundreds having been closed. Moreover, he had learned from more reliable sources that, although the severe persecution of the past had been modified to a degree, it was nonetheless still gravely inhibiting, especially for non-Orthodox religious communities.

This intervention did not, however, discourage the British Ambassador to Washington, Lord Halifax, from suggesting to the Minister of Information in London, Brendan Bracken, in late 1943 that a visit to America by the Archbishop could be useful to the Allied cause. Bracken agreed and Garbett accepted the idea with alacrity. In order to avoid arousing suspicion about a possible propaganda element in the visit, it was arranged that the Presiding Bishop of the Anglican Church in the USA should offer a formal invitation to the Archbishop.

Halifax was aware that President Roosevelt had for some time been seeking to gain wider support for America's involvement in the war by presenting it as a religious crusade against evil forces in Europe. Garbett had no difficulty in supporting such a view and toured the United States, emphasizing the need for a strong alliance of America, Britain and Russia to defeat the common Nazi enemy. Russia was now spoken of as an essentially Christian nation and, although Stalin was not a believer, God had in the past shown that he was able to use such a leader for his own good purposes. Garbett's portrait appeared on the cover of *Time* magazine.

The Foreign Office was well pleased with Garbett's efforts and, until the end of his life, encouraged him to undertake overseas visits, providing careful briefings on the different political situations he would find, and usually meeting his costs. The end of the war required, however, a different strategy inasmuch as the Soviet Union, 'our great ally', had been transformed into 'our dangerous enemy' supported by the newly installed Communist rulers of the other Eastern European states. The Archbishop immediately adjusted to this new situation, since he had a hatred, as well as a fear, of Communism and felt able to separate the Christian people of Russia from their leaders.

Thereafter he became the chief spokesman, in company with Pope Pius XII, in voicing the religious dimension of the Western involvement in the Cold War. In a fairly substantial book, *In an Age of Revolution* (1952), he wrote, 'in the conviction that mankind is now in the midst of one of the greatest crises in history'. The immediate secular answer, he said, was loyalty to Western ideals, coupled with effective rearmament and increased production, but only the revival of Christianity could deal with the long-term threat – Communism being one of its components.

The scale of his ostensibly church missions to parts of the world where politicians could not easily tread increased, and, although the religious character of these was never in doubt, he usually found it possible to meet heads of governments and reported on his conversations to the Foreign Office in London. One such visit to several Balkan countries was deliberately timed to follow a tour by Hewlett Johnson, the 'Red Dean' of Canterbury, and thus undo any harm to British interests that his unusual views might have caused.

In Britain, Garbett came to be seen as the Church's principal, well-informed authority on international affairs – a role that Archbishop Fisher was more than happy to support – and his reputation abroad became considerable. He spoke frequently in the House of Lords, addressed his Diocesan Conferences on particular issues, went about the country and cultivated the press with unusual skill.

Therein lay a problem. His erastian view of Church–State relations, the inter-relatedness of faith and patriotism, the necessary religious and moral components of true freedom and democracy, made him particularly vulnerable to exploitation by secular interests and ideologies. His readiness to support the retention, and in extremity the use, of nuclear weapons, together with his denunciations of peace movements, attracted criticism in Britain. Bishop George Bell and some other bishops were anxious about his uncritical association with the government.

Without doubting in any way Garbett's sincerity, he might in the end be judged to have himself been more influenced by the secular powers than he was able to influence them – a point made by Dianne Kirby in her revealing and important analysis of Garbett's activities from 1942 to 1965, published as *Church, State and Propaganda* (Hull University Press, 1999). He died, aged 80, on 31 December 1955, shortly before his announced retirement was due to take effect.

In complete contrast was Hewlett Johnson. He was born in a fashionable suburb of Manchester in 1874. His father was the prosperous owner of a wire works. When the family moved to a large house in Macclesfield, young Hewlett attended the local grammar school and went from there to take a BSc at Owen's College, which would grow to become Manchester University. Three and a half years working for a railway engineering firm made him aware of the social and economic gulf between workers and managers, and this attracted him to Socialism.

But he now offered for overseas service with the Church Missionary Society and was sent to Wycliffe Hall, Oxford, for a year to study Theology. In the event, he stayed for three and took a degree in Theology as a member of Wadham College. By now, however, CMS judged him unsuitable for missionary work, and, after launching, editing and financing a monthly magazine *The Interpreter*, he was ordained to a curacy at Altrincham, where Manchester's richest citizens resided.

There his Socialist views proved to be no impediment to a highly effective ministry, and when, after three years, the Vicar moved to other work, the leading lights of the parish petitioned for Johnson to succeed him. Sixteen more years of dynamic ministry followed, during which his activities were by no means confined to preaching and pastoral work. He frequently intervened in Manchester's social issues and organized a petition to the city council about insanitary slums. In 1917, he chaired a public meeting to welcome the Russian Revolution, and after the war wrote a book, *Socialism and Social Credit*. In this, he declared 'Capitalism had war at its heart from the first' and went on to look forward to a time when service would replace profit, and planning personal whim. Invitations to speak and preach on the subject took him to all parts of the country, but a sermon in Westminster Abbey in which he praised the developments in post-Revolution Russia provoked angry protests, and the churchwardens at Altrincham became anxious. But not for long. In 1924, the Labour Prime Minister, Ramsey MacDonald, prompted by William Temple, the young Bishop of Manchester, appointed their Vicar Dean of Manchester Cathedral.

Without in any way neglecting the ministry of the cathedral – in fact, invigorating it in many creative and imaginative ways – Johnson used his office to engage even more in Manchester's civic life. Housing continued to be a major concern and Dean and Chapter land was made available for the building of accommodation for the poor. Pubs were bought and closed to reduce the drink problems, and during the 1926 General Strike the Dean sided with the miners. Soon afterwards he congratulated 'our socialist brother' Mussolini for his improvements to Italy's roads and railways. The railways and bus companies of the North West were urged to follow this example.

Johnson was, however, knocked off his stride somewhat by the death of his wife in 1931, and William Temple believed it important that he should get away from Manchester and make a fresh start elsewhere. He therefore put his name forward for the vacant Deanery of Canterbury. Archbishop Lang readily agreed. King George V, who had been impressed by his preaching, was enthusiastic, and Ramsey MacDonald was only too ready to accept the suggestion. Soon after his installation at Canterbury he was accepting what became regular invitations to the Soviet Embassy in London, as the guest of the Ambassador, Ivan Maisky, and the course was set for the appearance on the national stage of 'the Red Dean of Canterbury'.

This improbable character claimed public attention and either embarrassed or annoyed leaders in both Church and State for the next 31 years. He did not retire until he was 88. His Socialist opinions were unacceptable to some, but no one contested his right to hold them. The Canons of Canterbury did not like the large 'Ban the Bomb' placards later erected outside the Deanery, and they were furious when Mahatma Gandhi stayed there as a guest. But eccentric deans are not rare, and in any case are not subject to a higher ecclesiastical authority. Johnson's relations with the archbishops of his time varied.

No one could have disagreed more with his views than Lang, but their relationship was warm and friendly. Temple was not unsympathetic to his Socialist outlook and in any case his two wartime years at Canterbury demanded cordial relations with the Soviet Union as the price of national survival. Fisher was, however, outraged by his views and behaviour and often said so, being the more irritated by confusion abroad concerning the titles of Dean and Archbishop. Eventually he was driven to add his name to a House of Lords-sponsored petition calling on the Crown to remove him from office, but this was to no avail.

Johnson first went to Russia in 1937 as the guest of the Soviet government. There he was entertained lavishly, shown some of the alleged successes of the Soviet system, shielded from its appallingly destructive excesses, and, like many other visitors in the 1930s, left with the impression that he had been in touch with a wonderful new order that promised a solution to all the twentieth century's social and economic problems. Visits to Spain during the Civil War confirmed this in his mind.

On all his visits to Eastern Europe, Johnson was accompanied by Alfred D'Eye – a Marxist who lectured on history, politics and economics for the Workers' Educational Association. Whenever teaching in Kent he stayed at the Deanery, where he assisted his host with the facts and figures and intellectual arguments for his speeches and articles on Communism. His influence was considerable. Whether or not he was a Soviet agent will never be known – he always denied this – but the ease with which he moved in Communist circles, inside and outside Russia, created deep suspicion.

On his return to England, Johnson travelled extensively commending the virtues of the Soviet system and began writing his 350-page *The Socialist Sixth of the World*. This was published in December 1939 and brought him instant world fame. Several million copies in 22 editions and 24 languages were sold. Its reception in Britain was, however, hostile and he said later, 'Few could have endured greater vilification or endured more violent attack. Rare was the critic who could be found to say kind words about it.'

His readers were told that the Soviet peoples were activated by a moral purpose and working for the common good, being motivated by Christian morality, even though they denied this. There was only the briefest of references to the war against religion, which he justified on the grounds that the Russian churches had failed to observe the ethical demands of the Christian faith and were understandably regarded as an enemy. He had evidently failed to notice that, during Stalin's reign of terror, execution and deportation had reduced the number of Orthodox bishops from 165 to about four, and the number of other clergy from over 51,000 to some hundreds. The number of churches open had been similarly reduced and the academies and seminaries all closed. Stalin was portrayed as one of humanity's greatest heroes.

Earlier in 1939, Johnson had published a pamphlet, *Act Now! An Appeal to Heart and Hearth*, in which he advocated close collaboration between Britain and the Soviet Union and the embracing of Socialism to provide effective opposition to the menace of Hitler's Nazism. When in August of that year the Soviet Union and Germany signed a non-aggression pact, most of the left-wing leaders in Britain became disenchanted with Russia, but Johnson tried to justify the pact on the grounds that the Western powers had consistently rejected Russian overtures for friendship. He came to believe that if *The Socialist Sixth of the World* had been published just six months earlier, these overtures would have been responded to favourably and thus brought about the vanquishing of Hitler without resort to war.

Three days after the German attack on the Soviet Union in 1941 Johnson launched an appeal for a National Anglo–Soviet Medical Aid Fund and travelled the length and breadth of the country, appealing on its behalf. There was a huge response, and, in addition to £1.25 million, a vast number of blankets and clothes were collected. The unexpected wartime alliance led to the reopening in 1943 of the banned Communist newspaper the *Daily Worker*, to which he had been a frequent contributor, and at a meeting attended by 1,600 delegates to celebrate the event he was elected an honorary member of its board. He continued to write for it until the end of his life.

From 1941 until the end of the war in 1945, Johnson's pronouncements caused much less concern, and he was himself greatly preoccupied with the protection of his cathedral and the safety of its community during the German air attacks on south-east England. A total of 445 high-explosive bombs and 10,000 incendiaries fell on Canterbury, killing 115 people, injuring another 380 and destroying or damaging over 6,000 houses, including the Deanery. Throughout the onslaught Johnson stood as a pillar of faith and courage, and for most people in Canterbury it was this, rather than his view on Communism, that was most remembered.

On VE Day 1945 he was in Moscow and preached at a Thanksgiving Service there before accompanying Patriarch Alexi to the Orthodox Cathedral. Later he had a 50-minute meeting with Stalin and Molotov, during which the Soviet leader complained about the attitude of the British press. Johnson explained to him that the British newspapers were all owned by millionaires and that the only honest journal was the *Daily Worker*.

During the Cold War years and beyond his retirement in 1963 he continued to travel widely, mainly to Eastern Europe but also to America and China, though he was for a time refused a visa for America. Wherever he went he had meetings with national leaders, including President Truman in Washington, Tito in what was then Yugoslavia and Chairman Mao in China. On his ninetieth birthday, greetings came from Khrushchev, the Soviet leader. His support of the Communist world never wavered.

In a somewhat turgid autobiography, *Searching for Light*, completed with the aid of his second wife and Alfred D'Eye shortly before his death in 1966, he explained that the aim of his life and work had been to create a World Brotherhood – modelled on the family in which he had lived as a boy, a large happy family, not all equal in ability, but all equal in consideration and opportunity. Canterbury Cathedral was crowded for his funeral and among the congregation was the First Secretary from the Soviet Embassy in London and the General Secretary of the British Communist Party – of which he had never been a member.

Although the Soviet Union found Johnson a useful tool of its propaganda, his views were so extreme, to the point of silliness, that his influence in Britain was negligible. The sudden collapse of the Soviet empire and the end of the Cold War in 1989 came through economic weakness and the refusal of oppressed peoples to tolerate continued restrictions on their freedom. The isolation and military demands of the previous 40 years contributed much to the denouement.

14

The Church and the Bomb

The dropping of atomic bombs on the Japanese cities of Hiroshima and Nagasaki on 6 and 9 August 1945 caused the deaths of 200,000 people, great suffering to many more, and the immediate ending of the final phase of the Second World War. It changed for ever the context of international relations and the destructive potential of warfare. The planning and execution of the American attacks was conducted in the utmost secrecy, so that the majority of senior politicians on both sides of the Atlantic were taken unawares when the news broke.

It is not surprising therefore that neither the churches nor anyone else had given consideration to the moral issues involved in this astonishing development. In one sense these were not essentially different from those raised by Bishop George Bell of Chichester and a few other courageous witnesses at the time of the carpet bombing of German cities, which had in total caused equal destruction and many more casualties. Yet the mushroom clouds that rose over the Japanese cities caused an atmosphere of anxiety to spread across the entire earth, never to be completely dissolved.

The immediate aftermath of their rising was not, however, a good moment for looking to the future and engaging in dispassionate discussion of the fine points of morality. The sudden ending of a six-year world war that had caused unprecedented human suffering brought almost inexpressible relief to the victors and probably to most of the vanquished as well. Although the number affected by the two bombs was huge, the war might well have continued for at least another 12 months, with even more casualties – the Japanese being relentless and ruthless warriors. The way in which they had fought thus far evinced little sympathy for the victims of the nuclear holocausts.

Church leaders were nonetheless immediately called upon to pronounce on the morality of what had happened. Bishop Bell was naturally appalled, as also was the now forgotten Dean of St Albans, Cuthbert Thickness. Amid the end-of-war euphoria, he explained in a letter to *The Times* that there would be no Thanksgiving Service in St Albans Abbey – 'I cannot honestly give thanks to God for an event brought about by a wrong use of force by an act of wholesale destruction which is different in kind over all acts of open warfare hitherto, however brutal and hideous.'

Bishop Wilson of Chelmsford and Bishop Chavasse of Rochester were inclined to agree with the Dean, though they did not go as far as forbidding Thanksgiving Services in their dioceses. But from the earliest days of peace there arose a moral dilemma that would henceforth prevent the Church of England and virtually all other public institutions from speaking with one voice on the most dangerous ever threat to human civilization.

Within a few months of his Enthronement as Archbishop of Canterbury, Geoffrey Fisher – still regarded by many as bearing the conscience of the nation – was deluged with letters and telephone calls, mainly from those outraged or distressed by the way in which the war had ended but also from a significant number of parish clergy, seeking guidance. But, as Bishop of Chester, then of London, Fisher had not been accustomed to making public statements on national issues of any kind, so he hid for a few days in order to escape the attention of the press and to have time to think.

When he emerged, he made his views known in letters, a tabloid news-paper article, a speech in the House of Lords debate and the September issue of his diocesan magazine, the *Canterbury Gazette*. This was soon re-published as a pamphlet for wider circulation. Its opening sentences were not reassuring to the protesters – 'Of the victory God has granted to us and our Allies I will say no more here. We have celebrated it with humble gratitude and reserve.' He went on to say that the nation should be grateful that the Americans had discovered 'the method' before the Germans. He acknowledged the existence of a sharp division of opinion as to whether or not the bomb should have been used, but believed the issue now was how humanity could extract itself from the possibility of future conflicts involving the use of nuclear weapons. 'The way of deliverance is the Charter of the United Nations. Every nation that signs it must live by it, and between them there must be no military secrets.'

Fisher said much the same in his House of Lords speech and went out of his way to absolve scientists from blame for the way in which their aston-ishing discoveries had, rightly or wrongly, been used. He shared the hope that the possession of nuclear weapons by the great powers would make future wars unlikely, but there must be inspection and control.

A year later, he wrote to the American Secretary of State pointing out that rockets were being tested in Central Australia on land set aside as a reserve for Aborigines, but received only the brush-off assurance that his representations would 'be borne in mind'. Taken more seriously was a letter to the Prime Minister, Sir Anthony Eden, in 1955, in which he said there was a growing opinion among the churches that the British and American governments must take a fresh initiative in the field of nuclear disarmament if the situation was to be kept under moral control. 'The moral case for the bomb daily decreases.' He believed that Britain should work for a general reduction in armaments, the prohibition of certain classes of weapons and to make a distinction between strategic and tactical weapons.

The Prime Minister responded by setting out at some length the government's current policy. It was, he believed, still necessary to retain nuclear weapons as a deterrent power, since both sides possessed them in quantity. 'The West will never be the aggressor – a position recently reaffirmed by Washington – and the best hope was for the West', said Eden, 'to remain "strongest armed".'

A dialogue between Fisher and Eden's successor, Harold Macmillan, was rather less cordial. Towards the end of a meeting of the International Affairs Department of the British Council of Churches, Fisher expressed surprise that there had been no official British response to a 'remarkable' statement by President Khrushchev of Russia calling for total disarmament with full international control. This was, he said, what people had been praying for for years, and Mr Khrushchev 'could not more effectively have read the New Testament'.

Widely reported by the press, this drew many protests and the Prime Minister wrote to express surprise that the Primate was apparently unaware of a similar, more detailed proposal made by the British Foreign Secretary. Equally, he might not be aware of the use which the Communist newspapers were making of the Primate's statement – 'I do not mind this so much in this country, but throughout the Commonwealth and in every uncommitted country it will be used as the basis for unscrupulous propaganda.' Fisher was now close to retirement, and in retrospect it is apparent that he had done his best over the nuclear issue within a limited range of options.

No such limitations had existed when the Suez Crisis arose in 1956, and he conducted a fierce cross-examination of the Lord Chancellor in the House of Lords. His strong denunciation of Britain's connivance in the invasion of Egypt was almost certainly the last occasion on which an Archbishop of Canterbury felt able to deliver so stern a public rebuke to the government of the day.

The British Council of Churches (BCC), still in its infancy at the end of the war, had been quickly off the mark with the appointment of a commission which published a report in 1946, *The Era of Atomic Power*. This provided a careful analysis of the theological and moral issues, without reaching agreement on the possession of nuclear weapons. When it was brought to the attention of the Church of England's Church Assembly (the precursor of the General Synod), it was immediately passed to a special commission chaired by the Dean of Winchester, E. G. Selwyn – a distinguished New

Testament scholar. Their report was published in 1948 under the title *The Church and the Atom*.

Again it was necessary to report a division of opinion on the now familiar grounds, but its recommendation went further than those of the BCC document. Not only might it be necessary to have nuclear weapons to deter would-be aggressors, it could be morally justifiable and in certain circumstances a 'defensive necessity' to use them against an unscrupulous aggressor. The basis offered for this judgement was the traditional doctrine of the 'just war', the validity of which was now being seriously questioned by moral theologians who doubted if the impact of nuclear weapons could ever be regarded as a lesser evil of any conceivable kind. When the report was debated in the Church Assembly, more spoke against it than for it, but in the end, by the slimmest of majorities, 211 votes to 209, it was 'commended to the earnest attention of the Church'.

The report was then subjected to a good deal of hostile criticism, someone suggesting that a better title would have been *Up Church and At 'em*. Bishop Bell said that it displayed a lack of realism and any sense of urgency. He added that it might easily have been written and signed by any men of goodwill, and noted that in a long chapter on 'Morality and Warfare' the name of Christ was never mentioned. By and large, however, it was accepted, even if a little uneasily, by the Church of England's leaders and those of its members who read about it in the press.

The serious breakdown in relations between the Western Allies and the extended Soviet empire, which had become apparent even before the war's ending and soon led to what became known as the 'Cold War', did nothing to encourage a reappraisal of either the strategic value or the morality of nuclear weapons. On the contrary, it created a climate of fear on both sides that stimulated an arms race in which these weapons began to be stockpiled in large numbers. This absorbed massive scientific and financial resources, and in the end a certain stability was maintained based on a 'balance of terror' in which neither side dare risk taking an aggressive first step. It was a precarious balance, but it ensured no major war during the next half-century and remains the most potent deterrent against large-scale aggression.

Britain's contribution to Western policy, exercised through the North Atlantic Treaty Organization (NATO), has always been relatively modest, though not unimportant. In 1955, the Conservative government proposed the manufacturing of a hydrogen bomb, and two years later its first tests were carried out, surely inappropriately, on Christmas Island in the Pacific. In due course, Polaris submarines with long-range nuclear armaments were stationed on the west coast of Scotland, and the Bishop of Chester, Gerald Ellison, who had been a wartime Royal Navy chaplain, conducted a dedication service for one of them – arousing sharp criticism from opponents. These weapons were later replaced with more accurate Trident missiles. Later still, Britain was called upon to provide bases for an American strike force capable of creating destruction far in excess of that experienced in Japan in 1945 and thus achieved the unenviable distinction of housing the largest concentration of nuclear weaponry in the world.

It can hardly be surprising that significant objections were raised to this development and the policy that undergirded it. But not by the Church of England – at least not officially – since it had joined what amounted to a national consensus supporting government policy. The outstanding Christian figure in the anti-nuclear movement was John Collins, a courageous Canon of St Paul's Cathedral. The son of a Conservative-supporting master builder, he was born in Kent in 1905, and an encouraging academic achievement at Cambridge suggested a teaching career. He was for a short time chaplain of Sidney Sussex College, Cambridge, then combined a lectureship at King's College, London, with a minor canonry of St Paul's, where he had responsibility for the worship. From 1934 to 1937 he taught at Westcott House, Cambridge, and during this time not only shocked some with his liberal–modernist theological views, but also came under the influence of one of his pupils, Mervyn Stockwood, a future notable Bishop of Southwark, who converted him to Socialism.

When Stockwood eventually became a Vicar in Bristol, he introduced his former tutor to a local MP, Sir Stafford Cripps – a leading figure in the Labour Party who would become Chancellor of the Exchequer in the post-war Labour government. A friendship resulted, and this proved to be of critical importance in determining the character of Collins' post-war career. Meanwhile, having decided that Westcott House was too ecclesiastical an establishment for his taste, he moved to Oxford to be Fellow, Chaplain and Dean of Oriel College. While there, he met Diana Elliott, an undergraduate at Lady Margaret Hall, whom he soon married. More able in many ways than her husband, she became an important partner in all his subsequent enterprises.

In 1940, not long after Dunkirk, Collins joined the Royal Air Force as a chaplain and spent the next three years at Yatesbury – a large and dull training station in Wiltshire. There he became increasingly concerned that the Church should make the social, political and economic implications of the gospel effective in local, national and international affairs. To encourage thought about these matters he began to invite distinguished speakers to address camp meetings. Archbishop William Temple was the first to accept and was followed by Sir Richard Acland, MP, on 'The Christian and Politics'. Hewlett Johnson, the 'Red Dean' of Canterbury, spoke on 'The Christian and Communism', and there were several others.

When news of this reached the Commander-in-Chief of Technical Training Command, however, he panicked and, fearing that socialism might be advocated, tried to get Collins to withdraw any outstanding invitations. He refused and the matter went as high as the Prime Minister, Winston Churchill, who minuted 'The chaplain at Yatesbury must be either a Communist or a dupe'. In the end, the matter was sorted out and invitations to speakers were continued, though there was a fuss when the Soviet ambassador in London accepted and addressed an audience of over 1,000.

In July 1944, Collins was posted to Bomber Command Headquarters at High Wycombe, when the attack on German cities was at its height. He was disquieted, but as a member of the RAF was unable to express this publicly. The same was true after the bombing of Hiroshima and Nagasaki, but he wrote to the Archbishop of Canterbury asking why there had been no official protest by the Church of England against the American action. Fisher's subsequent public statements did not satisfy him, and he became a nuclear pacifist – later an unqualified pacifist, a step he took with reluctance.

Advised by Sir Stafford Cripps not to be in too much of a hurry to accept any church appointments he might be offered after the war, Collins returned to Oriel College in January 1946, and, after being greatly impressed by Victor Gollancz's book, *Our Threatened Values* (1946), decided to hold in December of that year a public meeting in Oxford Town Hall to consider 'A call to Christian action in public affairs'. Bishop George Bell was in the chair, and the speakers were Victor Gollancz, Sir Richard Acland, Barbara Ward, a Roman Catholic economist, and Roger Wilson, the former secretary of the Friends' Relief Organisation in Europe. The Town Hall was filled to capacity, as was an overflow meeting in the University Church, and it was estimated that some 3,000 people had turned out for the event.

A small organization named Christian Action was formed to take matters further, various notables including Quinton Hogg, the future Lord Hailsham, Lord Halifax and Sir Stafford Cripps were recruited as patrons, and Collins directed its affairs from Oriel. An early decision to back a Gollancz-inspired 'Save Europe Now' campaign, designed to promote reconciliation between Britain and Germany, attracted 7,000 people to a meeting in London's Albert Hall; 4,000 other applicants had to be refused tickets.

When a canonry of St Paul's fell vacant in 1948, the Prime Minister, Clement Attlee, gladly accepted the suggestion of Sir Stafford Cripps that Collins should be appointed. Archbishop Fisher and the Bishop of London, William Wand, strongly objected on the grounds that he would spend most of his time on his outside commitments, and the Dean, Walter Matthews, was annoyed that he had not even been consulted. Nonetheless, he was installed on All Saints' Day 1948 and made an immediate impact by inviting the Berlin Philharmonic Orchestra to give its first post-war performance in

England at St Paul's. In the end, however, this had to be transferred to the Queen's Hall since the Chapter of St Paul's would not allow tickets to be sold for a performance in the cathedral.

During the next 33 years Collins carried out his cathedral duties conscientiously, preached many controversial and much-publicized sermons, invited to the pulpit notable preachers, including Martin Luther King and Paul Robeson, who chose to sing, and developed Christian Action into a sizeable organization that provided support for his own considerable work in the social and political fields. Most demanding were his leaderships of the Campaign for Nuclear Disarmament and the South Africa Defence and Aid Fund.

Unusually for a cathedral dignitary, the slogan 'Hang Canon Collins' was daubed on his house on Amen Court, together with several others of a similar sort at different times. He opposed in Chapter the translation of the Bishop of Peterborough, Robert Stopford, to London on the grounds that he had declared it better for the world to be completely destroyed, rather than fall under the hegemony of Communism.

Early in 1957, a small group met in Hampstead and formed a National Committee for the Abolition of Nuclear Weapons Tests, with Bertrand Russell, the philosopher, as chairman. Diana Collins attended its early meetings, but John believed that something much bigger was needed to campaign for the abolition of all nuclear weapons. Nonetheless, much publicity and propaganda was generated, and Diana chaired a mass meeting in Trafalgar Square.

In November of the same year, an article by J. B. Priestley appeared in the *New Statesman*. Its content was not pacifist but consisted of a plea for Britain to renounce any reliance on nuclear weapons. The response was considerable and the editor, Kingsley Martin, despatched all the letters to the Hampstead committee. This led to a meeting in John Collins' study at St Paul's at which it was decided to launch a Campaign for Nuclear Disarmament, with Collins as the executive chairman. Its aims were to:

1. Persuade Britain to abandon nuclear weapons unilaterally.
2. Work for disarmament negotiations involving other countries.
3. Ban nuclear tests, missile bases in Britain and the over-flight of aircraft carrying nuclear weapons.
4. Ban the exporting of nuclear weapons.

The launch meeting was held on 17 February 1958 in Central Hall, Westminster, where 3,000 people were packed in, and five overflow meetings had to be hastily organized. Three bishops were among the first sponsors. Groups sprang up in most parts of the country, and by the end of the first year there had been 290 meetings, picketings and minor demonstrations. A small group of enthusiastic activists arranged a march from Trafalgar Square to the nuclear weapons research station at Aldermaston in Berkshire.

This attracted sufficient attention to encourage Collins and his committee to make the march an annual official CND event at Easter. Thus began annual Aldermaston marches, which became a rallying point for CND supporters. Soon it was decided to start at Aldermaston and end with a mass meeting in Trafalgar Square. The number taking part was never fewer than 7,000 and sometimes reached 20,000, and for many years no Easter seemed complete without media pictures of a motley procession headed by Collins in his cassock and various left-wing intellectuals, trade union leaders and Labour MPs. A white-on-black banner bearing the CND logo identified them. For most of those who marched – a largely middle-class fraternity – it was an enjoyable occasion, combining high moral purpose with fun. A fairly large number of clergy of all the churches belonged, though for them Easter was not a convenient time for marching. Many more laypeople were involved.

Since, however, the cause was presented in terms of great urgency, with nuclear war an ever-present possibility, it was hardly surprising that some of the marchers began to show signs of impatience when none of their efforts made a scrap of difference to government policy. Eventually this led to a sharp policy disagreement between Collins and Bertrand Russell, who formed a 'Committee of 100' to engage in direct action, including such gestures as lying down in Whitehall until forcibly removed by the police. Infighting, some of it bitter, followed among the leaders of the Campaign and in April 1964 Collins, believing correctly that he could no longer hold the movement together, resigned from the chairmanship. CND then went into a fairly steep decline, though it enjoyed a significant revival in the late 1970s and early 1980s under the dynamic leadership of a Roman Catholic, Monsignor Bruce Kent.

It is not easy to discern what CND achieved during the first phase of its existence. It undoubtedly spread among the public a better perception of the danger and horror of nuclear weapons. Collins believed that this, combined with similar campaigns in other countries, helped to create the atmosphere in which the signing of a Test Ban Treaty became possible in 1963. At the personal level it provided him with one experience of being arrested, locked in a police cell and charged with a public order offence after a demonstration in Trafalgar Square. The Bow Street magistrate subsequently dismissed the case.

Apart from the personal witness of Collins and a few others, the Church of England remained silent until October 1978, when, briefly, it grabbed national and international attention with what proved to be a highly contentious report on the subject. The chairman of the responsible General Synod working party was a highly competent theologian, John Austin Baker, at that time a Canon of Westminster, Rector of St Margaret's Church and Chaplain to the Speaker of the House of Commons. By the time of the report's publication he was Bishop of Salisbury. He was joined on the enterprise by lecturers in War Studies and in Social and Pastoral Theology, a Roman Catholic lecturer in Moral Theology and two well-known pacifists, one of these being a Quaker.

Their report, *The Church and the Bomb: Nuclear Weapons and the Christian Conscience*, 186 pages long, was a comprehensive, well-informed survey and analysis of all the issues involved and of a quality not seen on its subject either before or since. The first section consisted of a survey of the technological, strategic and political aspects of the debate about nuclear weapons, and gave a clear impression that the members of the working party knew what they were talking about. The final recommendations, however, were more questionable:

> The United Kingdom should adopt a unilateral policy to reduce the nuclear weaponry of the NATO Alliance, in the hope of encouraging multilateral reductions: strength identified simplistically with the number of weapons a side possesses may actually jeopardise security.
>
> The UK should renounce its independent nuclear deterrent for moral reasons in the hope of putting new life into the Non-Proliferation Treaty and also to eliminate the destabilizing effect on the world situation of several independent centres of nuclear decision-making within the Western Alliance.
>
> The UK should cancel the order for Trident, phase out Polaris (including work on Chevaline), and negotiate a timetable with her allies for the gradual disengagement from other nuclear weapons of British manufacture; US made 'dual-key' weapons; US air and submarine facilities and the projected Cruise missiles from 1983.

Massive media coverage followed the publication of the report. *The Times* devoted a long editorial to analysis and strong criticism, while the Foreign and Commonwealth Office gave a considered response, the tone of which was set by a single sentence: 'Giving a moral lead may be good for the conscience, but it is not a valid proposition in the real world.' It doubted whether the Soviet Union was interested in moral considerations.

Since the Labour Party was at the time committed to the unilateralist position, it naturally welcomed the report, as did the CND, but the Church of England was a very long way from being so committed, and the General Synod refused an endorsement. It was disappointing that the controversy provoked by the recommendations stood in the way of careful study of the main body of the report, which had handled the fundamental issues – still unresolved – with considerable skill.

The four Archbishops who followed Fisher – Ramsey, Coggan, Runcie and Carey – spoke from time to time about the evil of nuclear warfare and the dangers inherent in the stockpiling of weapons, but none advanced any viable alternatives apart from the obvious one of multilateral disarmament, which was nowhere near the international agenda. The collapse of the Soviet empire in 1989 and the serious internal problems created by this also made the issue less pressing.

The appointment of Rowan Williams to the Archbishopric of Canterbury in 2002 brought someone quite different to the Primacy. Born in South Wales in 1950, he had a brilliant academic career at Christ's College, Cambridge, and completed an Oxford DPhil. before his ordination in 1977. Teaching appointments in Cambridge followed, and, aged only 37, he moved to Oxford as Lady Margaret Professor of Divinity, combining this with a Canonry of Christ Church.

Five years later, he returned to his native Wales as Bishop of Monmouth, subsequently becoming Archbishop of Wales. By this time, he was widely known and admired from his many books, lectures and sermons, and his translation to Canterbury in succession to George Carey was greeted in most parts of the Church with enthusiasm. However, in a sympathetic television documentary on his life, soon after the announcement of his appointment, his friend Angela Tilby noted candidly, 'His politics always seem to come out of the less sophisticated part of him.'

His position on nuclear weaponry, indeed on all forms of weaponry, was in fact long established as a matter of deep religious conviction. He was, and remains, an avowed pacifist opposed to any kind of military action – a conviction explained, though without great clarity, in a small volume, *The Truce of God*, commissioned by Archbishop Robert Runcie for his 1983 Lent Book. Runcie was not happy with the result.

In the event, the nuclear issue was never high on the international agenda during Williams' time at Canterbury. America actually went so far as to reduce its stockpile of weapons slightly. It was, however, fear that the dictator of Iraq, Saddam Hussein, was manufacturing nuclear weapons (he had once claimed to be doing so) that led to what turned out to be a disastrous Anglo–American invasion of Iraq in 2003.

Williams was naturally opposed to this, though surprisingly he did not mention it in his Enthronement sermon, when the war was imminent. Instead, he issued a joint statement with the Roman Catholic Archbishop of Westminster, Cardinal Cormac Murphy-O'Connor, questioning the moral legitimacy of an invasion and calling for the greater involvement of the

United Nations in the problem. He also went to see the Prime Minister, Tony Blair, in the vain hope of getting him to change his mind. Earlier, he had urged collaboration with neighbouring Arab states in a quest for a peaceful solution, which suggested a pragmatic, rather than a merely utopian, approach. But in the circumstances of the time this was unrealistic and, as always, it seemed easier to advocate peace than it was to suggest alternative ways of overcoming the evils that war and preparations for war might bring.

15

Racism and Injustice in South Africa

The landslide victory of the coalition of National and Afrikaner parties in South Africa's 1948 election, followed by their merging three years later, represented the triumph of the nation's Afrikaner community after a struggle extending over more than a century to express powerfully its identity and secure power. None of the country's 200 million blacks had been allowed to vote, and, among the 4 million whites, one-quarter of the Afrikaners had voted against their own party. Nonetheless, the Nationalists continued to consolidate their power, which they did not relinquish until compelled to do so 46 years later.

The Dutch East India Company provided the Cape of South Africa with its first settlers in 1652 and their number, increased by the importing of slaves from other parts of Africa, grew modestly. In 1795, however, the Prince of Orange, who was a refugee in England at the time, ceded dominion over the Cape to the British on condition that the company be allowed to continue its trading and the Dutch Reformed Church (DRC) its privileged status.

Successive British governments were for some years content to administer their newly acquired colony through a corps of civil servants and a small militia, but, in response to the high unemployment following the Napoleonic Wars, the British government facilitated the migration of 5,000 of its own citizens to join them. Nine chaplains of dubious quality were eventually appointed and the Bishop of Calcutta called in while passing by to perform episcopal functions. More British migrants followed, along with other Europeans, and this required the development of a fully organized colonial administration.

The Dutch settlers had, however, never been happy with what they regarded as the Prince of Orange's betrayal of their interests, and, now outnumbered among the settlers, they became passionately determined to preserve their own distinct identity. Membership of the Calvinist DRC was an integral element of that identity. The consequences were to be tragic.

A critical moment, and what proved to be a dramatic landmark in South African history, came in the 1830s, when a large body of their number (then known as Boers, later Afrikaners) decided to secure their

independence by migrating from the eastern Cape to African tribal territory 400 miles and more to the north. The immediate causes of the Great
Trek are complex but the trekkers were sustained on their epic journey by
identifying themselves with the biblical account of the Israelites, who were
led by Moses from slavery in Egypt to a land of their own. The outcome
was the formation of what became the independent republics of Orange
Free State, Natal and the Transvaal – all under Boer rule, with the DRC
as, effectively, the 'established' Church.

For many years there was no question of this Church engaging in missionary work among the indigenous population. The efforts of a Moravian
missionary, George Schmidt, who arrived from Germany in 1738, were
strongly opposed on theological grounds, but also because the conversion of non-whites to Christianity might well disturb social stability.
Settler/slave liaisons were now producing people of mixed race (later to
be known as Coloureds), and some Africans were being employed on
menial tasks.

During the remaining years of the nineteenth century, however, large
numbers of missionaries went from Europe to the Cape 'to convert the
heathen', and this soon led to conflict with the DRC, which still saw no
need for evangelism beyond the now expanded settler community. It is
significant, however, that in 1829 a Synod of the DRC decreed that Holy
Communion should be administered to all, irrespective of race – this
being 'an unshakeable principle based on the infallible Word of God'.
Membership of the Church was no longer exclusively white, some others
having elected to join its ranks. Several subsequent Synods reaffirmed the
inclusive policy over Holy Communion, but social division between the
white and indigenous populations led the 1857 Synod to declare that,
while it did not wish to depart from the inclusive policy, yet, 'owing to the
weakness of some' (the whites), it felt obliged to authorize the holding of
separate services.

The theological basis of the DRC's position was based on the belief,
derived from the early chapters of Genesis, that the differentiation of races
is no mere accident but part of God's plan for the human race and must
therefore be honoured. Few Christians would disagree with this. But the
DRC went further, believing that this honouring required the races to
develop their lives separately, lest their distinctiveness be lost. This was a
pragmatic rather than a theological judgement and derived from the early
development of colonial life in South Africa, when, for practical purposes,
European settlers and indigenous Africans had to live in separate communities. All the settlers believed this to be necessary, but only the DRC
produced a theological rationale to justify its continuation. It was also
widely believed that tribal Africans were an inferior race and therefore

'designed' to be servants. Economic and land tenure conflicts became increasingly common and significant.

In spite of the large number of missionaries arriving from Europe, it was not until 1848 that the Church of England appointed Robert Gray to a newly created Archbishopric of Cape Town and initiated a permanent Anglican presence. Even then the intention was to minister only to English-speaking people, though the appointment of an archbishop suggests wider aims.

Gray's jurisdiction extended over 20,000 square miles, and by 1853 there were sufficient English-speaking people settled in widely separated areas to require the appointment of Bishops of Natal and Grahamstown. Four years later, a first Synod was held, after which Gray reported to the Archbishop of Canterbury that he had 'transported the Church of England system to this land'.

The appointment of John William Colenso to the Bishopric of Natal had, however, consequences that shook the Anglican Communion. Born in humble circumstances in Cornwall in 1814, Colenso won a scholarship to St John's College, Cambridge, where he proved to be a brilliant mathematician. He then taught at Harrow School for three years before returning to St John's as a tutor. In 1846, however, and having been ordained, he moved to the rich college living of Forncett St Mary, in Norfolk, where he exercised an exemplary ministry and found time to study much theology, coming under the influence of F. D. Maurice.

During his first year at Natal, the diocese of which embraced Zululand, he made an extensive tour, then returned to England to recruit clergy and raise money. He also published the journal of his tour, *Ten Weeks in Natal*, in which he said that African culture was noble and that, given the proper opportunities, Africans would achieve as much as the members of other races. Missionaries should seek therefore to build on the indigenous culture and not attempt to replace it with European civilization. The gospel was to be preached not in order to convert the heathen but to set before them a pattern of love to follow. While not in favour of polygamy, he argued that it should be regarded as part of the Zulu social order and not necessarily immoral.

This caused a furore in England and consternation among his episcopal colleagues in South Africa when he returned to Natal to create a strong base for missionary work among the Zulus. He was also in trouble with his own flock for allegedly holding papist beliefs and practices. They burned his effigy in public in Durban, though he was no more than a middle-of-the road Anglican. A remarkable linguist, he engaged on a grammar of the Zulu language, a Zulu–English dictionary and a translation of the Bible into Zulu.

For this work he employed a Zulu assistant, and when the Genesis story of the Flood was reached, the assistant asked awkward questions about the narrative. This led Colenso to apply his mathematical skill to the alleged dimensions of Noah's Ark and the discovery that these were not feasible. It was not a very sophisticated approach to biblical criticism, but it caused him to embark on a seven-part criticism of the early books of the Bible, which appeared between 1862 and 1879. The major controversy that followed is not an appropriate subject for this book, but it involved, among many other responses, the calling of the first Lambeth Conference and an appeal to the Privy Council. Colenso was eventually excommunicated and deposed by Archbishop Gray.

This turned out to have been illegal and, although another Bishop of Natal was appointed, Colenso continued his episcopal work with the support of some of the white population. He now regarded his main task, however, as that of defending the Zulus against exploitation by the white settlers. He bitterly condemned the war of 1878–9 in which the power of the Zulu king was broken, and by the time of his death in 1883 was regarded by the Zulus as 'Father of the People'.

In South Africa, it was in fact Colenso's attitude to African people, rather than his beliefs about the Bible, that was the chief cause of concern to the white Anglican community. The Anglican Church's missionary work was from its outset officially multi-racial and in due course a number of Africans were elected to its synods. But in practice it was hardly less segregationist than the DRC. Much of this was due to locational factors, but there were divisive social and cultural elements that remained a problem a century later.

The Union of the separate South African states, achieved in 1910, did nothing to weaken ties with Britain or their subordination within the Empire. British flags continued to flank the altars in Anglican churches. But the Second Anglo–Boer War (1899–1902) and the atrocities associated with the British victory intensified greatly the nationalist feelings and ambitions of the Afrikaner population – both powerfully supported by the Dutch Reformed Church. The outbreak of the Second World War in 1939 therefore found South Africa divided in its loyalties. The English-speaking population and some Africans rallied to what was seen as an Empire cause and made an important contribution to the war effort, as did some Afrikaners, led notably by General Smuts; but a considerable number believed that South Africa should stay out of the war, and some even advocated support for Nazi Germany.

Meanwhile there had been an awakening of indigenous African consciousness, which led to the foundation of numerous independent African churches and what came to be known as the African National Congress, much of the leadership of which was Christian.

The Nationalist–Afrikaner electoral victory in 1948 was followed immediately by legislation that made apartheid (separate development) an integral part of South African life – enforced by draconian laws that caused immeasurable suffering to the non-white population and some others who championed their cause. Ostensibly the policy was designed to enable them to develop in their own ways and at their own speeds, until they reached the point at which they could share fully with white people in every aspect of the nation's life. In practice, it constituted the most blatant racial discrimination, with non-whites always at a major disadvantage in incomes, politics, housing, education and freedom of movement. It led to the withdrawal, under external pressure, of South Africa from the British Commonwealth and the constant condemnation of the civilized world.

All the Christian churches, apart from the Dutch Reformed Church, shared to varying degrees in this condemnation and within South Africa sought to undermine the policy and alleviate its effects. It was to be a long struggle and this chapter now concentrates on some of the Anglican leaders who played an important part in it. Which is not to undervalue the contribution, often heroic, made by others. Neither is it possible to ignore the fact that most of the all-English Anglican bishops believed that a less than militant approach to the problem would be most likely to yield the best results. In this, they were proved to have been wrong.

Their position was accurately reflected in the approach of Geoffrey Clayton, who became Archbishop of Cape Town in 1949. Before moving to South Africa he had been Dean of Peterhouse, Cambridge, then Vicar of Chesterfield, and he was elected to the Archbishopric after spending 15 years as Bishop of Johannesburg. There was never any doubting his firm opposition to apartheid and related government policies, expressed in personal and corporate statements, most notably in 1948, when the Episcopal Synod of the Anglican Church condemned the proposed apartheid legislation and declared that 'discrimination against men on grounds of race alone is inconsistent with the principles of the Christian religion'. It went on to assert that the only hope for the men, women and children of South Africa lay in the creation of harmonious relationship between the various racial groups. This could not be achieved if Europeans sought to preserve for themselves the exclusive benefits of Western civilization, allowing non-Europeans to carry merely its burdens.

But Clayton and most of his colleagues stopped at this point and were not ready to condemn the government as such or to encourage any opposition that might encourage violence. He strongly disapproved of the activities of Ambrose Reeves, Trevor Huddleston and other militant clergy, and in the 1950s wrote, 'I have done my best to make clear to fellow Anglicans in England and elsewhere how complex the situation in this country is, and to discourage pronouncements on points of detail and condemnation of particular persons.' He went so far as to tell the Bishop of Pretoria, Selby Taylor, in 1955, that he found the outspoken clergy 'unbalanced in judgement and given to exhibitionism'.

Among these was Bishop Ambrose Reeves, who had succeeded Clayton at Johannesburg in 1949 and for the next 12 years was at the storm centre of the new regime's destructive actions. The importance of his witness has yet to be fully recognized.

Born in Norfolk in 1899, he went from Great Yarmouth Grammar School to Sidney Sussex College, Cambridge, to read History and Moral Sciences. Preparation for the priesthood at Mirfield brought awareness of the Community of the Resurrection's deep commitment to work in South Africa, but ordination in 1927 took him to a curacy in North London's Golders Green – a post he combined with that of General Secretary of the then buoyant and influential Student Christian Movement. This was followed by a spell as Rector of Leven, in Scotland, then two years in Europe as General Secretary of the World Student Christian Federation. He was Rector of Liverpool Parish Church when elected Bishop of Johannesburg.

There he succeeded Geoffrey Clayton, who had been translated to the Archbishopric of Cape Town, and his contrasting dynamic style soon led to accusations of dictatorship by members of the white Anglican community. In the crisis now engulfing South Africa he embarked on a policy that included forthright opposition and the empowering of Africans by building new churches in their locations and recruiting from their number priests who could be trained for leadership. Half of the population of Johannesburg comprised 350,000 non-whites, half of these living below the breadline, and those not living in separate locations outside the city occupied huts at the end of the gardens of European-owned houses. The economy depended on black labour.

Reeves's annual charges to his diocesan synod during the 1950s now provide vivid evidence of the developing course of the apartheid policy, of the problems this caused the Church and of his own leadership at a critical time. Although he was frequently accused of being too political, the charges, informed by a deep incarnational theology, are models of the inter-relationship of Christian faith and social action. He condemned apartheid as 'the great immorality' while at the same time calling on his white congregations to embrace multi-racial church life. Those who heard were both edified and challenged.

In the first (1950), he expressed concern that Communists were being imprisoned without recourse to legal process – an action that soon deprived the African trade unions of effective leadership. In 1952, when 'the skies are darkened by clouds of uncertainty, bitterness and fear', he complained that, although 150,000 new houses were needed to meet black African needs in Johannesburg, only 83 had been built during the past year, no one in authority seeming to care.

At the 1953 synod, he devoted much time to the recently promulgated Bantu Education Act and the Western Areas Removal Scheme. The first represented a direct assault on the schools established by the Church for the education of Africans. There were over 4,000 of these, compared with just a few hundred state schools, and, although most were in need of refurbishment and government finance, there seemed no reason why the Church should not continue to run them.

The government, having concluded, however, that the teaching of racial equality was subversive of its policy and that some schools, in particular St Peter's in Johannesburg, were producing black dissident leaders, decreed that this must cease. The pupils must henceforth be taught to accept their 'proper' place in the new South African society, and the Minister for Native Affairs, Dr Verwoerd, who was handling the Act, left no one in doubt what this place was intended to be. He told the Senate, 'There is no place for the native in European society above the level of certain forms of labour.'

This became a major issue for all the non-DRC churches that had schools. Failure to comply with the edict meant closure, but Reeves declared that the Church could have no part in it even though the consequences would be dire. He urged his Synod not to accept the situation passively but to work for the repeal of the legislation. Although the government claimed to be defending civilization, they were in fact undermining its basic values. He appealed therefore for volunteers to undertake teaching in the Sunday Schools that would remedy in part the lack of Christian education in the day schools when the Church would be driven to relinquish them to State control. Reeves led the Anglican Church's response to the Act, which was condemned by all the South African bishops in 1954, but he was the only bishop who refused to compromise with the government. This was not an easy decision, since it meant losing all the diocese's schools, but Father Trevor Huddleston believed that history would show him to have made the right decision.

The Western Areas Removal Scheme, amplified by the Group Areas Act, applied legal compulsion to the existing arrangement by which peoples of differing races lived apart. Very large numbers of Africans lived in separate communities a few miles west of Johannesburg, but the rapid growth of the city led to the expansion of European-owned housing in this direction. The point had been reached when this expansion could continue no further unless the Africans were moved and their housing demolished. Reeves recognized that much of this property and the social facilities urgently needed improvement, but declared that the Scheme was based on nothing more than a particular racist ideology.

The banishment of Africans from the towns and cities also had serious implications for the churches, which found it impossible to encourage multi-racial worship. Leases for land on which to build new churches in African locations were granted only on condition that the clergy would not encourage attitudes and actions that would undermine government policy. The same conditions were applied when the leases of older church buildings were due for renewal. Reeves responded by insisting that 'the Church must teach the truth whatever the consequences'. In this, as also over the Bantu Education Act, he worked closely with Father Trevor Huddleston who was ministering heroically in the Sophiatown area of Johannesburg.

Another incident in which Reeves was deeply involved aroused international concern and is now seen to have been a turning point in the struggle against apartheid. In March 1960, the Pan African Congress, in an organized protest, encouraged Africans to hand in to the nearest police station their passes – an identity document used to control their movements within the country. The police were unwilling to accept these and when a large crowd gathered outside the police station at Sharpeville they responded by opening fire. Sixty-nine Africans, mainly women, were killed, and 186 were wounded. Nationwide demonstrations followed, Nelson Mandela, Albert Lutuli and other black leaders were arrested, the government declared a state of emergency, and news of the massacre provoked horror and fury around the world.

Reeves, who supported the Congress, went immediately to the hospital to minister to the wounded and the relatives of the dead, and at the same time gather first-hand accounts of what had happened. This was subsequently used to institute legal proceedings against the Minister of Justice. The patience of the government was now exhausted and orders were given for the bishop's arrest, but he slipped out of the country to Swaziland and thence to England. He returned to Johannesburg in September but after two days was, without legal process, put on a plane and deported.

This led to protest rallies throughout South Africa, but in Britain neither government nor the Church of England was prepared for confrontation with the South African government, believing it best to maintain good relations in the hope of exerting influence. The witness of Reeves was not therefore appreciated and no senior appointment in the Church was forthcoming. Instead, he returned to the Student Christian Movement to spend five years as its general secretary and at the same time campaigned vigorously for justice and freedom for all the South African peoples. He became president of the Anti-Apartheid Movement and the latter part of his life was spent as Vicar of a parish in Lewes and as Honorary Assistant Bishop in Chichester diocese. He died on 23 December 1980.

No satisfactory explanation has ever been offered for the decision of the Community of the Resurrection to withdraw Father Trevor Huddleston from South Africa in 1956 in order to become Guardian of its small Mirfield novitiate. It was as if at the height of a crucial battle a leading commander was withdrawn in order to take charge of a minor training unit. Huddleston was displaying no sign of fatigue, and only his monastic vow of obedience would have torn him away from the land and people he loved. Probably the Community pre-empted the arrest and deportation, and consequent damage to its South African work, that would almost certainly have followed the imminent publication of his international best-seller, *Naught for Your Comfort*. Archbishop Clayton had, some years earlier, refused to continue as Visitor of the Community in South Africa while Huddleston was in office as its Provincial.

Son of Captain Sir Ernest Huddleston, who became Director of the Royal Indian Marine, Trevor Urban Huddleston was born in Bedford on 15 June 1913. He went from Lancing College to Christ Church, Oxford, where he read History. During summer vacations he went on hop-picker missions in Kent and became interested in the Christian Socialist movement, particularly the work of the Anglo-Catholic priests in the slums.

Having felt called to ordination, he spent a year studying mission work in India and Ceylon before going to Wells Theological College. In 1936 he became a curate in Swindon and, when this ended, went to Mirfield in Yorkshire to test his vocation to the religious life. In 1941 he was professed as a member of the Community of the Resurrection and two years later was sent as priest-in-charge of its mission in Sophiatown and Orlando, four-and-a-half miles west of Johannesburg. He was there until 1956, and, although he became widely regarded as an aggressive agitator, he was in fact a gentle person, with a deeply religious nature who exuded warmth, joy and friendship and was perhaps happiest when in the company of children – who adored him.

Sophiatown, a not unattractive place when viewed from a distance, had been built in 1903 as a small township for a white population, but the building nearby of Johannesburg's sewage plant and other developments made it less attractive and by 1920 most of the whites had moved out. This led to an influx of other races, so that by the time of Huddleston's arrival there were about 60,000 black Africans, 5,000 Coloureds, 1,500 Indians and about 600 Chinese. House-building had failed hopelessly to keep pace with this growth, hence desperately serious overcrowding and lack of amenities. It became a huge slum, yet there was no more vibrant, joyful a community in South Africa, being the epicentre of jazz, blues and politics and producing some of the country's most famous musicians, writers, artists and politicians.

Standing at the centre was the large church of Christ the King, where Huddleston lived and ministered for the next 13 years. Large numbers attended the Sunday and weekday services – all in the colourful Anglo-Catholic tradition – and there was social work among people of all ages. The Huddleston Jazz Band became a vital element in the mission.

He was also constantly on the streets and in homes, caring compassionately for people irrespective of their race. An African Children's Feeding Scheme attracted support from far outside the parish, and a special fund was set up to support the Orlando Squatters in another African community nearby, where Huddleston also ministered. Desmond Tutu, the future Archbishop of Cape Town, recalled how as a boy in Sophiatown he was standing with his mother outside a hostel where she was the cleaner. A white priest, in cassock and large black hat, swept by, and, to the utter astonishment of the young Tutu, raised his hat to the black lady. This was Trevor Huddleston.

The removal of Africans from Sophiatown to Meadowlands, eight miles away, and the Coloureds, Indians and Chinese to separate locations, began on 9 February 1955 and was heralded by the arrival of a fleet of lorries and 2,000 policemen, most of them armed with rifles or automatic weapons. The vacated houses, often owned by their occupiers, were quickly demolished. Huddleston was on the streets advising and consoling the fearful people, accompanied by Nelson Mandela and other activists. In an attempt to secure a change of policy, he joined the African National Congress on visits to the white suburbs aimed at persuading the residents to understand the consequences of what was being done in their names. But this was in vain, and he often complained that 99 per cent of Europeans had not the faintest idea of how Africans were required to live. The government spoke of 'clearing filthy slums'.

The town having been flattened, it was then rebuilt to house white working-class people and renamed Triomf – its original name – but this proved to be unsuccessful and it now houses poor Afrikaners. The name Sophiatown was restored in 2006.

As in most anti-apartheid moves, Huddleston worked closely with his Bishop, Ambrose Reeves, and when the Bantu Education Act was published he compared it with the policy of Adolf Hitler, who had demanded that German schools should teach the superiority of the Aryan race, a doctrine that led to the Holocaust. Of particular concern to him was St Peter's School in Johannesburg (the 'Black Eton of South Africa'), which was the only school to provide African boys with high quality second-ary education. The fact that it produced rebellious leaders such as Oliver Tambo had not escaped government notice. Faced with the Act's require-ments, the school chose closure but immediately set up again as a private institution, financed in part by small fees. It was soon oversubscribed and produced more African leaders.

In 1949, Huddleston was made responsible for overseeing all the Community of the Resurrection's work in South Africa, which involved travel beyond Sophiatown and enabled him to encourage other Mirfield monks and their congregations in the struggle against apartheid. He was also active in other parts of Johannesburg, addressing meetings of Africans, usually on Sundays after Mass, this being the only time they were free to attend, and outdoor protest demonstrations. He was among the few in South Africa who advocated sports boycotts of the country. At the same time, he was always aware of the high level of racism that infected the Anglican white congregations in South Africa, which he denounced even more frequently than he did the attitudes of the Dutch Reformed Church, sometimes accusing Anglican leaders of conniving with the government.

All of which, and much else, was vividly presented to the outside world in *Naught for Your Comfort*, which came as a revelation to most of its many readers. Essentially, it consisted of simple accounts of his own experi-ences in Sophiatown, which spoke for themselves, but it also, in the name of Christian faith, included powerful assaults on the doctrine of apartheid and those who implemented it without regard to its human cost. Neither was he afraid to suggest that violence might be necessary to overcome it, though the book ends on a moving note of confidence that God's loving will and purposes will one day liberate his African people.

On his return to England, Huddleston's supervision of the Mirfield novitiate was brief. In 1958, he moved to be Prior of the Community's house in London, which facilitated his considerable public speaking ministry, though two years later he was elected Bishop of South-West Tanganyika, soon to become Tanzania. There he worked closely with President Julius Nyerere and also prepared the way for an African to suc-ceed him in the Bishopric. Subsequent appointments included the suffragan Bishopric of Stepney in London diocese and the Bishopric of Mauritius, which he combined with the Archbishopric of the Indian Ocean. But he will be best remembered for his work in South Africa, which made him a legend in his own lifetime.

Also prominent among Anglican opponents of apartheid was Joost de Blank, who became Archbishop of Cape Town in 1957. He was driven by ill-health to resignation in 1963, but during these six years declared, uncompromisingly and with great courage, that apartheid was inhuman, un-Christian and fundamentally wrong. This resounded throughout the world.

Until his arrival in Cape Town the other bishops, while having no truck with apartheid, believed that the best form of opposition lay in quietly working behind the scenes to mitigate its worst expressions while trying to cultivate relations with the DRC that would eventually undermine its foundations. Yet the conditions of non-Africans were continuing to deteriorate, and South Africa was about to withdraw from the Commonwealth in order to be free from external pressure.

De Blank's attitude was made plain in his Enthronement sermon: 'It is my conviction that racial discrimination is a form of blasphemy and that those who condone it or allow it without protest place their souls in eternal peril. Sin is sin, and has to be repented of and forsaken completely – here and now.' This was not what many white South Africans wanted to hear, but the new archbishop became a beacon of hope for the millions of apartheid's victims, and thereafter it became much more difficult to advocate the 'discretion' approach, though some of his episcopal colleagues continued to favour it.

De Blank had never expected to become Archbishop of Cape Town and was in fact unaware of the vacancy until the call came to fill it. Of Dutch ancestry, he was born in Rotterdam in 1908 but brought up in London where, with his family, he attended a Presbyterian church. By the time he reached Queen's College, to read English and Law, he had become an Anglican, and, after spending a year in journalism, returned to Cambridge to prepare for Holy Orders at evangelical Ridley Hall.

He became a curate at Bath Abbey in 1931, and while there was attracted to the growing Moral Rearmament Movement (MRA), and his move to another curacy, at Bredon in Worcestershire, left him free to become its organizer for the West Midlands. This ended when he was appointed Vicar of Emmanuel Church, Forest Gate, in east London, where he exercised a vigorous ministry in a parish of 12,000 and gradually lost interest in MRA. In 1941, he enlisted as a wartime army chaplain and served with distinction in the North African campaign before going in 1944 to the British Liberation Army in Germany as a senior chaplain. He was among the few survivors when a German V2 rocket fell on a building in Antwerp in which a Confirmation service was taking place, and suffered disfiguring facial injuries.

On demobilization de Blank joined the staff of the Student Christian Movement, but this was not really his forte and in 1948 he became Vicar of St John the Baptist Church, Greenhill, Harrow. This already had a strong life and soon became one of the Church of England's most dynamic parishes, drawing inspiration from the burgeoning Parish and People

Movement with its emphasis on the centrality of the Eucharist and the need for the Church to be involved in every aspect of community life. This was encapsulated in an influential book, *The Parish in Action*, which made its author more widely known. Appointment to the suffragan Bishopric of Stepney followed in 1952, and during the next five years east London's often depressed parishes experienced his dynamic, creative leadership.

News of this reached South Africa where, following the sudden death of Archbishop Clayton, the English-born and educated bishops were unable to agree on a successor among themselves. A Dutch background and name was not without its attractions, but it is doubtful whether the bishops knew quite what they had voted for. He took Cape Town by storm and told the 2,000 people who crowded a Welcome gathering after his Enthronement that he was 'colour blind'. An attack on the government was not long in coming, and he informed the Church that episcopal ministrations would be withdrawn from any parish that practised racial discrimination. This attracted worldwide publicity and the first of many rebukes from the government.

Large crowds gathered to hear him preach in the cathedral or speak in meeting halls, where they often heard a call to mutual penitence as the only way to true reconciliation. His acceptance of the British-based Campaign Against Racial Discrimination in Sport aroused further antagonism among the white population, as did news of a letter to the London *Times* in which he described apartheid as 'morally corroding, economically suicidal, politically senile and theologically indefensible'. In the same letter, however, he pleaded for South Africa to be kept in the Commonwealth, because he believed that more would be achieved by sound argument, rather than by what he called 'a senseless parade of passion'.

De Blank seemed to need ceaseless activity and apparently enjoyed it, but the price was paid in August 1962 in the form of cerebral thrombosis. After treatment in London he returned to South Africa, but it soon became evident that what were for him irresistible demands would never lessen, and he was driven to resign from the archbishopric on the last day of 1963, at the early age of 54.

His final years were spent as a Canon of Westminster, where he felt like a caged lion, but nonetheless contributed much to the Abbey's life and carried out a multitude of speaking and preaching engagements throughout Britain. He died, exhausted, on 1 January 1968, and the memorial tablet in the Abbey describes him as an 'Indomitable Fighter for Human Rights'.

Trevor Huddleston believed that the end of apartheid and the advent of freedom and democracy would await the emergence of outstanding African leaders. He lived long enough to see their arrival in the persons of two outstanding human beings – Nelson Mandela, who was released in 1990 after spending 27 years in prison, and Desmond Tutu, the first African Archbishop of Cape Town, elected in 1986 and widely recognized as the nation's moral conscience. Both occupied key positions of leadership at the time when the policy of apartheid was threatened by a combination of serious, often violent unrest, economic decline, reduction of the white population and mounting international pressure. Some Afrikaner theologians were also questioning its religious basis and the more far-sighted members of the government were becoming aware that the administration was doomed.

Desmond Mpilo Tutu was born on 7 October 1931 in a small town in Western Transvaal, but the family soon moved to Sophiatown, where he came increasingly under the influence of Trevor Huddleston, especially during the two years he spent in a sanatorium recovering from tuberculosis. This interrupted his education at the Western High School to which, in spite of his family's poverty, he had entered on a scholarship. He next trained as a teacher and proved to be a brilliant one, but felt frustrated by the government's racist control of the curriculum and went to St Peter's Theological College, Rosettenville, for training as a priest.

Ordained in Johannesburg in 1960, he served briefly two curacies before being selected for further theological education at King's College, London, where he took a BD and a postgraduate MTh. On his return to South Africa he joined the teaching staff of a theological college at Alice, in Cape Province, combining this with a university chaplaincy, where he took part in a student protest strike against government apartheid policies. This was followed by two years as a lecturer at the University of Botswana.

Next came a spell (1972–5) in London as assistant director of the Theological Education Fund, though most of his time was spent travelling in Africa funding education projects, but this ended when he was called back to become the first African Dean of Johannesburg. There he chose to live in the black township of Soweto, instead of in the official Deanery, and continued the work of his predecessor in the building of a multi-racial cathedral community. Before he could accomplish much, however, he was elected Bishop of the mountainous diocese of Lesotho, a ministry requiring horseback travel to the scattered parishes.

This ended in 1978 with his appointment as General Secretary of the South African Council of Churches, which was now a substantial ecumenical body at the forefront of the Christian witness against apartheid. Under his leadership it became a major force on the frontier of religion and politics, and he became the most widely recognized leader of South Africa's black community. He was jailed briefly after a protest march and was probably saved by his international fame from a more severe sentence. Election to the Bishopric of Johannesburg in 1985, followed a year later by his translation to the Archbishopric, was a clear indication of the Anglican Church's recognition of the impending national crisis and of the need for a leadership that only he could effectively give.

That he did so is now firmly fixed in South Africa's history. He was fearless in his denunciation of government policies and supportive of all efforts to undermine them. While at Johannesburg, he had helped to found a National Forum to oppose a proposed new Constitution designed to blunt anti-apartheid action, and at the funeral of a murdered Communist leader, Chris Hani, in 1993, led a crowd of 120,000 in chanting 'We will be free. All of us, black and white, will be free'.

In all his utterances Tutu emphasized the need for reconciliation rather than division, and after the African National Congress, under the leadership of Nelson Mandela, had decisively won South Africa's first democratic election in 1994, he was instrumental in setting up a Truth and Reconciliation Commission that did much to heal the racial division which had tormented non-Europeans for so long. He retired from the Archbishopric in 1996 but not until 2010 from a public life devoted to the difficult and still unfinished task of creating what he called a Rainbow Nation.

He was awarded the Nobel Peace Prize and many other prestigious international honours, and Nelson Mandela said of him – 'Sometimes strident, often a teacher, never afraid and seldom without humour, Desmond Tutu will always be the voice of the voiceless.'

No one outside South Africa did more to support those engaged in the struggle against apartheid than Canon John Collins of St Paul's Cathedral. As early as 1950, when there was little concern in Britain over the matter, he packed Central Hall, Westminster, for a meeting to hear about it at first hand from an unusual Anglican priest, Michael Scott, recently expelled from South Africa for encouraging Indians to use non-violent methods of opposition.

Under the umbrella of Christian Action, which he was leading, Collins next established a Race Relations Fund to assist black students and immigrant workers in London, and at the request of his friend Trevor Huddleston, the families of men who were being imprisoned for their non-violent opposition to apartheid. In 1956 this was extended by the launching of a Treason Trial Defence Fund which raised £170,000 for the defence of black and white people whose opposition to government policy had led to them being charged with high treason. The trial lasted four years and all were acquitted.

The fund eventually became a separate International Defence and Aid Fund through which the Swedish and several other governments, as well as the United Nations, channelled money for the defence and assistance of apartheid's victims. Collins, who was banned from entry to South Africa, remained at its helm for many years and was honoured with a Gold Medal by the United Nations. The King of Sweden made him a Commander of the Northern Star. He died on the last day of 1982, and Trevor Huddleston gave the address at a Service of Thanksgiving in St Paul's.

16

A New Morality

The intimate relationship between Church and State existing in England at the beginning of the nineteenth century was most powerfully experienced in the sphere of marriage. Despite the upheaval of the sixteenth-century Reformation, the nation retained the long-established custom by which the Church controlled the terms under which marriages were contracted and applied the disciplines demanded by deviation from these terms.

The basis of marriage was, naturally, that of the Christian belief in marriage as a fundamental part of a divinely created human order, involving a lifelong commitment of the parties involved. The Bible, in particular the teaching of Jesus, was cited as the ultimate authority for this belief, reinforced by long experience of marriage providing the natural, and therefore the best, environment for the nurturing of children. It presupposed a Christian social order and the Canon Law of the Church as the law of the State.

That such an arrangement would inevitably produce happy marriages is defied by the evidence: infidelity and illegitimacy kept the church courts busy. Yet there was no provision for divorce, except by the extreme and highly expensive means of securing an Act of Parliament. Dating back to the seventeenth century, this was rarely attempted, though between 1830 and 1857 they averaged about three a year. The Church of England had in fact the strictest of marriage laws. It had abandoned the pre-Reformation provision for granting decrees of nullity but not embraced the Eastern Orthodox tradition of allowing divorce and second marriage in some circumstances.

A small procedural change to marriage procedures came in 1836 with the introduction of civil marriage and freedom for Dissenters to contract marriages in their own churches, though it was necessary for these to be recorded in the Church of England's registers. Far more significant was the passing in 1857 of a Matrimonial Causes Act which allowed divorce on the grounds of adultery, though not for women unless they could prove additional cruelty. Many churchmen welcomed this, but there was sharp disagreement about freedom to remarry, and in any case the Church was unwilling to conduct such ceremonies. The argument of the opponents was concerned not so much with the indissolubility of marriage as with the likelihood of the proposed legislation undermining its stability and that of the social order generally.

The Bishop of St David's predicted, with what turned out to be remarkable prescience, that it would pave the way for further concessions until divorce was brought within the jurisdiction of the county courts and made available to all who felt they needed it. He recognized nonetheless that, although the Christian position was binding on all believers, it should not necessarily be imposed on others by legislation. This was a point made by F. D. Maurice after the passing of the legislation and thereafter became the basis for the Church's involvement in a growing debate about marriage and divorce. The good bishop did not, however, live to see his prophecy fulfilled. In 1910, there were no more than 910 petitions for divorce, and, although the figure rose somewhat as a result of the First World War, it was only 3,396 in 1929.

The possibility of widening the grounds for divorce had, however, continued to be discussed, and a Royal Commission reported in 1912 that the majority of its members favoured the addition of wilful desertion, cruelty, incurable insanity, habitual drunkenness and imprisonment under a commuted death sentence. This worried the clergy in the Lower House of the Convocation of York, who resolved 'that the law of the Church of England, being what it is, namely that marriage is indissoluble, we cannot give our support to any increased facilities for any divorce other than judicial separation.' The Lower House of the Convocation of Canterbury followed suit.

War now intervened, and the report of the Royal Commission gathered dust until the 1930s, when its majority recommendations were picked up by the writer and Independent MP for Oxford University, A. P. Herbert, and incorporated into another Matrimonial Causes Act, which passed into law in 1937. Most of the Church of England's bishops opposed this, but, not having distinguished clearly between rules for Christians and rules for a wider community, were left defending what most people regarded as indefensible, namely the retention of adultery as the sole grounds for divorce. It was now beyond doubt that the law of the Church could no longer be determinative of the law of the nation.

Once again war intervened, but in 1951 an entirely new approach was proposed. Mrs Eirene White MP introduced in the House of Commons a Private Member's Bill designed to make divorce possible to either party after seven years of living apart. No longer would a 'matrimonial offence' be required. Her speech expressed a widespread and growing concern that the current legislation encouraged 'offences' by those seeking to end their marriages, together with the sleazy activities of private detectives and hotel chambermaids, and the taint of 'guilty parties'. The legal emphasis was now moving, inexorably as it proved to be, from contract to relationship.

Recognizing that there was no possibility of it passing into law, Mrs White withdrew her Bill and the government responded by setting up a Royal Commission to consider the issues that lay behind it. The Church of England submitted a memorandum to the Commission in which it strongly opposed the abolition of the 'offence' requirement and concluded that there would be injustice if one of the parties to a marriage were to be divorced against his or her will. This drew sharp, detailed criticism from an evenly divided Commission, notwithstanding which its report in 1955 endorsed many of the Church's recommendations, including retention of the 'offence'. There was, however, a minority statement by Lord Walker proposing plainly that matrimonial offence should be abandoned in favour of irretrievable breakdown of the marriage. Several factors might contribute the evidence for this and the absence of a declared guilty party would indicate shared responsibility for the breakdown.

The next move came in 1963 from another MP, Leo Abse, who proposed a Bill incorporating Mrs White's ideas and adding measures to promote reconciliation. This was discussed in the House of Lords in April of that year and, though the Archbishop of Canterbury, Michael Ramsey, opposed the proposal, he added, significantly:

> My Lords, this is not to say that I am content with the present law on divorce and the operation of the divorce courts . . . If it were possible to find a principle and a law of breakdown, of marriage which was free from any trace of the idea of consent, which conserved the point that offences and not only wishes are the basis of the breakdown and which was protected by a far more thorough insistence on the reconciliation procedure first, then I would wish to consider it. Indeed, I am asking some of my fellow churchmen to see whether it is possible to work at this idea, sociologically as well as doctrinally, to see if anything can be produced.

These fellow churchmen constituted one of the most able bodies the Church of England has ever brought together to consider a matter of national importance, and its report, *Putting Asunder: A Divorce Law for Contemporary Society*, published in 1966, remains a classic example of Christian social thinking. Meeting under the chairmanship of the Bishop of Exeter, Robert Mortimer, himself a moral theologian, were a number of eminent scholars, lawyers, social workers, psychiatrists and a member of the government.

The report began by emphasizing – 'in the reddest of red ink' – that it was concerned only with the marriage law of the State:

> How the doctrine of Christ concerning marriage should be interpreted and applied within the Christian Church is one question; what the Church ought to say and do about secular laws of marriage and divorce is another question altogether. This can hardly be repeated too often. Our terms of reference make it abundantly clear that our business is with the second question only.

There followed a well-informed discussion of the issues involved, and it reached the conclusion that 'irretrievable breakdown' was a lesser evil than 'matrimonial offence' and should therefore become the basis of reform. It argued that, in spite of the best initial intentions of the parties involved in a marriage, including lifelong commitment, a union could die, with or without a matrimonial offence. In these circumstances, judgements concerning 'guilty parties' should be replaced by verdicts on the state of the marriage.

The report, which also included recommendations about procedures and the welfare of children, emphasized in the strongest of terms the need for reconciliation agencies to be expanded and improved to meet whatever demands might be made on them, and that these should be generously subsidized. Courts must be certain that the agencies had been conscientiously used before making decisions.

This was sufficient to satisfy Archbishop Ramsey and the majority of the bishops. It was also considered to have made a significant contribution to the public debate, and a Marriage and Divorce Act, incorporating the 'irretrievable breakdown' principle, was enacted by Parliament in 1969.

There was a failure, however, to take seriously the Church's recommendations about reconciliation agencies, and fears that the divorce rate would escalate were quickly realized, though other factors were involved in this. There were also important consequences for the Church.

In spite of the *Putting Asunder* emphasis that its concern was simply and solely with the State's attitude to divorce, a carefully argued statement that marriage relationships could actually die was bound to challenge the theological and sacramental bases of indissolubility and therefore of the Church's unwillingness to acknowledge the possibility of divorce and remarriage for its own members.

This point was quickly taken up by a commission which had been appointed by Archbishop Ramsey in 1968 to examine the wider question of the Christian Doctrine of Marriage. Chaired by Canon Howard Root, a Cambridge theologian, and including several other theologians, its report, *Marriage, Divorce and the Church*, was published in 1972. Having examined the medieval roots of the doctrine of indissolubility, it concluded:

> The notion of a metaphysical or ontological bond existing independently of any empirical features was satisfactory enough to philosophers and theologians in what is known as the Realist tradition. The difficulty today is to persuade ourselves of the existence of such a bond when everything observable in the relationship and dispositions of the persons concerned points to its non-existence. In other words, we can entertain and accept the idea of a complete breakdown of marriage, and when faced with this the Church community is driven to determine its pastoral response.

The Commission believed that this pastoral response could include the possibility of re-marriage in church, under certain conditions, of Christians who had been divorced. The report was, however, heavily criticized in the Convocation of Canterbury, and no action was taken. It is not the purpose of this book to discuss the tortuous journey that took the Church of England to acceptance and implementation of the Root Commission's suggestions in 2002. By this time, other pressing issues concerning sexuality and marriage had become more controversial.

By the middle of the twentieth century, the Church's ability to influence the nation had declined almost to the point of insignificance as the cultural change ushered in by the so-called 'Swinging Sixties' found it at the mercy of events, rather than determining them. A heady optimism, new hopes and aspirations, an emphasis on youth and its new music, a questioning of authority and a decline of deference all contributed, at least in the south of England, to a liveliness and creativity that the Church's leadership found puzzling and sometimes threatening. This was especially so in the sphere of sexuality, where the widespread availability of a new contraceptive pill, for the first time in history, gave women control of their fertility. Removal of the fear of unwanted pregnancy, combined with a disinclination to accept traditional values, led to the complete breakdown of an already declining belief in chastity before marriage.

The Church of England had, however, within its ranks a significant number of younger clergy and laity who were more than ready to look again at the moral issues involved and anxious to do this in the context of a re-examination of traditional Christian doctrine and the reform of the Church. Chief among these was John A. T. Robinson, whose short paperback *Honest to God* (1963) provoked huge controversy and eventually sold more than one million copies in many languages.

He was in many ways an unlikely source of such an upheaval. The most recent offspring (born in 1919) of a dynasty of distinguished Anglican scholars and churchmen, he had been reared in the precincts of Canterbury Cathedral, gone from Marlborough to Jesus College, Cambridge, where he secured a First in Theology, then to nearby Westcott House to prepare for ordination. A wartime curacy at St Matthew, Moorfields, Bristol, had given him inner-city parish experience and also friendship with its dynamic, left-wing Vicar, Mervyn Stockwood. This was followed by a spell of teaching at Wells Theological College and, his academic credentials recognized, appointment in 1951 as Dean of Clare College, Cambridge.

Although a group of distinguished young Cambridge theologians was now beginning to raise questions about the credibility of Christian belief as traditionally formulated, Robinson was not prominent among them, his chief interest being reform of the Church's liturgy and institutional life. It was on the strength of this that Mervyn Stockwood, who had moved from Bristol to the University Church at Cambridge and on to the Bishopric of Southwark, invited him to join him as suffragan Bishop of Woolwich. Archbishop Fisher of Canterbury raised objections, chiefly on the grounds of Robinson's youth and academic background, but gave in to Stockwood's insistence. He soon had reason to regret this.

The prosecution of Penguin Books in 1960 under an Obscene Publications Act for their publication of the first unexpurgated edition in Britain of *Lady Chatterley's Lover* became a cause célèbre, and the appearance in court of the recently appointed Bishop of Woolwich for the defence shocked many in the Church of England, including the Archbishop of Canterbury. They were troubled by his support for the book, and, perhaps chiefly, by the content of his support. While in no way condoning the kind of adulterous relationship portrayed by Lawrence, he had spoken of the author trying 'to show the sex relationship as something essentially sacred, akin to holy communion'.

Following the jury's 'Not guilty' verdict, which had a profound effect on the future of publishing, Lambeth Palace was flooded with telephone calls and letters protesting against Robinson's action, and the Archbishop felt constrained by what he called his pastoral responsibility to rebuke him in public for becoming 'a stumbling block and a cause of offence to many'.

When, therefore, *Honest to God* appeared three years later, its author's name was not unknown. The fuss now was mainly focused on Robinson's not altogether original suggestion that the traditional images of God 'up there' were no longer credible, and needed to be replaced by images of God near at hand 'in the depths of our being' (a phrase borrowed from

Paul Tillich). There was, however, a brief chapter at the end on 'The New Morality' in which it was suggested that understandings of morality, as well of transcendence, were also in the melting pot. He expanded on this in three lectures given later in the year at Liverpool Cathedral and subsequently published as *Christian Freedom in a Permissive Society*.

The gist of his argument, which drew heavily on the work of the American Joseph Fletcher in his *Situation Ethics*, was that the Sermon on the Mount is not to be seen as a law (even if St Matthew so interpreted it) but as an illustration of what love *may* require but not what it always demands. Therefore, Robinson wrote, 'Nothing can of itself be labelled "wrong". One cannot for instance start from the position "sex relations before marriage" or "divorce" are intrinsically so, for the only intrinsic evil is lack of love.'

Greater weight was added to this view by a symposium on *Christian Ethics and Contemporary Philosophy* edited by Bishop Ian Ramsey, who said in his introduction that 'Christian morality is no morality of rules, no morality of mere obedience to commands'. Ramsey later affirmed the need to recognize principles, some of which might be sacrosanct, but these must always be interpreted in the light of particular human situations.

What this might mean for sexuality caused considerable alarm among church leaders and others for whom behaviour in this vital area of human life was subject to what were believed to be divinely given, and therefore binding, rules. Feeding into what was already becoming known as 'The Permissive Society' and influenced by the spread of the then deadly HIV infection, there were accusations of betrayal of the Christian cause. The concepts of the New Morality were therefore never openly accepted by the Church, but by the end of the century it had become almost normal for those whose marriages were conducted in parish churches and cathedrals to have previously cohabited for some time. No eyebrows were raised. A much more substantial assault on the institution of marriage was now on its way.

From the time of Saint Paul until the middle of the twentieth century, the Christian attitude to homosexuality, shared by the Church of England, was one of uncompromising hostility. As late as 1800, two labourers were reported by a Bristol newspaper, without comment, to have been executed for homosexual offences. So also in 1822 was an army trooper caught with none other than the Irish Bishop of Clogher. The Bishop escaped to Scotland. The armed forces had their own harsh laws, and four sailors on HMS *Africaine* were hanged in 1816.

In 1826 there were in London more death sentences for sodomy than for murder. After 1861, however, penal servitude for life was substituted for the death penalty in cases of sodomy, a maximum of ten years for indecent assault. As always, detection was obviously necessary, and provided that homosexuals exercised discretion they were reasonably safe.

The law had at all times the full support of the Church of England. The Criminal Law Amendment Act of 1885, with its abolition of the compulsory medical tests, the outlawing of brothels and the better protection of women, was rightly seen as a triumph for Josephine Butler's long campaign on behalf of what were then known as 'fallen women'. But, having originated in the House of Lords and passed all its stages, the Bill was being considered in committee in the House of Commons when at a late stage a Liberal–Radical MP, Henry Labouchere, secured the approval of a sparsely attended House for the insertion of an additional clause which provided that: 'Any male person who in public, or private, commits or is a party to the commission of, or procures or attempts to procure the commission by any male person, of any act of gross indecency with another male person shall be guilty of a misdemeanour.' It is believed that the intention was simply to afford to young boys, who were also being widely trafficked in London, the same protection as that now proposed for girls. But the Bill did not say so, and the phrase 'gross indecency' was patient of such wide interpretation that it could embrace all manner of inter-male activity. The maximum prison sentence was reduced to two years.

When the Bill returned to the House of Lords for final approval, a few members objected to the additional clause on the grounds that it was ill considered, but it was nonetheless passed. The Bishop of Winchester, Edward Harold Browne, speaking, he said, on behalf of all the bishops, was enthusiastic in his support and the homosexual clause was included in subsequent legislation, where it remained a dire threat for the next 72 years. 'The blackmailers' charter' it proved to be, and, besides those who were prosecuted, many more men were, over the years, discreetly removed from teaching, clerical and other public positions without recourse to the law.

In 1921 a Scottish MP, who was also a lawyer and chanced to be the son of a Church of Scotland minister, was horrified to discover that lesbianism was not covered by the 1885 Act. He took the opportunity therefore to add to a new Criminal Law Amendment Bill that was then going through Parliament a clause that would deal with what he described as 'this horrid grossness of homosexual activity': 'Any Act of gross indecency between female persons shall be a misdemeanour and punishable in the same manner as any such act committed by male persons under section eleven of the Criminal Law Amendment Act 1855.' Although this ran into difficulties during the debate, the House of Commons accepted it by 148 votes to 53, but opposition was greater in the House of Lords, where the subject was introduced by the Bishop of Norwich, Bertram Pollock, deputizing for the Bishop of London, Arthur Foley Winnington-Ingram.

In general, the Church of England did not pronounce on the subject of homosexuality, since it was believed to be self-evidently wrong and adequately dealt with by the law. Sometimes, however, there were controversial public events that raised the issue and brought episcopal intervention.

One of these involved Sir Roger Casement, an Irish nationalist who had done distinguished work in the British Consular Service, but on the outbreak of war in 1914 went to Berlin in the hope of securing German help for a rebellion in Ireland. In 1916 he was landed on the east coast of Ireland from a German submarine but soon arrested. Sent to London and tried for High Treason, he was sentenced to death. At this point the contents of his private diaries were brought to light and these revealed that he was an active pederast. A number of public figures pressed for a reprieve, and among these was the Archbishop of Canterbury, Randall Davidson, who wrote privately to the Home Secretary and the Lord Chancellor. His main case was that the execution of Casement would be politically and diplomatically unwise, but he also indicated some knowledge of the diaries and believed these to indicate a man who was 'mentally and morally unhinged'. The Lord Chancellor considered the letter important enough to take it to the Cabinet, where it was fully considered, but Casement was nonetheless hanged. The Archbishop had conceded no moral ground, but there was a hint that psychological factors might be involved, if only to suggest mental instability.

Many more years passed before this non-moral possibility was given more attention, though during a Parliamentary debate on Divorce Law Reform in 1937, when homosexuality was considered as a matrimonial offence, Lord Dawson of Penn, a distinguished physician, told the House of Lords:

> I am not at all sure that in the future it [homosexuality] may not be regarded as an insufficiency disease, and although it is true that the law must take recognizance of it and punish it in order to act as a preventive to potential offenders, the more reasonable view is gradually being adopted that it at any rate has one foot in the realm of disease and is not wholly in the realm of crime.

This was still a very long way from acknowledging that it might even be a natural, God-given condition. The Archbishop of Canterbury, Cosmo Lang, certainly thought not. When, in 1938, the former Headmaster of King's School, Taunton, who had recently been convicted of homosexual offences, wrote to him pleading for a better understanding of his condition, Lang replied that, having had much experience of clerical misconduct, he could not believe that the position of homosexuals was particularly tragic. Indeed, 'I am not at present ready to suggest that offences of this kind should be put in the same position as indulgence of sexual instincts with the other sex.'

The recipient of this letter fared no better when, 15 years later, he raised the matter with Archbishop Geoffrey Fisher and was told:

Homosexuality is against the Christian law of morals and is rightly regarded as a social menace if it becomes in any sense widespread. Quite obviously society must protect itself against this as against any other anti-social moral perversion. I hope that all homosexuals will start at once to realise that, whatever their physical infirmities or natural tendencies, any indulgence of them is against Christian morals and the public welfare. They should seek priest and psychiatrist for help.

In the event, the major assault on the 1885 Act which came in the early 1950s focused on the issue of whether or not the law had any place in the governing of private behaviour. It was provoked by a sharp rise in the number of homosexuals being arraigned before the courts – explicable only by a toughening of police policy. The consequent prison sentences handed down to several public figures, and widely reported in the media, increased concern, and in April 1954 Desmond Donnelly MP asked in the House of Commons for a Royal Commission to be set up to 'investigate the law relating to and the medical treatment of homosexuals'. The government responded by announcing its intention to appoint a Home Office departmental committee to examine and report on the laws relating to homosexual offences and also to prostitution.

The Church of England's Moral Welfare Council was, however, ahead of the State. At the end of 1952, when the number of arrests was being discussed in the correspondence columns of the *New Statesman*, Graham Dowell, a young ordinand who would one day become Vicar of Hampstead, wrote to the magazine *Theology* questioning the wisdom of prison sentences and asking what the Christian conscience had to say to those homosexuals who wished to be active and healthy members of the Christian community.

The editor, Canon Alec Vidler, who was also Dean of King's College, Cambridge, where homosexuality was not unknown, commissioned a responsive article from Dr Sherwin Bailey, a priest-doctor who had recently been appointed as a lecturer on the staff of the Church of England's Moral Welfare Council. In his previous post as chaplain of Edinburgh University he had been stimulated to undertake research into homosexuality and quickly provided *Theology* (February 1953) with what proved to be a ground-breaking article, 'The Problem of Sexual Inversion'.

After pointing out that all the available evidence pointed to the widespread incidence of homosexual behaviour among women as well as men, Bailey asserted that the complexity of the problem precluded 'indiscriminate moral judgement'. He had no doubt that society must 'demand of the invert the same restraint in sexual matters as that demanded of the heterosexual, protecting the young and all from assault, nuisance and indecency'. He went on to express his belief that English law, by intruding into the privacy of the invert's sexual life, was grossly unfair and conducive to crime. Therefore:

> It is without doubt a Christian duty to press for the removal of this anomalous and shameful injustice which has done untold harm, and achieved no good whatever, and it is to be hoped that those who look to the Church for a lead in this matter will not be disappointed.

These were at the time brave words, and, after receiving many private letters of support and gratitude, Bailey persuaded his Council to initiate a study of the subject. This it did by convening a small group of doctors, lawyers and clergymen – an unofficial body that was to meet privately.

On 3 December 1953, the Education Secretary of the Council, Canon Hugh Warner, reported that the group had been meeting for a year and produced a draft interim report. By coincidence, the Council met at St Albans on the same evening that questions were being asked in the House of Commons about the increased police activity. It was decided therefore to ask the Home Secretary, Sir David Maxwell Fyffe, who regarded homosexuals as 'exhibitionists, proselytizers and a danger to others, especially the young', to set up an official enquiry into the whole question of homosexuality. Included with their letter was a list of subjects requiring attention:

1. The penalties to which a homosexual is liable and the wide diversities of penalties actually imposed for identical offences.
2. The implications of new psychological knowledge in assessing guilt and imposing punishment.
3. The adequacy of treatment available in prison and the effect of normal prison regime upon the homosexual prisoner.
4. The validity of the right given to the State to take cognisance of the moral private actions between adult male homosexuals to which no such right is given in the case of female homosexuals or in cases of heterosexual immorality between adults. The duty of the State to protect the young is self-evident.

5. The effect of this right of State interference on the whole question of blackmail.
6. The factors contributing to some forms of inversion which are due to wrong attitudes developed in childhood and the responsibility of parents and teachers for the emotional, moral and spiritual development of their children.

The 27-page-long Interim Report, which had been written by Sherwin Bailey, was printed a month later under the title *The Problem of Homosexuality* and with a foreword by the Bishop of St Albans which emphasized that the views expressed in it were only those of the study group. The front cover was marked 'Private, not for publication'. Comments were invited.

The most substantial chapter dealt with 'The Moral and Religious Aspects'. It firmly rejected any suggestion that homosexual and heterosexual love-making were equally natural, spelling out what was believed to be a fundamental difference. It then discussed the situation of the homosexual, indicating a pastoral rather than a judgemental approach to his or her problems. Any idea that a physical expression of personal desire might be permissible was hardly considered. Homosexuals should behave precisely the same as those heterosexuals who, for a variety of reasons, are denied marriage – acceptance, sublimation, avoidance of temptation, spiritual or psychological counselling.

The final chapter was concerned with 'The Law and the Male Homosexual'. After insisting that any changes in the law should not reduce the responsibility of the State for protection of the young from seduction and assault, it went on to discuss various anomalies in the existing law, concluding that the most serious of these was that 'in no other department of life does the State hold itself competent to interfere with the private action of consenting adults'. It added that the law did not regard fornicators and adulterers as criminals, even though the consequences of their actions were often serious. The age of consent in any new law should be 21.

After an initial circulation of 500 copies to selected individuals and groups, the Moral Welfare Council decided in March to distribute it more widely to potentially interested parties, including members of both Houses of Parliament. Within two months, 3,000 copies had been issued, even though it had not been on sale to the public. *The Times*, *The Spectator*, the *New Statesman* and *The Lancet* commented favourably, and when the Council met in November, 1,570 comments and case histories had been received.

Desmond Donnelly, MP, quoted from the report in his House of Commons speech asking for the appointment of a Royal Commission, and there seems little doubt that its circulation in influential circles played an important part in the 1954 decision to appoint a Departmental Committee of Inquiry under the chairmanship of Sir John (later Lord) Wolfenden, Vice-Chancellor of Reading University and a former Public School Headmaster.

The Moral Welfare Council gave oral and written evidence to the Committee, drawn in part from its Interim Report (a fuller report was thought to be unnecessary), together with a summary of the comments made on the report. It recommended that those aspects of the 1885 Criminal Law Amendment Act dealing with homosexual acts should be repealed and replaced by a new law that would 'penalize any male or female person who commits any homosexual act with a person under the age of consent, or in circumstances constituting a public nuisance or infringing public decency, or involving assault, violence, fraud or duress'. It also suggested that better facilities be made available to provide those charged with specialist treatment, and that the age of consent should be 17 years. Sherwin Bailey, who had by this time published a study, *Homosexuality and the Western Tradition*, was frequently consulted by the Wolfenden Committee.

The 14-strong Committee consisted of doctors, lawyers, politicians, a leader of the Girl Guides, Canon Victor Demant, the Regius professor of Moral and Pastoral Theology at Oxford, together with the Minister of St Columba's Church of Scotland in London. At the first meeting the chairman announced that, for the sake of the ladies on the Committee, homosexuals would henceforth be referred to as Huntleys and prostitutes as Palmers – the names of a well-known Reading firm of biscuit manufacturers. Considerable difficulty was encountered in persuading fearful homosexual men to appear and give personal evidence, but eventually a few were, and their names were concealed.

The report was published in 1957, with only one dissentient – the Procurator Fiscal for Scotland – and, after stating that homosexuality should not be regarded as a disease, it went on to assert that, while it was the duty of the State to preserve public order and decency and protect the young, it was no business of the State to intervene in areas of private behaviour that had no adverse social consequences. Homosexual activity involving consenting adults over the age of 21 in private should therefore be decriminalized.

In general, it was regarded as a good piece of work and its conclusions were strongly supported by many. Thirty-three distinguished supporters, including the Bishops of Birmingham and Exeter, wrote to *The Times* urging the government to prepare the necessary legislation. But it was not until November 1958 that it reached the House of Commons for discussion, and the Home Secretary, R. A. Butler, was at pains to stress his opinion that 'there is at present a very large section of the population who strongly repudiate, and whose moral sense would be offended by an alteration in the law which would seem to imply approval or tolerance of what they regard as a great social evil.' There was therefore no possibility of a Conservative government introducing legislation, and, although a number of attempts were made to reintroduce the Report in the House of Commons, and the moral theologian Bishop of Exeter, Robert Mortimer, told a public meeting organized by the Homosexual Law Reform Society that the present law was 'a monstrous injustice', nothing much happened until 12 May 1965.

By this time a much wider sexual revolution was under way and there was talk of a 'permissive society and the maximization of personal freedom'. Lord Arran was thus emboldened to put down a motion in the House of Lords calling attention to the Wolfenden's recommendations on homosexual offences and proposing their implementation. The day before the debate, the Bishops of London, Exeter, Birmingham, Bristol and St Albans joined a number of Law Lords in signing a supportive letter to *The Times*. In the debate itself, the Archbishop of Canterbury, Geoffrey Fisher, began by saying: 'I believe that homosexual acts are always wrong in the sense that they use in a wrong way human organs for which the right use is between men and women within marriage.' However, recognizing the complexity of the causes and expressions of homosexuality, he concluded:

> I think there is a real cogency in the plea of the Wolfenden report that not all sins are properly given the status of crimes, not even the adulterous conduct of a man or woman that can smash up the life of a family and bring misery to a whole family of children. If a line can reasonably be drawn anywhere, homosexual acts in private between consenting adults fall properly on the same side of the line as fornication.

At the end of the debate only three Peers opposed the motion.

A year later, the Labour government not wishing to express an opinion on the matter, it was left to a backbencher, Leo Abse, to sponsor a Sexual Offences Bill in the House of Commons. The Prime Minister, Harold Wilson, allowed a free vote, and in 1967 the Bill passed easily into law.

This proved to be one of the twentieth century's major social advances, overturning millennia of cruelty, injustice and persecution. But for the Christian homosexual a most serious problem remained. If he expressed his sexual desires, he might no longer be a criminal, but he was certainly a sinner. His Church had told him so in the clearest, uncompromising terms. It said that, although he should not now be held responsible for his orientation, he was nonetheless psychologically disordered, and, with or without counselling, must keep his emotions under strict control. He was not to be despised or shunned, but if he belonged to a Christian congregation he had better keep his condition secret, since many of its members were still a long way from accepting even the Wolfenden distinction between sin and crime.

Another 22 years passed before the Church, in the form of a General Synod Board of Social Responsibility working party, was prepared to have this discussed. Its report, which suggested that homosexual relationships involving Christians might be acceptable, deeply divided the Board and was published only as 'A Contribution to a Discussion'. Since then the problem has proved to be intractable, dividing not only the Church of England but the entire Anglican Communion, threatening its organic future.

The worst fears of those in the Church of England opposed to homosexual relationships were realized in 2003, when the government, having declared its intention not to move in the direction of 'gay marriage', produced a consultation document designed to prepare the way for a Bill that would allow homosexuals to enter into legally binding partnerships, with most of the financial responsibilities attendant upon marriage.

The Archbishops' Council responded with a commentary that recognized the importance of justice for homosexual couples but expressed unease that 'the proposals risk being seen as introducing a form of same-sex marriage with almost all of the same rights as marriage'. When a Bill embracing these proposals was presented in the House of Lords the following year, eight bishops voted in its favour and two against. Within the Church more widely, opposition came mainly but not exclusively from its Evangelical wing.

That the unease expressed by the Archbishop's Council was not without foundation became clear in 2012, when a recently elected Coalition government declared its intention to produce a Bill that would legalize the marriage of homosexual partners. This proved to be hugely controversial and was strongly opposed by all the mainstream religious bodies.

Nonetheless when a Marriage (Same Sex Couples) Bill was taken to the House of Commons in May 2013 it was, on a free vote, passed by 366 votes to 161 – most of the opposition coming from the Conservative benches. When it reached the House of Lords a month later it was again passed, this time by 390 votes to 148. Among the opponents were nine bishops, led by the Archbishop of Canterbury, Justin Welby who said in his speech that he would have welcomed a Bill that introduced alongside traditional marriage a new and valued institution for same-gender relationships.

17

Into the Heart of Industry

It did not occur to any of the Church of England's nineteenth-century leaders, nor indeed to many since then, that the challenge to Christian mission posed by the consequences of the Industrial Revolution might not be met simply by the extension of the thousand-year-old parochial system forged to meet the needs of stable, agrarian societies.

Recognition that something different was needed led, however, to the founding in 1877 of the Navvy Mission Society. The brainchild of a philanthropist, Mrs Garnett, it was designed to minister to the spiritual and moral welfare of the great army of navvies engaged in the construction of Britain's new railway network. The extent of the achievement of these men remains visible and beneficial in the vast number of tunnels, cuttings, embankments and other essential features of the current railway system – all carried out by pick and shovel and without modern earth-moving machinery or drills. The men who carried out this gruelling work were physically strong, illiterate, relatively well paid, addicted to gambling, heavy drinking (often for several days) and worked off any surplus energy in prize fights. Of necessity, they and their families were nomadic and generally regarded as a class apart, outcasts almost.

Huts with basic church furnishings were therefore erected in the villages or settlements where they were working and lay preachers – sometimes converted navvies – were appointed to conduct services, run Sunday Schools for the children and undertake much-needed pastoral work. These were organized and financed by local committees, and in 1877 it was decided to form a national society to provide simple co-ordination, raise funds and spread information.

The degree of success that attended this pioneering form of industrial mission is impossible to discover, but welfare work alone must have been significant. By the end of the century, most of the railway network was completed, and the working conditions of the navvies had greatly improved. Many of them moved on to assist in the construction of reservoirs and other major public works projects, some to railways work overseas and, after 1914, to the digging of trenches in the Army Labour

Corps. So the Mission still found some work to do, but when the war ended in 1918 it merged into a new Industrial Christian Fellowship (ICF), where it was soon joined by the greatly weakened Christian Social Union, also seeking a future role.

A Committee of Inquiry appointed as part of the 1916 National Mission of Repentance and Hope had showed some awareness of the need for radical change in the Church's approach to an industrialized society. It suggested, for example, that workers should become involved in the management of firms in order to prevent mass unemployment and secure living wages for all. Clergy should be recruited from the industrial and business classes, and not only from the middle and upper classes, as had been the long-established tradition. Moreover, ordinands in training should be confronted by the challenges of social and economic theories and problems.

Nothing much came of this, and the formation of the ICF was stimulated mainly by the experience of wartime army chaplains who had been made painfully aware of the vast gulf existing between the Church's life and message and the lives of the soldiers in the trenches. Among these was P. T. R. Kirk, who had been Vicar of a large London parish before the war and was now specially concerned by the failure of the Church to bear witness to the Lordship of Christ (echoing the language of the Christian Social Union) over industry and the working life of men and women.

Kirk recognized that this could not be remedied through the Church's parochial life, so with the encouragement of William Temple, at that time Bishop of Manchester, and others he set up a special organization to undertake the task. He served as its General Director for more than 30 years. Area Directors, usually clergy, were appointed to promote the work in the English regions and they, together with lay missioners, often drawn from industry, visited factories and other industrial enterprises to address workers and managers in canteens at lunchtime.

Other opportunities, including sermons in churches, were taken to spread the message, which did not seek personal conversions, but rather to declare the sovereignty of God over the world, the Lordship of Christ over every part of it, and the gospel and its values as essential to the proper ordering of society and the securing of harmonious relations in industry. While not avowedly Socialist, the implications of the message were a more just and equal sharing of God-given resources.

Chief among the missioners during ICF's early years was Geoffrey Studdert Kennedy – 'Woodbine Willie' – already a national figure by reason of his distinctive and heroic ministry as an army chaplain in the trenches. He was demobilized not long after the end of the war and spent six months on the staff of St Martin-in-the-Fields, in Trafalgar Square, working alongside its equally famous Vicar, Dick Sheppard.

When, scandalously, the Church found no appointment in which he could exercise his unique gifts, he returned to the Worcester parish he had left to join the army and remained there for the next two years. This was not a satisfactory arrangement, since he was in constant demand for speeches and sermons and became involved in the development of the ICF. In 1922, however, he was appointed Rector of St Edmund, King and Martyr, in Lombard Street, and this small London city parish gave him a base and time for a major contribution to the ICF.

This was to occupy the remainder of his life – just seven years. Much of this time was spent in trains, carrying him to every part of the country to undertake an unceasing round of speaking engagements. His effect on audiences was almost mesmerizing. Dark, sad eyes and a friendly voice gave individuals the impression that they were being addressed personally, and William Temple and his wife confessed to becoming 'under his spell'. While about to deliver a course of Lent lectures in Liverpool Parish Church in 1929, he became ill and died within a few days.

In spite of all the ICF's efforts, however, which included the idea and organization of the 1941 Malvern Conference, there was no real engagement with the industrial masses nor any significant challenge to those aspects of industry and commerce that might be considered inimical to Christian faith and ethics. A different approach was needed, and the initiative for this came soon after the end of the Second World War from the Bishop of Sheffield, Leslie Hunter.

Born in 1890, the son of a famous Scottish liberal Congregational preacher, Hunter was the most wide-ranging and prophetic church reformer of the mid-twentieth century. When William Temple died in 1944, his mantle of social concern and church reform fell on Hunter, whose effectiveness owed nothing to charisma or gifts of speech. After taking a First in Theology at New College, Oxford, where he was much influenced by the thought of F. D. Maurice, he was on the staff of the Student Christian Movement for a few years. In 1916, however, he was ordained and seconded to the YMCA to serve the soldiers in France for a few months.

This was long enough for him to become aware of the vast gulf between the Church and the working-class soldiers – a fact confirmed by involvement in a two-year interdenominational enquiry into the problem, the report of which was published in 1919. He remained on the staff of the SCM until early in 1923, when Dick Sheppard invited him to move to St Martin-in-the-Fields.

A year later, however, he left to become a Canon of Newcastle-upon-Tyne Cathedral. Initially, it was intended that he should concentrate on work among students and other young people, but he was soon concerned by the acute poverty of post-war Tyneside – particularly bad housing and ill health – and became involved in social work. After two years, this was ended by a call to become Vicar of Barking – once a small country town in Essex but now with a population of over 50,000 and incorporated into east London. Four years of intensive ministry led, however, to ill health and to resignation, but in 1931, partly recovered, he returned to Tyneside as Archdeacon of Northumberland.

Once again, he became deeply involved in social work, mainly among the unemployed – over 75,000 Tynesiders being out of work. As chairman of the local Council of Social Service, he led a major effort to alleviate the consequent distress, and in a letter to *The Times* in support of the 1936 Jarrow March, he pointed out that this was a clear expression of a whole community's deep sense of frustration and despair. He added:

> The march from Jarrow ought therefore to impress those who live in happier areas that, while there has been much talking and some window-dressing on the part of the government, little has been done to remove the burden – while depression and unemployment remain on a vast scale.

When the Bishopric of Sheffield fell vacant just three months before the outbreak of war in 1939, Leslie Hunter was the obvious choice for the succession, though initially he was reluctant to accept the offer. But he was there for 23 years, leading the diocese through the testing wartime years, when the city was heavily bombed, and in the post-war era, attracting to its service an unusual number of gifted priests to implement a notable programme of reform and renewal.

From the outset, he was made aware that contact between the Church and the steelworks of Sheffield and Rotherham was insignificant. Efforts to bridge this gap had some success at the management level, but most of his attempts at the shop-floor level were rebuffed by workers who, with good reason, were distrustful of the Church. In 1944, therefore, he created an opportunity to appoint E. R. (Ted) Wickham for a period of two years to discover whether or not there might be a full-time job for a priest on the shop floor of Sheffield's major steelworks.

Born in humble circumstances in London in 1911, Wickham never lost his assertive Cockney style. Small of stature, decidedly scruffy, with tousled hair and a no-nonsense manner, many were surprised to discover that he was a priest. He left school early, worked in industry for a time, experienced standing in a dole queue, then, feeling drawn to Holy Orders, taught himself Latin, Greek and Hebrew, took an external London BD and completed his training for the priesthood at St Stephen's House, Oxford.

In 1938 he became a curate in a poor Tyneside parish, but this was more or less flattened by a single night's bombing in 1941, and he moved to become chaplain of a Royal Ordnance factory in Staffordshire. This vital component in Britain's war effort employed 25,000 people, and Wickham experimented with chaplaincy methods that extended beyond pastoral work into discussions with the workers of current social and ethical issues. It was this that led to Bishop Hunter's invitation to undertake an exploration of possible openings for similar ministry in Sheffield.

Initially Wickham was, for financial reasons, obliged to combine his factory work with the half-time chaplaincy of an almshouse, which was hardly appropriate to his gifts and interests, but, through the good offices of the managing director of a major steel works, he gained access to a sphere in which he was able to establish an experimental pattern of mission that remained for the next 12 years.

With the agreement of the trade unions, he wandered around the shop floor, talking to the steelworkers as opportunity arose, getting to know them and learning about the issues that concerned them. He was to remember always that he was a guest, with neither status nor rights. The aim was to build a modest bridge between the Church and industry, and, before long, Wickham found himself involved in a great deal of pastoral work among men who had never before encountered a priest and who would never have contemplated taking their problems to their local vicarage.

Next came the arranging of informal gatherings in snap-breaks. The steel-making processes at that time allowed breaks during which workers could eat sandwiches or simply pause for a smoke, and Wickham used these to initiate discussions on a variety of subjects. Some were suggested by himself, others by the men, some with a direct religious dimension, many raising social, ethical and political issues. Anything from 20 to 100 would gather and quick-witted Wickham was adept at stimulating discussion and encouraging involvement. And, since many subjects were too big to be dealt with in 15–20 minutes, further meetings were held out of working hours in a home, a pub or a hall – occasionally at weekend residential gatherings. Managers as well as workers were often involved, and the small number of active Christians were encouraged to regard their primary sphere of witness not in their parish churches but in the factory, where they might become shop stewards or trade union officials or simply demonstrate with sensitivity their love of their fellow workers. Wickham saw this not so much as the mission of the Church to industry but rather as an expression of the Church's life within industry.

News of the development spread quickly, and soon he was invited to visit other companies. Long before the exploratory, experimental period was completed it became evident that there was scope for this kind of mission, and the work continued to develop. In 1949 a meeting of 142 industrialists, convened by the Master Cutler, agreed on the need for urgent expansion of the mission and its financial support. On the following day this was endorsed by a meeting of trade union officials and in 1950 the Sheffield Industrial Mission was formally inaugurated. Wickham moved from the almshouse to a residentiary canonry of Sheffield Cathedral in order to be able to devote more time to its leadership.

As the work expanded, more chaplains, including a woman, were recruited, and the steelworks at Rotherham, as well as the Sheffield railway depot, were added to their responsibilities. Theological students came in large numbers for pre-ordination courses which included work experience on the shop floor. During the late 1950s chaplains moved from Sheffield to Teesside and Manchester to establish missions there. Others were started in Detroit and Nigeria. Southwark diocese had already established its South London Industrial Mission, under the leadership of Colin Cutell, and many other dioceses appointed industrial chaplains, though there was nothing on the Sheffield scale.

Wickham had taken some time off in 1955 to reflect on the Sheffield experience and this resulted in a seminal book, *Church and People in an Industrial City* (1957), which revealed him as a considerable theologian as well as a mission pioneer. Two years later, Industrial Mission was considered important enough to require a Church Assembly report on *The Task of the Church in Relation to Industry*, and this proposed that a national secretariat should be established to co-ordinate and promote the work. Wickham would have been the obvious person to head this, but the report proved to be highly contentious, and there was never the remotest possibility of the bishops agreeing to relinquish responsibility for Industrial Mission in their dioceses.

Wickham had not sought the post, but was now in need of a wider responsibility, and the rejection of the proposal left him high and dry. For want of anything better, he accepted appointment in 1959 as suffragan Bishop of Middleton in Manchester diocese. He was suited neither by temperament nor inclination for such a post, and his low view of parish clergy, frequently expressed in Sheffield, was well known about in Lancashire. So the early years of his episcopal ministry were not easy, but in time he learned how to minister effectively to clergy and people in inner-city parishes and found ways of carrying out his long-held belief that bishops should serve local secular communities as well as the structure of the Church. He played a large part in the development of a new Salford University, serving as chairman of its Council and as a Pro-Vice-Chancellor, and he wrote three more stimulating books – *Encounter with Modern Society* (1964), *Growth and Inflation* (1975) and *Growth, Justice and Work* (1985).

Meanwhile, his successor in the Industrial Mission and a new, evangelical Bishop of Sheffield sought to link the work more closely to the diocesan structures and to emphasize its pastoral and evangelistic aspects. Most of the chaplains who had been appointed by Wickham either left or were dismissed, and his pioneering creation was more or less dismantled. He died in 1994.

The Sheffield pattern was, however, now firmly established and prospering on Teesside. The Senior Chaplain there, Bill Wright, had spent four years on the staff at Sheffield before moving in 1959 to start new work among chemicals and heavy engineering workers in the North East. The initiative for this had come from the recently appointed Bishop of Jarrow, Mervyn Armstrong, who had himself been involved in industrial management before his ordination and had recently written a British Council of Churches report, *The Church and Industry*.

Wright was the obvious choice for this pioneering work. Born in 1927 and brought up in the North East, he never lost the marks of his artisan beginnings or his regional accent. Tall, energetic, informal, always enthusiastic and often autocratic, he exercised leadership by getting alongside people, winning their confidence and usually their admiration. At St John's College, Durham, where he prepared for Holy Orders in the late 1940s, he took a good degree in Theology and was senior student. But then, to the great consternation of the conservative Principal, R. R. Williams, who later became Bishop of Leicester, he announced that he believed the Church to be so out of touch with industrial society that, instead of being ordained, he proposed to work as a labourer in Sunderland's shipyards, which he did for three years, becoming a shop steward.

He was greatly impressed, however, by a visit to the Sheffield Industrial Mission in its heyday in 1954 and was subsequently ordained to join its now large chaplaincy staff. By 1959 he was well equipped for a new challenge, albeit in surroundings very different from those of a Sheffield steel mill. His first approach was to the management of ICI's huge chemicals plant at Billingham on Tees, where he was heard sympathetically but without encouragement to believe that there might be a role for him among their highly organized operatives.

Nonetheless, he continued to meet them and also a number of trade union officials, and eventually it was agreed that he might start to visit the plant on an experimental basis. He also gained entry to a heavy-engineering works at Thornaby on Tees and to the British Rail depot at Darlington, and in these very different spheres both sides of the industries quickly came to recognize that he had something valuable to offer.

In 1961, opportunities came to expand the work to the south bank of the Tees, where ICI had another rapidly expanding plant, and, besides a number of smaller factories, there was a major steel works at Redcar. With the support of the Bishop of Durham and the Archbishop of York, the Teesside Industrial Mission was now formed to work across diocesan boundaries. More chaplains were recruited, a Methodist minister worked part-time in Darlington, and later a chaplain was appointed to serve in a large steelworks at West Hartlepool. By the time of his retirement in 1992, after 33 years of service, Wright had created an ecumenical team of 11 chaplains, including a professional theologian, and also a group of Durham University theologians offering advice.

Until the 1970s, the Mission's work remained modelled on that of Sheffield, with the adjustments demanded by a variety of different industries. Factory visiting continued, and meetings of workers, trade union officials and managers were held, usually off-site, to discuss, in the light of the Bible, the various social and ethical issues that arose from their relationships and objectives. Chaplains contributed extensively to apprentice and junior management training schemes. Managers and head teachers of schools were brought together to consider how best school-leavers might be prepared for employment. Meetings were held in parishes to acquaint churchgoers with industrial matters and Christian responsibility within industry.

From 1970 onwards, the emphasis changed in two ways. The larger firms had by now discovered that chaplains could be very useful in furthering relations between management and workers, and they were increasingly involved in various schemes concerning organizational structure, problem-solving techniques, team-work skills and other managerial ploys. Wright, because of his growing experience, was sometimes invited to attend, as an observer, official negotiations between managers and workers, and, if necessary, to explain to each the other's positions.

He was among the first to recognize the likelihood of industrial decline in the North East and the certain consequences of this both for individuals and community life. These proved to be devastating, as ICI alone eventually reduced its payroll from 16,000 to 1,000, and heavy engineering virtually disappeared. In these circumstances, the chaplains were drawn increasingly into the handling of large-scale redundancies and the effects on families and communities.

Groups were now formed to investigate whether the problems were the result of a deep depression or permanent de-industrialization caused by government policy, and the results were communicated to Whitehall. Educationists, employers and trade unionists were brought together to consider what forms of education were now appropriate for young people who would no longer have jobs waiting for them when they left school or within the foreseeable future. Manpower Services Commission finance was used to develop youth training schemes, community programmes and volunteer projects. Collaboration with companies pursued early-retirement schemes and split or shared jobs, especially for the young.

A long-term plan to develop self-employment among young people and an immediate effort to help people working in the black economy to get the business skills necessary for setting up legitimate businesses were among other projects. Centres were established where older people who were unlikely to benefit from these initiatives could determine their own future without paid work, creatively and without stigma. The approach was entirely professional and said by the chaplains to be an appropriate response by the Church to the teaching of Jesus about the Kingdom of God.

But was it? That it was laudable work and entirely appropriate for the Church to undertake is indisputable. The theologians from Durham University became deeply involved, and a short book of biblical reflections and descriptions of experimental work in many parts of the North East was published. Yet over this and the entire Industrial Mission enterprise there hung a major question as to whether or not the activities of the chaplains and the lay people who worked with them were engaged in what could accurately be described as Christian mission.

From the time of its formation in Sheffield in 1950, there had never been any shortage of people at every level of the Church of England's life who scorned the efforts of Ted Wickham, his colleagues and successors in many other parts of the country. It is unfortunately the case that Wickham, Wright and other leading chaplains were no less disdainful of the ministry of the parish clergy and often expressed their views in terms that caused offence. There was rarely any meeting of minds and sharing of experiences between the two. This failure was exacerbated by the ad hoc character of the initiatives that led to the formation and maintenance of Industrial Missions. They were the result of personal decisions by bishops, responding to their own insights or to pressure from others, and never integrated into any overall diocesan mission strategies. There were in fact rarely strategies into which they might have been integrated.

These, and other related issues, were the subject of an important analysis of the Teesside Industrial Mission made by a theologian–sociologist, Canon Michael S. Northcott, and published as *The Church and Secularisation* (1989). During his studies at Durham University, Northcott, like Bill Wright 30 years earlier, became aware of the vast gap between what he was being taught in the theological faculty and the industrial life of County Durham just over its walls. After three years as a curate in Manchester and five as a missionary in Malaya, he embarked therefore on intensive field-work research into the diocese of Durham's engagement with industry on Teesside and its attempt to inaugurate new patterns of ministry in Sunderland.

While entirely supportive of the desire to engage closely with industrial society, Northcott was driven to conclude that, while the Industrial Mission had certainly established strong links with certain elements in Teesside's industries, mainly management and trade union officials, it had not succeeded in bringing any significant Christian influence to bear on the serious issues facing those industries. On the contrary, in order to win and maintain a place in the factories and plants, it had itself become secularized. Northcott linked this to the fact that its starting point had been the theological outlook of the 1980s, which he believed to have been a secularizing of the Christian faith rather than a true engagement between religion and society.

The concept of chaplaincy was, he suggested, flawed inasmuch as it indicated a dependence for its existence on an Establishment, in this case company management. This rendered Industrial Mission impotent in situations, increasingly common as decline set in, that called for firm prophetic criticism. Indeed, it often found itself used in the implementing of questionable management techniques, and, although much of its work among the casualties of decline was valuable, this did not exhaust the Church's responsibility for evaluating the ethical aspects of the decline.

A better approach, according to Northcott, would be to concentrate more seriously on the resources still available to the Church of England in its parishes and, by more intensive education of the laity in the interrelation of faith and action, equip those involved in industry at every level to bring Christianity to bear on personal relations and decision-making. Unfortunately, he did not give any indication of who might carry out such training, though he thought that specialist ministries within industry might well be still useful.

Northcott's analysis and criticisms, which received scant attention by church leaders at the time of their publication, had been voiced earlier by a Japanese academic who visited Britain in 1983 to study Industrial Mission. She identified what she regarded as serious dangers – 'clericalism, conformism, and reductionism, all three of which are associated with the chaplaincy model'. In Germany, the renowned theologian Jürgen Moltmann, who had a particular concern for the social impact of the Christian faith, concluded that 'Only in the gathered Christian congregation does the believer become ready for action and capable of resistance.'

In the meantime, Industrial Mission nationally has moved on. Although the Sheffield and Teesside Missions were for many years the largest and most influential of the pioneering initiatives, most other dioceses eventually employed one or more industrial chaplains. In 1960 there were ten teams, and by the early 1970s there were 140 full-time and many part-time chaplains. There was now an Industrial Mission Association and close collaboration with chaplains appointed by other churches.

Most were employed in smaller-scale industries and some in commercial enterprises, including large retail centres and airports. Workplace visiting still predominated but alternative methods were applied when this was not possible.

Some chaplains began to criticize the radical economic policies carried out by Margaret Thatcher's Conservative administration in the 1980s, which were leading to widespread factory closures and large-scale unemployment, especially in the north of England. The majority, however, followed the Teesside line of seeking to mitigate the worse effects of the destruction and some became involved in the work of a Manpower Services Commission. The rapidly changing shape of British industry inevitably involved movement by Industrial Mission into different spheres of work, including the service industries.

During the 1990s, however, the combination of growth of the Church's Evangelical wing, which had always been critical of Industrial Mission, and a decline in the Church's financial resources, brought the enterprise under considerable pressure. Cuts in diocesan income normally led to the reduction or closure of frontier work, and, although some chaplaincy remains, it is nationally only a shadow of its former presence. Nonetheless, Industrial Mission was the most substantial and sustained effort by the Church of England in the twentieth century to engage with a major component of society. It was, however, never adequately resourced, the lessons learned have yet to be absorbed, and the Church is no nearer to bridging the gulf between its own life and that of industrial and commercial Britain.

18

A Sorry Tale of Too Many Cities

During the immediate post-war period of reconstruction, successive Labour and Conservative governments accorded the highest priority to the provision of much-needed housing, most of it to be located on large Local Authority estates on the edges of towns and cities. Wartime experience suggested that a major project of this kind could be carried out effectively only by the State, equipped with the necessary powers and resources.

An unfortunate consequence of the concentration on new housing was the complete overlooking of the needs of the inner areas of towns and cities which had, of necessity, been neglected during the war years and were now decaying rapidly. From the mid-1950s onwards some of these areas, particularly in London and Birmingham, attracted substantial immigrant populations from Commonwealth countries, drawn by cheap accommodation and job opportunities. Modest attempts by the State through Local Authorities to deal with the situation made little impact, and, by the 1970s, it had become scandalous.

It was not until 1977 that a Labour government produced a White Paper on *Policy for the Inner Cities*. This was a serious attempt to diagnose the basic cause of the problem, which it located in poverty and lack of resources. The need was for a co-ordinated programme of planning, building and renovation plus industrial development, all of which required partnership between the government and private enterprise. The inner cities should now be given the highest priority. Steps were taken by the government to implement the recommendations, but before much progress could be made it went out of office and was replaced by a Conservative administration which, under Margaret Thatcher, had other priorities.

During the weekend of 10–12 April 1981, however, serious rioting broke out in Brixton – a run-down area of south London with a large African–Caribbean population. By this time the nation was in severe economic depression, and the consequent unemployment had exposed clearly the social inadequacies of Brixton and the fragility of its community life.

The immediate cause of the rioting was anger at police tactics, which were believed to be unnecessarily tough and also racially biased. Widely used 'stop and search' methods were applied almost exclusively to black people and created widespread resentment. This ignited discontent related to unemployment, poverty, inadequate housing, lack of social amenities and a high crime rate.

The police were, however, the chief target of the rioters, whose numbers were estimated to be about 5,000. During the course of the weekend, 299 police officers were injured, as were 65 members of the public. Approximately 117 buildings were damaged and looted, some set on fire. Over 100 motor vehicles, 56 of which belonged to the police, were burned. Chaos replaced order and the nation's shock was increased in early July by outbreaks of rioting in Liverpool, Nottingham, Birmingham, Manchester and the Southall district of west London. Unrest was reported from a number of other towns.

Two days after the Brixton riots the Archbishop of Canterbury, Robert Runcie, who had been in office for only just over 12 months, met six of the leading clergy of the area to hear their verdict on the weekend's events. They expressed their own concern at the tactics of the police, both generally and during the riots, and also emphasized that the government should listen to what the local community leaders had to say about Brixton's problems. The frequent changing of social objectives and tampering with projects was causing much frustration among those trying to improve the situation.

Runcie immediately communicated this to the Home Secretary, William Whitelaw, with whom he had served in the Scots Guards during the war, and concluded his letter:

> You can imagine that I am under some pressure to give a moral spiritual lead in what may become the central issue for our society in the coming months and years. I am eager to respond but not by rushing into generalised and unconstructive comments on highly complex issues. Nevertheless, I regard this letter to you as a first step in my responsibility for spiritual leadership in the face of a deteriorating situation in community relations which is not confined to Brixton.

Whitelaw thanked the Archbishop for his 'kind and helpful letter' and arranged to meet him and representatives of the Brixton Council of Churches to hear their views.

The violence experienced three months later in the Toxteth district of inner-city Liverpool was on a scale much larger than that experienced in Brixton. Police reinforcements were drawn from other parts of the country, and on 6 July, 25–30 CS gas canisters were fired to disperse a crowd – the first time these had been used in Britain apart from in Northern Ireland.

After nine days of rioting, 468 police officers had been injured, 500 people arrested and 70 buildings so damaged by fire that they had to be demolished. Looting of shops had been widespread. Later estimates suggested that the number of police officers injured and buildings damaged was about double that of the official figures.

The Home Secretary, William Whitelaw, responded by commissioning a Public Enquiry, conducted by Lord Scarman, a senior and highly respected judge. Addressed to the Brixton events, but with Toxteth also in mind, this moved with unusual speed and published its report in November of the same year. There was criticism of certain police methods and some changes were recommended, but without any significant relaxing of strict control.

The report's main diagnosis, however, centred on the economic, social and political factors that created the underlying discontent. Urgent action was, it asserted, needed to remedy the problems of racial disadvantage and inner-city decline, and not only in Brixton, otherwise they would generate 'an endemic and irradicable disease threatening the very survival of our society'.

The report was well received by the political parties, the media and community organizations, and some of its proposals relating to the police were implemented. Archbishop Runcie commended it to the churches and said he hoped that after careful study they would be able to make a joint response indicating the part they could play in the rebuilding of trust and confidence. But the Inquiry had been in no position to recommend solutions to the underlying problems, and among politicians there was disagreement as to their significance.

Little action followed, except in Liverpool, where the situation was deemed serious enough to prompt the Prime Minister, Margaret Thatcher, to despatch the Minister for the Environment, Michael Heseltine, to investigate and make recommendations. Runcie also went to Merseyside to learn and to encourage the churches, only to be told in no uncertain terms by a forthright evangelical that he was disqualified from talking to them since 'You represent the church of the Shires, and we shall never make progress here as long as we are wedded to the church of the Shires.'

Heseltine was so appalled by what he found that he secured, against the wishes of many of his government colleagues, the Prime Minister's approval for a Task Force to remedy some of the problems. Applying considerable drive and energy to its work, he succeeded over the next few years in implementing a major programme of urban renewal for the whole region. The Labour-controlled Liverpool City Council showed its gratitude by granting him the Freedom of the City.

Meanwhile, the Church of England was preparing its own considered response. While on pilgrimage to Santiago de Compostela in Spain, at the beginning of July 1981, the Archbishop read in *The Times* an article by the paper's Religious Affairs correspondent, Clifford Longley. In this, he looked back on the life of the Church of England since the 1960s and, noting the statistics of decline revealed in falling numbers of baptisms, Easter communicants and weddings, interpreted this, correctly, as 'the progressive decline of Anglicanism as a pillar of national life'. He doubted if the Church's leadership would regard the 'incontrovertible facts' in this way.

Runcie immediately despatched a postcard to Canon Eric James, the then Director of Christian Action, requesting a substantial letter of response. James, who was fully acquainted with inner-city issues, having himself ministered in south London, obliged and in his letter expressed surprise that Longley had not referred to the Church's inner-city problems. He went on to urge the Archbishop to set up a commission to consider the Church's role in these crisis areas, with appropriate attention to causes.

Runcie moved quickly and, in consultation with James and several urban bishops, convened an 18-strong commission under the leadership of Sir Richard O'Brien, who had recently retired from the chairmanship of the Manpower Services Commission. The Bishop of Liverpool, David Sheppard, was appointed vice-chairman and the other members made up a remarkably distinguished, knowledgeable and experienced company of no known party-political allegiances. Their remit was:

> To examine the strengths, insights, problems and needs of the Church's life and mission in Urban Priority Areas and, as a result, reflect on the challenge which God may be making to Church and Nation, and to make recommendations to appropriate bodies.

It was explained that the term 'Urban Priority Areas' (UPAs) should include not only inner-city districts but also large council estates and other areas of social deprivation. Six advisers, including Eric James and representatives of resource bodies, attended the Commission's meetings and, significantly, the secretary was a civil servant seconded from the Department of the Environment.

Seventeen meetings of the full Commission were held during the next two years, together with many meetings of specialist sub-committees and weekends spent in more than 40 cities, towns and London boroughs, where local opinion was garnered at public meetings. The result was a 398-page report, *Faith in the City: A Call for Action by Church and Nation*, which Professor Adrian Hastings, a church historian, described in his biography of Runcie as 'the most important venture of his whole archiepiscopate, the enterprise in which he affected the most people, was most attacked and most justified, the venture for which he is in the long run likely to be most remembered'.

The report's opening chapter states in robust terms its view of the causes of the problems of UPAs, which, it declared, have emerged not simply as a result of decisions by their inhabitants but from the decisions of political authority, business management or individual choice. It goes on to become specific:

It would be wrong to assume that a market economy *necessarily* leads to inequality . . . Our own time has witnessed a more or less crude exaltation of the alleged social consequences of individual self-interest and competition. The inner city may justly be seen as the disfigured battleground of this modern phase of an age-old conflict . . . poverty reflects the structural inequality of the nation and the UPAs reveal it in its most intractable forms.

Had Archbishop William Temple been still alive, this would, without doubt, have received his full endorsement. But he would have insisted on a stronger theological basis for the initial statement and all that followed. This, it turned out, was the report's one weak point, and the lack of serious theological undergirding left it exposed to the criticism of those who did not like its analysis and recommendations. There is, in fact, some attention given to the Bible and the doctrine of the Kingdom of God, but this lacks the depth of Temple's work, and part of the explanation seems to be that the Commission was suspicious of theological propositions 'applied' to situations – 'Theology has always arisen from and reacted to new situations.' None, however, arose from the UPAs, though Bishop David Sheppard saw the force of the Latin American liberation theologian's insistence that the Bible displays 'a bias to the poor'.

The first part of the report, occupying about 150 pages, was addressed primarily to the Church and contained proposals for radical reform that were unfortunately largely overlooked in the controversy provoked by the social, economic and political material. Many visits to inner cities and housing estates had made a considerable impact on members of the Commission, who were appalled by much of what they found, yet were often impressed by the quality of much of the church life. The size of this was always small and for the overwhelming majority of the large populations the Church's activities were not seen as relevant to their daily experiences. It was noted, however, that black-led churches were fast growing.

The Church of England's mission in these areas was, it seemed, handicapped by two main factors, the first being its middle-class ethos. The social background of its clergy suggested an institution identified with authority and wealth. The second involved the buildings – 45 per cent of the churches and 40 per cent of the ancillary buildings were said by their users to be inappropriate to current needs.

The Commission's reaction to this was, 'The Church must change. The traditional approach is no longer viable. Things cannot be allowed to continue as they are or there will be further alienation.' There followed a long list of proposals for change, with considerable emphasis on the need for the Church to be both local and outward looking. It must become immersed in different aspects of community life – secular organizations, community centres and groups pressing for change in the environment – and see this as an integral part of its mission, evangelism and service. The Church's life should not run parallel to that of the wider community but be part of it.

Informal expressions of church life outside its buildings – house meetings, 'good neighbours' schemes and the like – were needed, and serious attention should be given to baptisms, weddings and funerals that still involved many not otherwise in touch with the Church. Additional, more appropriate, liturgical resources were required. Collaboration with other churches in the area was essential, leading often to the sharing of buildings, worship and action in the community. Serious local consultation was also essential whenever the closure of churches is envisaged.

The Commission recognized that prescriptions for the renewal of church life in UPAs, which had been largely prompted by existing examples and suggestions gathered during their visits to these areas, would require substantial support by the wider Church (diocesan and national) and some policy changes at all levels. Church leaders were urged to give a positive lead 'to overcome inertia, insecurity and prejudice in local congregations'.

A basic requirement, which it ought not to have been necessary to state, was that dioceses should identify their UPA parishes and, in collaboration with them, devise appropriate strategies. This might require boundary changes to enable parishes to accord with real neighbourhoods. In urban areas, the Deaneries should have a clear role as units of planning and support, additional financial resources would need to be allocated and the deployment of clergy adjusted to meet special needs.

It was recognized that the clergy serving in UPAs would continue to be drawn from a different social background. Hence the need for some ordinands to be introduced to these areas and trained in their needs, as well as specialist post-ordination training for all involved in them. Many more men for local ordained ministry were needed and non-residential courses provided for their training. The number of black clergy should be increased substantially, there being no more than 100 of them in the whole Church.

The second half of the report, addressed 'To the Nation', began by stating that it intended to give special attention to unemployment and housing since it believed these to be at the heart of the problem. It then turned to the 1977 White Paper on *Policy for the Inner-cities*, which it considered to be on the right lines, but no sustained effort had been made to put its proposals in to effect. Indeed, since the arrival of the Thatcher government, there had been a reduction in public expenditure on UPAs and private enterprise zones, and less money for Local Authorities: 'If the problem of urban deprivation lies in the fundamental structure of the economy (as we believe it does in large part), the public policy response is clearly open to the charge of being inadequate and superficial.' Seeking to be constructive, the Commission then urged on the government a better response, summarized in the following terms:

1. The policy response to the UPAs should embrace both the area-based approaches and the adoption of policies directed towards reducing social and economic inequalities whenever they exist.
2. A greater priority should be given by government to the problems of the outer housing estates of many towns and cities, which on many indicators are now in urgent need of attention.
3. There is a regrettable lack of will on the part of central government to support local government and to devote adequate resources to UPA local authorities in the face of the problems.
4. A co-ordination of programmes is needed, and the concept of partnership needs to be developed to promote greater participation at local level, to combat the pervasive feelings of powerlessness.
5. The potential for small businesses to regenerate the UPAs (particularly the outer estates) is limited. Education and skill-training programmes are necessary to increase UPA people's chances of creating and gaining 'new jobs'. Better housing and environmental improvements are needed to encourage growth enterprises to locate in the UPA; neighbourhood action programmes are also needed.
6. Finally, not least, what the inner cities need more than anything else is a vote of *confidence*. It must be for the government first and foremost to demonstrate this confidence through a sustained programme of public investment on both current and capital account, as has happened in the docklands areas of the UDCs. In this way it will give greater confidence to the private sector to invest.

The implications of all this were then developed in some detail and criticism of government policy, or lack of it, was intensified. There had, it said, been serious inconsistencies in financial policy, which had often caused UPAs to lose grants for projects that were just getting established. Nonetheless, the Commission had been 'enormously impressed with the work undertaken by Local Authorities and voluntary bodies with help from the Urban Programme'.

All in all, however,

We have lost a decade. We urge that policy-makers return to the 1977 White Paper and to what it argued was the necessary first step in responding to the inner-cities' problems: 'The first essential is a *specific commitment* on the part of central and local government to the *regeneration* of the inner areas . . . both central and local government will be judged by their willingness to *implement new priorities, to make funds available, to change policies,* and *to adapt their organizations.'* (our emphasis)

Turning next to the issues of unemployment and poverty, of both of which there was more in UPAs than elsewhere, the Commission began by pointing out that in recent years legislation had led to lower-paid workers paying more in taxation, while the highly paid were paying as much as 15 per cent less. Moreover, pay differentials had also widened sharply, so that three and a half million people now had total earnings (including overtime pay) that fell below the £100 per week definition of low pay.

It is the poor who have borne the brunt of the recession, both the unemployed and the working poor. Yet it is the poor who are seen by some as 'social security scroungers', or a burden on the country, preventing economic recovery. This is a cruel example of blaming the victim.

Wealth creation was essential, but so also was its fair distribution, and there was no reason for believing that the benefits of business success would automatically 'trickle down' to the less well-off, since there was no mechanism to enable it to do so.

The Commission acknowledged that the Church had no instant or potent solutions to the current economic and social problems. Nonetheless –

[The Church of England] is in the position of being the national Church. It has a particular duty to act as the conscience of the nation. It must question all economic philosophies, not least those which, when put into practice, have contributed to the blighting of whole districts, which do not offer the hope of amelioration, and which perpetuate the human misery and despair to which we have referred. The situation requires the Church to question from its own particular standpoint the *morality* of these philosophies.

Notwithstanding the disclaimer about the Church's competence to offer long-term solutions, the Commission felt able make eight 'Recommendations to Government'. These included more support for small firms in UPAs, an increase in job-creating expenditure in these areas, expanding the programme of community projects to provide employment for a further 500,000 people who had been out of work for a year or more, and increasing the level of Child Benefit as an effective means of assisting, without stigma, families in poverty.

Further chapters dealt with housing, health, and social and community work in UPAs, again adding sharp criticism of some current policies and making a number of recommendations. The final chapter was devoted to the thorny issue of order and law, noting first that certain forms of crime were more prevalent in UPAs – robbery, burglary, theft, vandalism, theft from or of cars. These were invariably committed by local people and the victims were also local people; therefore it should be recognized that the impact of petty crime was more serious for those living in conditions of social deprivation. The fear of crime is another form of discomfort.

In spite of popular demands for the imposition of law and order, the Commission was convinced that intensifying of policing was not the answer. Evidence proved that this yielded few positive results. The basic causes of the breakdown of social order needed to be tackled. Meanwhile, Community Development projects involving local people and supported by the churches, offered the prospect of some success. Changes in policing methods, especially in UPAs, was particularly important because

> the fifteen years from 1964 up to 1980 witnessed in practice a steady accretion of power in society to the police, relatively free from accountability to 'government'. No other organisation of similar size could live without making some errors and so it unfortunately was with the police . . . In many urban areas the police to a degree lost the trust and support of the public.

Local consultative committees involving police and public were now urgently needed.

The report *Faith in the City* was published in December 1985 and it was hardly to be expected that so well informed and so sustained a critique of government policies and the political and economic philosophies that informed them would lead to its being warmly welcomed in government circles. It was not, and shortly before publication day an unnamed Cabinet

Minister denounced it as 'Pure Marxist theology'. The Conservative MP for Leicester East, Peter Bruinvels, who was also a member of the General Synod, agreed, adding that the Church was 'stabbing its own loyal flock in the back'. His colleague at Luton North, John Carlisle, failed to notice that the Commission was predominantly lay and declared, 'The Church of England seems now to be run by a bunch of Communist clerics.'

The Prime Minister, Margaret Thatcher, evidently resisting the temptation to launch a full-scale attack, expressed her preference for a Jewish analysis of the situation, in which the Chief Rabbi urged UPA residents not to look to the government for help but, after the example of nineteenth-century Jews, climb their own way out of poverty. Michael Heseltine, now Minister of Defence and still a Liverpool hero, told the Archbishop, 'Your bishops have got it wrong. Conditions in the inner cities are much worse than they say.'

The Daily Telegraph described it in an editorial as 'savourless salt', lacking 'a specifically Christian theology' and being 'intellectually inadequate'. Paul Johnson, in the *Daily Mail*, described it as 'a flawed gospel . . . intellectually beneath contempt' and the tabloid papers were generally dismissive. In marked contrast, the *Financial Times* said, 'These are not revolutionary proposals from a Church of Militants, but sober suggestions, mainly within the government's own terms of reference. They deserve a thoughtful reading.' It added that the government's intemperate attack would likely be more damaging to ministers as 'it gives the impression that they are rattled'.

As a result of all the controversy, 17,000 copies of the Report were sold during the first few months, and an abridged version sold over 66,000 copies. Translations were made into several European languages. Significantly, there was no serious challenging of the facts it contained, and some members of the Commission attributed this to Sir Richard O'Brien's insistence that every stated opinion should be supported by sound evidence. Just over a year later, in a debate in the House of Lords on inner-city problems, Lord Scarman described *Faith in the City* as 'the finest face-to-face analysis and description of the problems of the inner-city and of other urban priority areas we have yet seen. In the long run it will take its place, I believe, as a classic description of one of the most serious troubles in British society.' The Archbishop immediately accepted the report, owned it and gave it his unwavering support, pressing for the implementation of the proposals relating to the Church. An officer for UPAs was appointed and advisory groups were set up in every diocese, each with an officer to maintain contact with the national office. Some dioceses produced their own local reports and the General Synod appointed a Committee for Black Anglican Concerns.

A Church Urban Fund, recommended by the Commission, was established, with a target of £18 million to be spent over a number of years on community projects in UPAs. The Queen became its patron, a share of the target figure was allocated to each diocese and the money came in remarkably quickly. Soon more than 200 projects were being financed and the Fund has remained in existence, having by early 2013 granted a total of £65 million to 2,500 projects and initiatives.

This was the Commission's chief legacy, for, although *Faith in the City* stirred the Church of England to useful action, not many of its recommendations for church reform were implemented. In most UPAs, the Church itself still struggles to survive and is able to make only limited contributions to the mitigation of social problems. On the other hand, the report placed the inner cities high on the national agenda, so that even the Thatcher administration could no longer ignore them. Over the next decades, considerable efforts were made, with some success, to regenerate the worst examples of decay and brokenness, but many serious problems remain for both nation and Church.

Faith in the City was followed in 1990 by the important but less controversial *Faith in the Countryside*. The former was, in fact, just one, albeit the most significant, element in a confrontation between the leaders of the Church of England and the Thatcher government during the 1980s. The issues concerned essentially economic justice, and commitment to co-operation rather than aggressive competition – challenges offered by the New Right and resisted by Archbishop Runcie and many other clergy of all the churches. The Labour Party being very weak during this period, it was often said that the Church of England had become the opposition. This was an exaggeration, but it meant that the Church of England could less easily be described as 'the Tory Party at Prayer', at least as far as its clergy were concerned.

19

Whither Prophecy?

Although the Church of England is now beset with a number of serious internal problems, and, for several reasons, less influential in public life than at any other time during the past two centuries, it nonetheless retains a deep social commitment and a concern for the well-being of the nation as a whole. Its involvement in social and community work is impressive. Moreover, the statements of its leaders on political, economic and social questions continue to attract media attention, and government ministers often feel obliged to respond publicly to criticisms of their policies. There is no reason therefore for the Church to reduce its prophetic witness, and the only issues for discussion concern the forms this witness should take and the resources available to make it effective in an increasingly complex and secularized society.

The 1941 Malvern Conference, followed quickly by the publication of Archbishop William Temple's *Christianity and Social Order* marked the end of an era of Anglican visionary social thinking that began with the theological work of F. D. Maurice in the mid-nineteenth century, developed through the witness of the Christian Social Union in the late Victorian and Edwardian periods, and reached its climax at the COPEC Conference in 1925.

Malvern added nothing new to this but helped to carry the movement of thought forward into the heart of the most appallingly destructive war in human history. The chief recommendations of this conference, which included matters such as adequate housing, education, working conditions, wages and leisure, were in significant measure met by the provisions of the Welfare State and the growth in national prosperity which, with a few ups and downs, characterized the remainder of the twentieth century. These years witnessed social changes, including less respect for religious institutions, that radically altered national life and culture.

Meanwhile, the Church of England's leaders were becoming preoccupied by their own institution's needs and problems. Much time was devoted to liturgical and synodical reform, both against the background of declining church attendance. This decline accelerated quickly after the 1950s, creating distracting financial and clerical manpower pressures.

Circumstances, which also included the lack of a commanding figure such as Temple had been, and little development in the field of Christian social thought, conspired therefore to inhibit further comprehensive critical commentary on the nation's life. Which is not to say that the voice of the Church was silent.

Several chapters in this book provide evidence of substantial initiatives by individuals and groups of Anglicans during this time, and there were others for which space could not be allocated. These included abolition of the death penalty, child poverty, ecology, immigration and nationality as well as major enterprises of aid to the developing world. Here it is to be noted that these were addressed to particular issues, rather than to broad programmes of reform, and that they were tackled with expertise – often a great deal of expertise.

This characterized the many reports produced by the Church of England's Board of Social Responsibility which, over a long period, used the resources of its own staff and a large number of others, often distinguished in their fields, who were willing to devote a good deal of time to serious projects. *Putting Assunder*, *The Church and the Bomb*, *Faith in the City* and *Faith in the Countryside* attracted much attention, and the titles of just a few others indicate the range – *Ought Suicide to be a Crime?* (1959), *Punishment* (1963), *Abortion: An Ethical Discussion* (1965), *Not Just for the Poor* (1986), *Growth, Justice and Work* (1986).

It must be a matter of the utmost regret that the majority of these were, after a flurry of publicity attending their publication and some synodical debate, consigned to gather dust on unvisited shelves in Church House, Westminster. In most cases, fewer than 100 copies were sold. The dioceses and parishes hardly noticed them, and, even more seriously, they did not find their ways into the hands of the statutory bodies responsible for policy in their areas of concern. In these circumstances, it is perhaps hardly surprising that when the General Synod was faced with serious financial constraints, the resources previously available for such projects were savagely cut and the reports reduced to a trickle.

Yet the need for the Church's pronouncements on political, social and economic matters to be informed by accurate information concerning the facts and the likely outcome of any decision-making by those responsible becomes ever greater. William Temple's criticisms of bankers in the 1930s drew the not unjustified response that he simply did not understand the workings of the banking system. How much more difficult then to understand its complexities today when many of the bankers themselves are baffled?

A distinction has to be made between general statements of moral principle, which are part of the Church's calling, and attempts to apply these principles to particular issues which nearly always involve multiple factors and require compromise.

Compromise has some bad connotations and needs to be used cautiously, but refusal to deal with it may be tantamount to withdrawal from serious decision-making. It may have either responsible or irresponsible manifestations. The former has belonged to the Christian ethical tradition from the earliest days of the Faith. It is, for example, doubtful whether Jesus intended the absolute ethical demands enshrined in his Sermon on the Mount to be treated by his followers as a precise guide to their future behaviour. Rather they were held up as shining examples of love in action, the spirit of which must infuse all their choices.

The evangelical counsels of perfection, as they are called, can in fact be obeyed only within the sheltered life of a closed religious community, and even there failure is not unknown. Elsewhere, the discipline of the Christian life consists in a constant Spirit-guided attempt to let Love take control and in the many situations where the issues are not clear-cut make the most loving, and therefore the most life-enhancing, choices, even when these may be less than ideal.

The Church's moral theologians have often offered guidance in this area of Christian obedience, and individual believers have often found this helpful. But much greater challenges attend Christian decision-making when this is required in corporate, rather than individual, spheres, and only limited assistance can be offered by those who are remote from the complex factors involved. Some can nonetheless point to principles of great importance shared by other religious and moral traditions.

In his seminal *Moral Man and Immoral Society* (1932), Reinhold Niebuhr, one of the great American theologians of the twentieth century, called attention to the obvious, but frequently overlooked, fact that individuals in a crowd tend to behave differently, and often worse, than when on their own or in small family groups. His particular concern was to discuss the implication of this for politics, though it has a wider relevance. He concluded that it is unwise, sometimes dangerous, to attempt to apply directly to corporate decision-making those Christian values which are an imperative for the individual believer. It is always necessary to take account not only of human potential for good, but also of the limitations of human nature, particularly those which manifest themselves in humanity's collective behaviour – 'The moral obtuseness of human collectives makes a morality of pure disinterestedness impossible.'

This note of sober realism is bad news inasmuch as it suggests that little in the way of social improvement can be hoped for. But Niebuhr saw the whole of life in terms of a perennial paradox. Christians judge themselves and the world in the light of the eternal, yet work ceaselessly to transform society while under no illusion that society can ever be perfected. Christians will find no ultimate fulfilment in society, but neither will they find salvation apart from social and political engagement.

The shades and shadows of human life are therefore as important as the contrast between the radiance of the divine holiness and the darkness of the world. Hence, again, the need for compromise in most decision-making. The question now arises: Does the Niebuhrian paradox provide sufficient dynamism for constructive social and political action, and the right context for activists to discern the frontier between constructive compromise and destructive capitulation to action that will not further human welfare?

One Anglican who thinks so is Archbishop John Habgood, formerly Bishop of Durham, then Archbishop of York, who, in company with Ronald Preston, a Manchester professor and cathedral canon, made the most substantial contribution to the Church of England's social thinking during the second half of the twentieth century. Habgood's training as a scientist has never permitted him to overlook facts or the possibility that these might be differently interpreted, neither does his temperament ever incline him to off-the-cuff judgements. He found, therefore, in Niebuhr a theological depth and social realism that illuminated many of the new social challenges facing both Britain and the wider world which a church leader could not ignore.

His work has never therefore so much as hinted at a comprehensive programme for the building of a new and better world. It has consisted of serious intellectual analysis of problems, sometimes influenced by membership of interdisciplinary working parties, and expressed in sermons, addresses, papers and lectures. This, together with his heavy responsibilities as a bishop and an archbishop, precluded long spells of research and writing. Some of his work has, however, been brought together in books, and a six months' sabbatical, after ten years at Durham, enabled him to write *Church and Nation in a Secular Age* (1983).

Among the subjects claiming his attention at various times were 'Technology and Politics: Ethical Reflections on the Arms Race', 'The Christian Tradition and Medical Ethics', 'The Human Fertilisation and Embryology Bill', 'Finding a Moral Heart for Europe', 'The Gulf War' and 'The Ethics of Resource Allocation' – all highly topical at the time and stimulating in their analysis, but too nuanced to provide easy pickings for hurried journalists.

Neither was Habgood often tempted into making off-the-cuff comments on current political issues, but this did not exempt him from the disapproval of Margaret Thatcher, who saw him as a potentially dangerous opponent who could not easily be undermined. When, during the 1983–4 miners' strike, a Labour MP accused her of disregarding the advice of the bishops over colliery closures, she replied, 'I am not prepared to tangle with His Grace the Archbishop of York.' He once described himself as a conservative liberal, and that seemed right. His biography is appropriately titled *Living with Paradox.*

Also firmly in the Niebuhrian tradition is Richard Harries, who was born in 1936 and after some parish experience and teaching posts in theological colleges and as Dean of King's College, London, became Bishop of Oxford. The heavy responsibilities of that large diocese did not stand in the way of an immense output of writing and broadcasting, both exceeding by a long way that of any other bishop. An early concern was the need to end loans to the South African government, which in the 1980s was still pursuing its apartheid policy. He was chairman of a campaigning group and related to this was a personal attempt to persuade the Church Commissioners to cease investing in South Africa. Not long after he became a bishop he argued in a much-publicized High Court Action that the Commissioners had an over-riding duty to promote the Christian faith and not merely maximize their income. This failed, but the point was powerfully made.

The issue of the 'just war', and, related to this, arms control, was another important concern about which he wrote much and also served for five years on the Council for Arms Control. He then turned to medical ethics, acquiring sufficient expertise in various fields to lead to memberships of the Human Fertilisation and Embryology Authority (chairing its Ethics and Law committee) and the Nuffield Council on Bioethics, as well as chairmanship of the House of Lords Select Committee on Stem Cell Research. He was also a member of a Royal Commission on the Reform of the House of Lords and his membership of that House was so valued that, on retirement from his bishopric, he was made a Life peer to enable it to continue, which it still does.

At a quite different level has been the contribution made by Harries over the course of more than 40 years to the 'Thought for the Day' feature in the BBC's news-orientated *Today* programme. In this challenging secular setting, his three-minute comments are models of how a Christian liberal mind may be applied to topical issues without being platitudinous.

In the life of the Church, he was chairman of the Board for Social Responsibility and also did much to promote Christian–Jewish relations. In 2003, considerable controversy surrounded his recommendation of Jeffrey John, a Canon of Southwark, for the suffragan Bishopric of Reading. The Archbishop of Canterbury, Rowan Williams, was aware that John was a homosexual living in a chaste relationship with a male partner, but accepted the recommendation. Subsequently, however, he yielded to pressure from within the Oxford diocese and other parts of the Anglican Communion and persuaded John to withdraw his acceptance. Much damage to the Church resulted.

The question of whether or not Harries should have given greater weight to the likely consequences of his recommendation remains open. He continued to defend his choice and attacked what he called 'a cruel homophobia in the Church of England'. This was not an issue where compromise was possible, though he was driven to accept a different Bishop of Reading.

Quite different, and altogether more radical, has been the contribution of Charles Elliott, a distinguished Development Economist, whose life's work has involved study of the gulf between the world's rich and poor and of how best this gulf might be bridged – the most important and most difficult of the modern world's problems. Born in 1939, he became a scholar of Lincoln College, Oxford, took his Doctorate in Economics at Nuffield College, then began his teaching career in that subject at Nottingham University in 1963 and was ordained in the following year.

Specializing in Development Economics, he has travelled widely in the developing world, held several chairs in the subject, also taught Christian Ethics, was Director of Christian Aid from 1982 to 1984, was a senior consultant to the Overseas Development Institute and ended his full-time ministry as Fellow and Dean of Trinity Hall, Cambridge.

He argued forcefully in *Comfortable Compassion? Poverty, Power and the Church* (1987) that the world's poor are trapped in political and economic power structures that make the elimination of their poverty impossible. The problem is structural and not one that can be solved by minor adjustment and generous aid. Viewed in a Christian perspective, 'The prevailing development policies (which have not changed since he wrote this) fall short of the Gospel.' His word to the Church was severe, and this is a recently resigned Director of Christian Aid speaking:

> In responding to mass poverty in an age of plenty, the churches have become stuck in a specific concept of the problem and their role in response to that problem . . . The response is not false but inadequate and largely self-defeating. It has led the churches into a cul-de-sac of well intentioned but largely ineffective gestures, while leaving the real issues either unidentified or neglected.

The fact of poverty, says Elliott, is the outworking of the power of some over others, and 'it is in the nature of that relationship – of the powerful over the powerless – that it distributes wealth to the former at the expense of the latter . . . The use of power is in its essence a religious question – so fundamental in human wellbeing that it is a recurrent theme in the biblical record of God's love for his people.' He believes that power needs to be confronted and transformed by the truths of the Christian faith, and, until the Church itself has been converted by these same truths in respect to its own life, the witness is most likely to be made by small communities within the Church. This was 'the voice of one crying in the wilderness' and has yet to be taken seriously.

Rowan Williams, who was enthroned in the chair of Saint Augustine in Canterbury Cathedral in 2003, is Britain's finest theologian, and, more widely, one of the nation's foremost public intellectuals. As an Archbishop, he was in a class of his own, and it might be thought that a Church capable of producing such a leader had little to fear. It had been necessary, however, to import him from Wales, where the previous 12 years were spent as Bishop of Monmouth and Archbishop. Before that, he was engaged almost exclusively in academic work, becoming at the early age of 36 Lady Margaret Professor of Divinity and a Canon of Christ Church, Oxford.

His outlook on life bears the marks of an erudite, albeit fairly conservative, biblical theology, a deep sacramental spirituality and a sensitive, wide humanity. Of his concern for political and social matters there was never the slightest doubt. While a Cambridge University don he had taken part in student demonstrations, and a luxuriant beard had encouraged the description of him as 'a hairy Lefty'.

How such a combination of intellectual, spiritual and social awareness would be employed in the office of Primate of All England was bound to be interesting. It was, though it soon became evident that he was not well equipped for handling the serious problems in the Anglican Communion's own life. Trying but failing to satisfy all sides in often bitter disputes over biblical interpretation, homosexual clergy and women bishops, Williams underwent a decade-long personal 'crucifixion'.

During the course of these years, Williams commented frequently in statements, sermons and lectures on a wide variety of contemporary issues. His substantial offerings were often awesome in the brilliance of their analysis, yet sometimes so complex in their argument that even experts were left baffled about their meaning. The sheer quality of his achievement was confirmed by the publication, on the eve of his retirement in 2012, of a collection of 26 of his lectures under the title *Faith in the Public Square*.

An introductory chapter made plain his faith starting point:

If it is true that the world depends entirely on the free gift of God, and that the direct act and presence of God has uniquely appeared in history in the shape of a human life two millennia ago, this has implications for how we think about that world and about human life. The risk of blundering into unforeseen complexities can't be avoided; and the best thing to hope for is that at least some of the inevitable mistakes may be interesting enough (or simply big enough) for someone else to work out better responses.

He added that he was not offering 'a compendium of political theology, but ... a series of worked examples of trying to find the connecting points between various public questions and the fundamental beliefs about creation and salvation from which (I hope) Christians begin in thinking about anything at all'.

These 'worked examples' include subjects such as 'Has secularism failed?', 'Do human rights exist?', 'Renewing the face of the earth: human responsibility and the environment', 'The gifts reserved for age: perceptions of the elderly', 'Ethics, economics and global justice', 'Big society – small world', 'Theology and economics: two different worlds'. All are illuminating, visionary, challenging and infused with hope, but they stop short of grappling with the conflict of choices that politicians, economists and other decision-makers are required to make daily.

This is not necessarily a criticism, but the evidence of Williams' Primacy is that when he attempted to handle specific political and social issues he trod much less securely. At the time of his appointment to Canterbury, one of his Monmouth archdeacons spoke of 'a streak of holy naivety in him'.

In the event, many of his interventions on contemporary events seemed out of touch with reality, and this was demonstrated vividly in a lecture (not included in the book) given to leading London lawyers in February 2008. In this, he expressed the view that the incorporation of some aspects of Sharia law into the English legal system 'seems inevitable'. A major controversy ensued. The leaders of all the political parties rejected the suggestion, the chairman of the Equality and Human Rights Commission described it as 'muddled and unhelpful', and even the Muslim Council of Great Britain insisted that most members of its community did not want Sharia. What might have made an interesting subject for discussion in a private meeting was introduced into the realm of delicate and potentially explosive racial and cultural tension. Throughout his Lambeth years, he appeared to lack advice as to the likely impact of his public utterances and he was wont to complain that the government no longer took Christian opinion seriously.

His successor, Justin Welby, disclaims intellectual gifts but 11 years as an executive in the oil industry have given him a grasp of finance and business good enough to take him into membership of a Parliamentary

Commission on Standards in Banking, where he is more than capable of questioning bankers on their own terms. This is a unique technical qualification in an Archbishop of Canterbury, and it remains to be seen how well it can be transferred to other secular spheres.

What, then, of the future of Christian prophecy, which involves a declaration and a call to action? The declaration is that the universe and therefore the world is the creation of a transcendental power conceived and described by human beings in terms of a personal God with whom they enjoy a relationship. This God is ceaselessly renewing the created order, and, since all was born of Love, the renewing process is always benevolent. Human life in its fullness is therefore both a response to and an expression of love. It has a sacramental character.

Christians discern this within the pages of the Bible, most specially in the life, death and resurrection of Jesus Christ, whose openness to God made him a unique channel of divine revelation. To this is added reflection on the course of human history and on personal experience, both of which provide unmistakable evidence that Love is denied by human self-centredness – remedied only by spiritual redemption.

This is how things are. This is the context in which human life is lived, and, in order that this life, personal and corporate, may be enjoyed and redeemed, Love is translated into terms that influence behaviour. The starting point is a conviction that every human life is of infinite worth and that relationships must be characterized by justice, equality, freedom, compassion and mutual responsibility. The further translation of these ethical principles in order that they may influence corporate behaviour is a task that the faith community cannot ignore, though it will never be alone in carrying it out.

It is necessary therefore to distinguish between two expressions of Christian prophecy, the first of which is the declaration of foundation beliefs and broad ethical principles. In the main, this is the responsibility of those in the Church who address the public in word or writing at several different levels – archbishops, bishops, scholars and other clergy. Statements of principle, while of the greatest importance, are nonetheless of limited usefulness in the modern world where there is no common ethical ground on which all stand.

The prophet must nonetheless go on to spell out what the principles could mean in the vision of a Good Society in which the fundamental needs of every man, woman and child are met, not as a privilege but as a right. Matters relating to health, housing, income, employment, leisure and provision for old age are obviously involved, and, at the risk of seeming utopian, the vision of such a society must be always kept alive. Reduced expectation will always lead to satisfaction with that which is less than the best. Or, in the words of Niebuhr concerning justice, 'justice cannot be approximated if the hope of its perfect realization does not generate a sublime madness in the soul. Nothing but such madness will do battle with malignant power and "spiritual wickedness in high places".'

The Church's task is to point society in certain directions, rather than to issue directives about the means of travel, and it had better avoid making pronouncements on complex policies requiring technical knowledge. At the same time, prophetic witness will always require the asking of questions. If particular government policies appear to be moving away from, rather than towards, a Good Society, the Church has a duty to point this out, and, constructively, ask for reconsideration. The welfare of the poor must always be a primary Christian concern. There are also much larger and not unrelated structural questions, of the sort Charles Elliott has raised in relation to world poverty, that need to be asked of British society. It may be necessary to question the socially destructive effects of over-large accumulations of wealth and power. So diocesan bishops, and most especially the Archbishop of Canterbury, need advisory groups of professionals with whom they can meet to discuss political, economic and social issues.

It is also the task of the Church, which it should be uniquely equipped to perform because of its divine calling, to remind the nation that transformation of society depends on the transformation of the individuals who make up that society and of the relationships that enable community life to cohere and flourish. The Christian faith offers insights into the meaning, purpose and inter-relatedness of human life that provide a perspective, a motivation and a liberation for behaviour which enhances rather than disfigures whatever it touches. Moreover, it offers a constructive, redemptive way forward whenever, as often must be the case, there is failure.

Other religious faiths have a no less important part to play in upholding the essentially spiritual and moral basis of human life at its most creative and fulfilling levels. Most moral philosophies point in the same direction and need to be heard. It is important therefore that all should with confidence speak out and indicate with some precision the differences that faith and philosophy can make.

The second expression of prophecy, not normally so conceived, lies with those who have time and ability to engage in interdisciplinary study of particular issues demanding national and international attention and requiring specific recommendations. A continuing episcopal presence, albeit on a reduced scale, but augmented by the representatives of other churches and faiths, will remain an important sphere of prophetic witness in the national legislature. The best church leaders are in close touch with the communities they serve and are particularly well qualified to judge and report on the effects of legislation on the lives of ordinary people.

All this acknowledged and strongly emphasized, it must remain the case that the overwhelming responsibility for Christian prophecy in society lies with those of the laity who are involved daily in the making of decisions that affect, for better or for worse, the quality of personal and community life. The need for such prophetic ministries cannot be open to doubt. Neither can the fact that in today's world where conflicting values and motives as well as powerful, impersonal forces are rampant, they can ever be easy vocations.

This inevitably raises questions concerning the scale and content of laity education – a long-neglected aspect of the Church's life which has in recent years been addressed, in terms of personal discipleship, by the evangelically inspired Alpha courses. But these are no substitute for other enterprises directed towards the application of Christian faith to the corporate environment in which all human beings seek to thrive. The renewal of the Church's witness in the world now urgently requires the allocation of spiritual and intellectual resources to grapple better with the issues that daily face lay men and women in the secular sphere.

Of particular urgency and offering scope for positive action is the role of the very large number of self-supporting clergy who have remained in their secular employment after ordination. All have received two or three years of training, usually on part-time courses, designed to equip them to conduct worship, preach and teach and engage in pastoral work in support of parochial ministry. Few, if any, have been trained to handle the hard ethical decisions frequently demanded of those who hold senior secular posts, and the wrong kind of training may be a hindrance to it. Even so, the recruitment of men and women for self-supporting ministry offers immediate opportunities for the extension of prophecy.

The unchanging demand of all Christian prophecy, most especially in times of uncertainty and fear, is to share with others the bright vision of a world in which every man, woman and child may live life to the full. And in the face of doubt and disenchantment to maintain the ray of hope that always lingers on the borders of despair and is derived ultimately from trust in the promises of God. That the life of the Church itself in every age fails to embody fully that which it exists to proclaim is only too evident, and never more so than at the present time. Hence, the desperate need also for prophets possessed by a vision of a Church as well as of a society renewed.

Further Reading

The church leaders referred to in these pages all have standard biographies, most of them available on the second-hand book market. There are, however, some more recent studies that include important reassessments:

Robert Beaken, *Cosmo Lang*, I. B. Tauris, 2012.
Owen Chadwick, *Herbert Hensley Henson*, Clarendon Press, 1983.
John Kent, *William Temple*, Cambridge University Press, 1992.
Dianne Kirby, *Church, State and Propaganda: The Archbishop of York and International Relations, A Political Study of Cyril Forster Garbett, 1942–1955*, Hull University Press, 1999.

The most perceptive biography of Archbishop Rowan Williams is Rupert Shortt's *Rowan's Rule*, Hodder & Stoughton, 2008, to which needs to be added Williams' own *Faith in the Public Square*, Bloomsbury, 2012.

Of particular importance for an understanding of the Irish problem is Alf McCreary's biography of Archbishop Robin Eames: *Nobody's Fool*, Hodder & Stoughton, 2005.

More generally:
G. K. A. Bell, *The Church and Humanity, 1939–46*, Longmans, 1946.
Ian Bradley, *God Save the Queen: The Spiritual Dimension of Monarchy*, Darton, Longman and Todd, 2002.
Malcolm Brown and Paul Ballard, *The Church and Economic Life, 1945–2006*, Epworth Press, 2006.
Chris Bryant, *Possible Dreams*, Hodder & Stoughton, 1999 (on Christian Socialism).
Owen Chadwick, *The Victorian Church*, A & C Black, 2 vols, 1966 and 1970.
Henry Clark, *The Church Under Thatcher*, SPCK, 1993.
Peter Coleman, *Christian Attitudes to Homosexuality*, SPCK, 1980.
John de Gruchy, *The Church Struggle in South Africa*, SCM, 2004.

David L. Edwards, *Leaders of the Church of England, 1828–1978*, Hodder & Stoughton, 1978.

Charles Gore, *Christ and Society*, Allen and Unwin, 1928.

John Habgood, *Church and Nation in a Secular Age*, Darton, Longman and Todd, 1983.

Richard Harries (ed.), *Reinhold Niebuhr and the Issues of Our Time*, Mowbray, 1986.

Richard Harries, *Christianity and War in a Nuclear Age*, Mowbray, 1986.

Adrian Hastings, *A History of English Christianity, 1920–85*, Collins, 1986.

Peter Hinchliffe, *The One-Sided Reciprocity: A Study in the Modification of the Establishment*, Darton, Longman and Todd, 1966.

Robert Lee, *The Church of England and the Durham Coalfield, 1810–1926*, Boydell Press, 2007.

G. I. T. Minchin, *Churches and Social Issues in Twentieth Century Britain*, Clarendon Press, 1998.

Jürgen Moltmann, *God for a Secular Society: The Public Relevance of Theology*, SCM Press, 1997.

Reinhold Niebuhr, *Moral Man and Immoral Society*, Scribners, 1947.

E. R. Norman, *Church and Society in England, 1770–1970*, Clarendon Press, 1976.

Michael S. Northcott, *The Church and Secularisation*, Verlag Peter Lang, 1989.

Bernard Palmer, *High and Mitred: Prime Ministers as Bishop-Makers*, SPCK, 1992.

Ronald H. Preston, *Religion and the Persistence of Capitalism*, SCM Press, 1979.

Maurice Reckitt, *Maurice to Temple*, Faber, 1947.

John A. T. Robinson, *Christian Freedom in a Permissive Society*, SCM Press, 1970.

David Sheppard, *Bias to the Poor*, Hodder & Stoughton, 1983.

William Temple, *Christianity and the State*, Macmillan, 1928.

William Temple, *Thoughts in Wartime*, Macmillan, 1940.

William Temple, *Christianity and the Social Order*, Penguin Books, 1942 (reissued SPCK, 1976).

William Temple, *The Church Looks Forward*, Macmillan, 1944.

E. R. Wickham, *Church and People in an Industrial City*, Lutterworth Press, 1957.

Alan Wilkinson, *The Church of England in the First World War*, SPCK, 1978.

Alan Wilkinson, *Christian Socialism: From Scott Holland to Tony Blair*, SCM, 1998.

Index

abdication 7–9
Abse, Leo 164, 175
Acland, Richard 139, 140
African independent churches 150
African National Congress 150, 155, 160
alcohol abuse 68
Aldermaston marches 142
allotments 66
Anglo-Boer War 66
apartheid 147–8, 150–61
Archbishops' Council 176
Armstrong, Mervyn 183
Arnold, Thomas 13–14
Asquith, H. H. 74–5
Auckland Brotherhood 48, 50

Bailey, Sherwin 171–3, 174
Baker, John Austin 143
Baldwin, Stanley 8
Balfour, A. J. 40, 41
banks 116–17, 200, 207
Baring, Charles 47
Barker, Ernest 94
Barnes, Ernest William 105–6, 112–13
Barrington, Shute 46
Barth, Karl 94, 95
Bathurst, Henry 13, 16
Beaken, Robert 8
Bell, George
  at Oxford conference (1937) 94

concern for Christians in Germany 100, 103–6
concern for Jews in Germany 100, 105
early sympathy for Nazism 98
and nuclear bombs 135, 138
World War II 4, 109–10
Bennett, Frank 103
Benson, Edward White 20
Beresford, Marcus 13
Beveridge Report 120, 124
bioethics 203
bishops
  against apartheid 148, 150, 152, 157–8
  against homosexuality 169
  in the House of Lords 3, 19, 107, 109, 112–13, 114, 127, 130, 136, 169, 175
  and House of Lords reform 203
  and the Reform Act (1832) 15–19
  should serve secular communities 182
  and social welfare 94
  support reform of law on homosexuality 175
  and university reforms 39–40
Blank, Joost de 156–8
Blomfield, Charles 3, 18, 37
Blunt, Alfred 7
Board Schools 40
Board of Social Responsibility 200